Bill Thomas

MORAG FRASER is the editor of *Eureka Street* magazine, a forum for public affairs, the arts and theology. She was educated by Brigidine nuns, and at Melbourne and La Trobe universities. In recent years she has been a regular contributing reviewer and commentator, in print and on electronic media. Morag Fraser was joint editor, with Joseph O'Reilly, of *Save Our ABC: The Case for Maintaining Australia's National Broadcaster* (Hyland House, 1996) and contributed a chapter, 'The Landscape of Father Lovers', to Susan Geason's *Regarding Jane Eyre* (Random House, 1997). She is married to Frank Jackson and has two daughters.

seams of light
best antipodean essays

a selection edited by
morag fraser

ALLEN & UNWIN

First published in 1998
Allen & Unwin Pty Ltd
9 Atchison Street, St Leonards, NSW 2065 Australia
Phone: (61 2) 9901 4088
Fax: (61 2) 9906 2218
E-mail: frontdesk@allen-unwin.com.au
URL: http://www.allen-unwin.com.au

 This project has been assisted by the
Commonwealth Government through the
Australia Council, its arts funding
and advisory body.

National Library of Australia
Cataloguing-in-Publication data:

Seams of light: best Antipodean essays: a selection.

Bibliography.
ISBN 1 86448 472 1.

1. Australian literature – 20th century. 2. New Zealand – 20th century.
3. Australian essays – 20th century. I. Fraser, Morag.

A824.308

Cover and text design by Beth McKinlay
Cover photo (diver)© Steve Niedorf/The Image Bank

Typeset in Giovanni by J&M Typesetting
Printed by Australian Print Group, Maryborough, Victoria
10 9 8 7 6 5 4 3 2 1

For Frances Mary von Allworden

Acknowledgments

This book would not have been possible without the cooperation of magazine and journal editors in Australia and Britain. It is a pleasure to acknowledge both their ordinary labours and their extraordinary generosity.

I would also like to thank the following individuals for their skill and indispensable encouragement: Jackie Yowell, Foong Ling Kong, Lynda McCaffery, Rachel Petro, Catriona Jackson, Juliette Hughes, Siobhan Jackson, Peter Steele SJ, Helen Daniel, George Papaellinas, Kerryn Goldsworthy and Frank Jackson.

MF

Contents

MORAG FRASER

# Matisse's Turban

An Introduction

IN 1916 HENRI MATISSE caught sight of himself in a mirror. Head wrapped in a white towel, glasses propped owlishly on the bridge of his nose, he looked like a rheumy, disconcerted Salman Rushdie.

'I find myself a bit Moroccan with my towel on my head,' he wrote to his friend Gustave Kahn, 'and this gave me the idea to sketch myself.'

The sketch—one of his most ironic—catches Matisse in essay mode. Here he is, swaddled against the snuffly cold of a Paris winter, deep in the privacy of his ablutions, when a fortuitous collision of memory, mirror and bath towel obliterates nationality, fractures space-time and whisks him back to Tangiers, to the cobalt intensities of a stronger sun and the patterned luxuriance that had changed his painting forever. Matisse had visited Morocco only twice, in winter and spring of 1912 and 1913. But the experience was pivotal. Four years later, on another continent, he takes pen and ink and draws himself into the picture.

The writers of these antipodean essays do as Matisse did: they let the world beyond their own borders mark them and mark what they make. And like him, they do so without surrendering the ground from which they launch their explorations. Matisse remained the quintessential Frenchman (one of the Moroccan drawings shows him perched on a camp stool in frock coat, hat and the owl glasses, like an undertaker in the Casbah), yet he allowed North Africa to seep into his eye, to re-order his spatial reflexes, his methods of abstraction. It was no simple matter of a few new or exotic subjects or a brightening of his palette: he was changed, permanently. And under his hand, so was Morocco.

Matisse made his short exploratory journey from the Parisian centre to the exotic periphery. At least that is how we have charted it, using inherited European cultural coordinates. Ludicrous, when you consider that it was in Morocco that Matisse encountered Islam. Nonetheless, that is how we have done it—through mind-sets born out of the shifting relativities of power. Australian, New Zealand and Pacific writers have conventionally made their imaginative odysseys the other way round, from the southern to the northern hemisphere, from the distant periphery—the antipodes—to what was regarded as the source.

We map differently now. We have for decades, though cultural shifts take a long time to stabilise into certainties. In 1959 historian and critic Bernard Smith gave the word 'antipodean' a positive, clarion charge when he used it, in 'The Antipodean Manifesto', to argue for a distinctive character—for the power of the image—in Australian art. Forty years later, a writer who ranges as widely as Robert Dessaix can adopt the term 'antipodean' to characterise his grounded cosmopolitanism. He picks up from both Bernard Smith and Peter Beilharz (who has traced Smith's intellectual career in his 1997 work, *Imagining the Antipodes: Culture, Theory and the Visual in the Work of Bernard Smith*) the idea of reciprocated traffic. He also realises on the singular advantage of antipodean isolation: the rest of the world may not know us, but we know ourselves, and we know them.

'In Smith's way of thinking,' Beilharz argues, 'to be antipodean is to be constructed into a relationship. The antipodes is not a place, though its image is often projected on a place away from Europe, like that which we inhabit.' Being antipodean, then, is also a condition of mind, and one that nurtures the refractory response. We are, in Beilharz's phrase, 'the bits that talk back'.

Seams of Light explores this idea of dynamic relationship, of the complex switching patterns that enrich the literature of this region. These eighteen writers, born south and north, are all beneficiaries of the intellectual hybridisation that is the benign legacy of colonisation. There are less benign legacies, as Denis Byrne notes in his essay on the Philippines, 'Intramuros's Return', and sometimes they yield more to the dispassionate eye of distance. Peter Walker's account of changes in the temperature of Maori–Pakeha relations in his native New Zealand is more stark for his long absence. 'Maori War' reads like a fresh scar on the face of a sister, got while your back was turned.

Walker, like his fellow essayists, is a globe wanderer: 'Antipodeans can spend years like this,' he says, 'wavering between hemispheres, unsure where to settle.' Well, there are advantages in that, and you can settle anywhere with a pen, or keyboard. At least for a while. All of these writers have occasional homes in remote places or other cultures: in Mexico, for example, or Australia's far north, in Ireland, Italy, China, France or Britain. They are also at home in many disciplines, holding day (or night) jobs as poets, historians, novelists, journalists, satirists, public servants and broadcasters. I didn't impose the term 'antipodean' on them: it emerged out of what they wrote, offering itself as the one term that could contain their heterogeneity and link them together in a way that made concerted sense of Peter Porter's trenchant passion for music, Chris Wallace-Crabbe's treading on the hem of Bloomsbury or Barry Oakley's immersion in a backyard pool.

The condition of cultural bilingualism, of being antipodean, suits the essay; it sits naturally with the ironic habit of mind that is one of the essay's hallmarks; it stimulates a necessary willingness to rub thoughts together and revel in the sparks. The wryness of antipodean experience sorts with ambivalence, with unexpected or doubled ways of seeing. And such binocular practice happily parallels that other famous interaction which Michel de Montaigne freely proclaimed in 1580, when he published his revolutionary *Essais*—the conversation between self and the world.

With the *Essais*, his antidote to melancholia, Montaigne gave posterity a name for the opportunist's ideal prose form. There had been personal writing before Montaigne, but never so systematic or so unattached to high motive or purpose, be it confession, instruction or exhortation. His was the classic assaying of his own mettle, a zig-zag between self and subject, between interior ruminations and the exterior world. 'I am myself the matter of my book,' he declared, with disarming and revolutionary frankness. He was neither statesman, memoirist nor historian, so he became literary analyst, speculating about his own humanity and satisfying a fundamental psychological need long before Freud. Montaigne was the dilettante who, in Robert Dessaix's adaption of the old phrase, 'loiters with intent'; the self-professed amateur who tries ideas out on himself, like Matisse's turban, to see how they fit.

His effect, of course, has been to toss twenty generations of readers into the crucible with him. Try hanging on to your abstract notions of what a habit is after you have read Montaigne: 'The power of habit was very well understood, it seems to me, by the man who first forged that tale of a village woman who had grown used to cuddling a calf and carrying it about from the time it was born: she grew so accustomed to doing so that she was able to carry it when it was a fully grown bull.'

That 'it seems to me' is the structural characteristic—almost a condition of sale, as it were—of the essay. The genre is an interrogatory one, bearing the implicit invitation to ponder alongside, to question, to read and, because you have read, turn your head in an entirely different direction and catch the view from there. Or not. Essays may persuade but they do not coerce. And of course you can write a splendid essay while remaining narrowly focused, exasperatingly provincial and venturing no further than your bed. One of my favourites, 'The art of the nap', by Joseph Epstein, begins with this sophisticated throw-away: 'Intellectual serenity in the United States, I have heard it said, consists in not giving a damn about Harvard.'

Epstein and Montaigne share more than a cultivated urbanity: they are both savourers of language and they know how to wield it. Not all essayists have followed them in that. But then not all essayists are volunteers. The form has had its perversions through its conscription to pedagogy. Duty displacing opportunity. No one with even a skerrick of schooling can have escaped such dread commands as these: 'Five hundred words on the electrolysis of water' or 'The postcolonial stance in Doris Lessing and Toni Morrison: contrast'. No wonder so much raw dough is produced. Indeed, Samuel Johnson in his Dictionary of 1755 glossed the essay as a rough experiment, 'an irregular or undigested piece'. Maybe he had set a few.

But there is nothing undigested or remotely dutiful about the essays in this selection. They have been chosen precisely because their writers are Montaigne's descendants—unruly perhaps, as you would want, but adepts of their craft. I selected them because they ask the question that we all must ask in this region as elsewhere— how may we live together? But in doing so they take the reader through the strata of antipodean experience, asking what stirs us to exult or protest, what tweaks our conscience or stirs the imagination. 'Dolphin of the mind' is Peter Steele's phrase for one wordsmith who delights him (in 'Stealing Poseidon's Trident'). These writers play like dolphins, breaking the surface of ideas. They do it in voices that are variously accountable. They dramatise. They own up. They look behind their backs and into the middle and far distance. They stretch the form. Brian Castro employs it to intrigue. Inga Clendinnen commits herself as the travelling companion of Mr G.A. Robinson, nineteenth-century Chief Protector of Aborigines, and writes a diary in response to his, layering document upon document. Kerryn Goldsworthy finds her essay, and her ramifying tale, on a tombstone in Port Vincent. In the hands of John Clarke, whose interviews with Bryan Dawe push the outer definitional edge of the genre, the dramatic essay becomes a feat of inspired ventriloquism. I know of no sharper reflection on the banal waywardness of late-twentieth-century leadership than Clarke's, and no other writer who manages to project such mordant integrity and Swiftian outrage behind the venalities of his characters. It might be enough, you would think, just to laugh.

These essays are not chosen on historical principles. Imre

Salusinszky's 1997 *Oxford Book of Australian Essays* and its predecessors more than supply that need. My criterion was simple: I
looked for supple thought and for writing that would both entice
and perhaps disconcert its reader. The essays are not thematically
arranged, although connections inevitably suggest themselves. It is
one of the occasional pleasures of editing that writers play into
your hands. I had not anticipated consonance between David
Marr's essay on the opening out of Sydney's pub windows and Les
Murray's call for splendour in public architecture. But it is there,
even though the two registers are distinct. Ivor Indyk unearthed
unmistakable seams of light—a kind of desperate anthracite radiance—in the poetry of Kenneth Slessor. (*Ex post facto* validation of
your gathering title is gratifying.) And in tracing Slessor's Jewish
heritage Indyk also lays a sombre ground for Shane Maloney's
experience of a Los Angeles Tolerance Museum. Bill Cope and
Peter Goldsworthy both write at the intersection of language,
science and anthropology. Goldsworthy is a poet who can't stay
away from linguistics and philosophy. Cope is a social scientist
who can't stay away from the poetry of myth.

Time has been the only other determinant: I wanted the essays
to give some account of these cauldron years we are living through
as the century goes down. With the exception of Helen Garner's
'Mr Tiarapu', all were published between 1990 and 1997.

Late in 1997 Germaine Greer gave a Melbourne Writers' Festival
audience what they'd come for when she lit a fuse under literary
taxonomies. Too many divisions, she declared. The moment was
exhilarating as moments are when fixtures suddenly seem vulnerable and you sniff cordite. But I'd fight for the division, for the
form of shapely thought this book celebrates, lest we lose a habit
of deft, civilised reflection to anonymity, or to merger. 'Montaigne
did swallow dives from one trapeze to another,' Peter Steele writes,
in the piece that closes this selection. That is the essay exactly—the
engaged mind in an acrobatics of serious delight.

1997

ROBERT DESSAIX

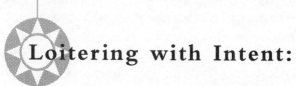# Loitering with Intent:

Reflections on the Demise
of the Dilettante

AT FIRST YOU HARDLY NOTICE IT. After a morning spent wandering through the dispiriting ruins at Eleusis under a fierce Attic sun it's easy to overlook the final words of the Brief Historical Survey: *Excavations to uncover the Sanctuary were begun at the beginning of the last century by the Society of Dilettanti. They were continued by the Greek Archaeological Society from 1882 until the present day.* A trifling misuse of tense in the last sentence, as the amateur philologist can't help noting in his inconsequential way, but that's not the striking thing about these two sentences.

To be precise, there are two striking things here: the first is the notion that a society of people calling themselves *dilettanti* should have undertaken such a serious scientific project as the restoration of the sanctuary at Eleusis—this was, after all, no minor temple to some insignificant Mediterranean deity, but the epicentre of the Eleusinian Mysteries, the most widespread religious cult in the world until Theodosius I and the Visigoths destroyed it; and the second is the way these sentences encapsulate the change in thinking about words like *dilettante*—how right it now seems that by the late nineteenth century a self-declaredly professional society should have taken over the diggings. Since I was roaming this rocky site in the petrochemical fug in an amateur, if not dilettantish, capacity myself, I fell to contemplating the fate of that intriguing foreign borrowing *dilettante*, with its faint aura of frivolous dabbling, ridiculous passion and moral failing—of Italy, in other words.

Gradually, over the last three centuries, the collective lip has curled more and more markedly whenever the word *dilettante* has been spoken. *Amateur* (another foreign import with a hint to it of Continental idleness) has hardly fared better. I wondered why. That is to say, I wondered what it is about our culture which has turned a word we once pronounced approvingly into a word we now pronounce with marked disdain.

When the Society of Dilettanti was founded in 1733, the word *dilettante* seems to have meant little more than someone who cultivated artistic pursuits out of a pure delight in them. (Not *mere* delight at this stage, notice, but *pure*, unmixed with any desire for pecuniary reward.) Their joy came principally from unearthing the civilisations of Greece and Rome, not from material gain. To be pure in this sense you obviously needed money, so it comes as no surprise to learn that the founding members were all wealthy, socially prominent young noblemen who had been on the Grand Tour. In no other sense was purity a prerequisite: Sir Francis Dashwood, for example, was a member of the scandalous Hell Fire Club, and Horace Walpole was of the opinion that, although the nominal qualification for membership in the Society was having travelled in Italy, the real qualification was being a drunk. It was your disinterested status as a gentleman that kept you pure, regardless of your behaviour. (At the end of the twentieth century, the idea of anyone, however rich, being 'disinterested' is so foreign to us that the very word has had to find something else to do: it has attached itself to 'uninterested', hoping no one will notice the difference.)

Since the Society of Dilettanti played a crucial role in assigning a particular meaning to the word *dilettante* in English and other European languages (even Lessing and Goethe were apparently influenced in their work by its activities), it is important to be clear about what sort of involvement in the arts its members considered appropriate to *dilettanti*. Above all, it was serious. What these knights, earls and other scions of the landed gentry actually did was to support high art forms from the sidelines (opera was one of their earliest enthusiasms) and foster a learned, methodical interest in classical architecture and archæology. Since no one else was doing it professionally—certainly not the universities—the Dilettanti over a period of some 150 years actually kept the serious study of classical antiquity alive in Europe, mostly through financing expeditions to the eastern Mediterranean and then publishing the findings.

At the very beginning, then, in the mid-eighteenth century, the word *dilettante* seems to have connoted a serious, disinterested passion for the systematic study and promotion of the arts. And the corollary of a disinterested passion in pre-industrial England was, of course, gentle birth and its attendant wealth. Nothing to sneer at in any of that in the mid-eighteenth century. Even if these titled gentlemen did not themselves sculpt, paint, play the violin or sing arias, except as what Jane Austen might later have called an 'accomplishment', what they did do was seen by anyone who mattered as valuable: they developed public taste. ('Greek taste and Roman spirit!' was in fact their toast.) *Both who they were and what they did were of consequence.* And consequentiality, I would suggest, is one of our culture's supreme values, the key to understanding why *dilettante*, dilettantish and dilettantism are now all uttered with a sneer.

As the Industrial Revolution got underway, the word *dilettante* understandably acquired a whiff of fecklessness in some quarters. It was not only barons and earls who now mattered or whose opinions about what was of consequence mattered. Despite the Society's real cultural achievements, by the mid-nineteenth century political, economic and cultural consequence attached more and more to the middle classes, and the idea of young blue bloods wandering around the shores of the Mediterranean rescuing buried statues and refining their tastes *from having nothing better to do* began to appear faintly ridiculous. Both Dickens and Ruskin use *dilettante* disparagingly, and in *Middlemarch* (1871), for example, Will Ladislaw is dismissed by his friend Naumann as 'amateurish and dilettantish' simply because he lacks a sense of determination, of manly 'brazenness', in finding out where the Casaubons are staying in Rome. James' Gilbert Osmond in *Portrait of a Lady* (1881) is of the opinion that Italy makes people 'idle and dilettantish, and second-rate', meaning by that, evidently, that it prevents them from getting on with the real business of life by distracting them with mere 'impressions'. When at the end of the nineteenth century the study of antiquities at long last became an academic discipline, it was clearly time for the Society of Dilettanti to redefine themselves: they were in danger of having nothing left to do but refine taste and pronounce—in other words, act like *dilettanti* in the modern sense. Knowledge and systematic study were now in other hands.

Particularly contemptible from the point of view of the expanding professional classes, who traded in certified knowledge, was any involvement in the arts on the part of non-professionals. For the professional classes, after all, status, not to mention income, depended on accredited competence. Nothing annoyed the upper middle classes more than the self-taught expert, the uncertificated, non-professional know-all—the grocer who had the effrontery to read military histories, the *arriviste* opera-loving bank-clerk who embarrassingly wanted to discuss with one the finer points of some diva's performance last night at Covent Garden. Such people were not erudite, they were dabblers, they were not connoisseurs, but impertinent nutters—the sort of people who probably knew the London–Nottingham train timetable off by heart. As we know, upper-middle-class writers in the early twentieth century such as Virginia Woolf, Graham Greene, T. S. Eliot and E. M. Forster reserved a particular kind of venom in their fiction for lower-middle-class upstarts with pretensions to significant knowledge. (Virginia Woolf couldn't bring herself to admire *Ulysses*, for example, because it was by 'a self-taught working man, and we all know how distressing they are'.)

The trading classes were also held in contempt, of course, as they still are—the bankers who assembled art collections, the wealthy factory-owners who saw themselves as patrons to the arts. Useful, worth grovelling to, but not professional, and therefore vaguely vulgar. In a peasant, self-improvement had a certain charm, being completely unthreatening to the professions.

The artist himself (very rarely herself) was also, intriguingly, to some degree exempt from ridicule—and perhaps still is. The actual production of art conferred a kind of aristocratic status on the artist which permitted amateurism in the pure sense—so long as his art was not mere craft, a money-making exercise too close to trade for comfort. In the artist the *dilettante* can (or could) live on. Even today we do not expect Thea Astley to engage in scholarly research of aged care before writing *Coda*—she is an artist.

Perhaps this is why living in a garret as you ground out your masterpieces was considered ennobling—it was, paradoxically, evidence of your aristocratic status, regardless of your class roots, a sign of your total dedication to what you loved and were skilled in, of your noble disregard for monetary advantage in your pursuit of beauty, taste and refinement—of your 'graciousness', as Barthes revealingly puts it in his note on *L'amateur*, hinting at the artist's willingness to engage with an art form without seeking recompense.

The artist's honorary aristocratic status may also be why amateur artists, for example, were exhibited with few qualms at the Royal Academy and 'Sunday afternoon painter' was a term of approval, not a supercilious put-down. At least as an actual artist you were, for a few hours a week, easily distinguishable from those other offensively self-assured 'gentlemen' who cobbled together eccentric, unscientific collections of Roman coins or forked out wads of grubby notes to support some would-be sculptor.

In nineteenth-century Russia, by way of contrast, where the industrial revolution had still not in any real sense taken place, gentlemen *dilettanti* retained their status: what were Tolstoy or Turgenev or Pushkin if not *dilettanti par excellence*? They wrote novels, plays and poetry without any literary training, naturally, and this would have been unexceptionable anywhere, but they also wrote unprofessionally on philosophy, history, aesthetics, economics, agrarian reform, religion and foreign policy—and were listened to and taken very seriously indeed by anyone who mattered because they mattered. What these aristocrats had to say on these topics was naturally of consequence. There was thought to be nothing *mere* about their dilettantism.

Attitudes to time, I would argue, are crucial to any understanding of consequentiality and therefore of the fate of the word *dilettante*. A pre-industrial gentleman (for all Tolstoy might have gone out scything with the peasants on occasion) had little need to distinguish between which of his daily activities were income-producing and which were not. Hosting a banquet, checking the accounts, attending a concert, selling a forest, reading Hegel, writing a love poem—it was all just part of being a gentleman. Money was often frantically important, it's true, but it was not linked to time.

In industrialised society, however, time for people of consequence is divided into two discrete categories: the serious hours spent creating wealth professionally (in some sense) and the frivolous hours spent resting and indulging in pastimes. To this day undirected eagerness for artistic pursuits is not tolerated at all in those classes where such pursuits must occupy non-professional time—particularly the lower middle classes. Their engagement with serious culture is, after all, literally *idle* and arguably parasitic. Over the last 150 years cultural activity has become more and more the exclusive province either of people of natural consequence (even Prince Charles' amateur architectural interests are accorded some grudging respect) or certified professionals (people whose interest has political and economic ramifications). *Mere* (and this is where the *mere* comes in) enthusiasm, learning, taste, dedication and skill are simply not enough in the kind of capitalist society we now live in. At the end of the twentieth century, when even pastimes have been largely professionalised in their management (everything from yoga to whitewater rafting, from stamp-collecting to surfing the Internet), the very words *pastime* and *amateur* have become terms of disapproval.

Today, in conditions of almost total professionalisation of everything across all classes, *dilettante*, now barely used, still has an aura about it of 'idle interest in improper imitation of the aristocracy', while *amateur* is generally directed by professionals as a scornful gibe at the non-professional (and therefore inconsequential) nature of an interest in any subject or activity. Increasingly, even the area of art production is less immune to judgments of this kind. This may be why, for example, the Australia Council now funds professionally run courses for writers around Australia to assist them in presenting themselves—selling themselves effectively—on television, on radio and in interviews in the press. You aren't just someone who writes any more—you are a marketable package and you must learn how to interact with professional arts personnel—TV hosts, journalists, bureaucrats.

This is also why, I would suggest, it is in the 'suburbs' that amateur activities are thought to properly take place—those middle- and lower-middle-class areas of a city where neither the artistic aristocrats nor professional intellectuals are concentrated. In Sydney, for example, amateur productions of *Private Lives* or *Lady Windermere's Fan* (typical choices because they evoke a world which, in real life, would legitimise these failed artists, if only they could enter it) seem proper to Kogarah and Castle Hill, but out of place in the inner-city. In Melbourne an amateur art-show might draw an unembarrassed audience in Macleod or East Bentleigh, but need repackaging as an Australia Council-funded independent artists' exhibition in Fitzroy, Carlton or St Kilda—that's professional territory.

There's a surreptitious gendering process at work here as well: it is above all the 'suburban housewife' who is idle (not employed as a professional) and whose engagement with the arts must therefore be amateur—and by extension frivolous, unresearched, inconsequential. The suburbs are supposedly riddled with women with time on their hands, listlessly attending life-drawing classes and turning out disarmingly misshapen coffee-cups. Effeminate men, too, as a sub-species of the female, also naturally infest certain amateur suburban groups in the popular imagination—one certainly doesn't picture them holding down positions of power and influence in the professional world.

Indeed, while attacks on non-professional commentary or management of the arts are now par for the course, it is the attempts to privilege the professionalised production of art which are setting off alarm bells. Writers are led to believe that a creative writing degree will turn them into professional writers, graffiti artists working with a Community Arts grant expect their murals to be treated with professional respect and every last photographer with a degree in Visual Arts expects a solo exhibition as a right. They've been certified as professional. In whose eyes, we might ask, however, is this of any consequence? Well, in the eyes of other professionals, the ring-masters in the public arena. *Their* validating gaze has the advantage of coming with money attached.

Some intellectuals in the 1990s are even loath to admit the existence of artistic activity until it has been consciously registered as existing by some professional organisation. Several years ago in an essay on the community arts movement the art historian Sandy Kirby wrote:

> *it has of course always been the case that people have engaged in cultural practices on a communal basis in different guises ... participat[ing] in a wide range of creative and cultural activities—song, dance, theatre, painting, sculpture, craft and music—and ... these have been based in diverse organisations ranging from ethnic clubs to factory associations, from women's groups to artists' societies. However, the impetus to organise and consciously engage ordinary people in the cultural life of this country has historically and consistently come from the left. ('An Historical Perspective on the Community Arts Movement', in Community and the Arts, 1991)*

What is striking about this paragraph, apart from its outlandish final claim, is the assumption that 'ordinary people' (not us, presumably) happily potting, singing, playing the piano and staging *Brigadoon* must be 'consciously engaged' (by us, we gather) before all that singing and dressing-up can be taken seriously (by us). Before we organised them—integrated them economically and politically into the community—they apparently languished in some sort of ungazed-upon limbo. That would not have been their point of view, of course, but then they were not, until we gazed upon them, of any consequence.

Now, the motive for writing this kind of thing was no doubt strictly honourable—in an age of total professionalisation, no one should feel excluded for class, gender or ethnic reasons. Everyone should feel eligible to play the game 'we' are organising. And, indeed, professionalisation of the arts and intellectual life has brought many obvious benefits at the public level—they are powerful industries now, diverse, influential, enriching. But the effect of total professionalisation is, I would argue, far from being totally beneficial.

In the first place, it has produced a situation where amateurism is permissible only in the consumer. Not only does no one mind if you spend your leisure hours as a reader skipping from Plato to Donne to Ruth Rendell, or as a concert-goer buying tickets to Madonna, *Rigoletto* and a (professionally produced) *butoh* play all in one week, your promiscuity is positively welcomed. Cultural consumers who spread themselves across a variety of fields keep the wheels of commerce ticking over nicely and do themselves no obvious harm in the process. The consumers' experience is literally inconsequential. The result is utter passivity, with consumers reduced to the level of paying voyeurs. Production, distribution, management, analysis and criticism are all firmly in the hands of professionals with credentials, marketing themselves to the consuming masses.

Secondly, professionalisation has induced a gnawing anxiety in most of us about the worth of what we do non-professionally. In a totally professionalised world, we are all amateurs in every area of life except one—and *amateur* is a rude word. This is troubling. Whether we're gardening, skiing, playing the flute, watching a movie, cooking, travelling or even walking the dog, we're doing so in the knowledge that this territory is already occupied by experts. Can what we're doing possibly be of any consequence? Is it just passing the time?

Oddly enough—and I'm sure to be misunderstood when I say this—I think part of the widespread disquiet over the academic discipline of Cultural Studies stems from these very anxieties over total professionalisation. While Cultural Studies courses serve a useful purpose, critiquing established assumptions, encouraging a diversity of interests and affording sometimes brilliant insights into why cultures function as they do (and who is to blame), it is difficult to overcome the suspicion that yet another area of legitimate and enlivening amateur activity has been fenced off for professional use only. (I know that Cultural Studies was supposed to be a Fourth Dimension, not simply a re-corralling of familiar elements from the old 3D world, but, if it is, the one is strangely indistinguishable from the other.) Whereas not so long ago the kind of dabbling in Wittgenstein, linguistics, the behavioural and cognitive sciences, quantum physics, literary theory, popular culture and post-Marxist philosophy which these courses offer was something any middle-class person might happily indulge in when not at the office, even this dabbling is now a degree course at universities all over the country. And whereas it was stimulating to discuss The Body as a site for deconstructing patriarchy around a dinner-table with scant knowledge of anatomy, neurophysiology or genetics, it is disconcerting to find professional teachers doing the same thing. Now even theorising without evidence is professionalised, a paid public activity. At darker moments it feels as if even thinking is something you may not do without authorisation.

In his fourth Reith lecture on public intellectuals, delivered on the BBC in 1993, Edward Said suggested that one way to counteract the negative effects of professionalisation may be through a return to amateurism, to a culture where, quite literally, intellectuals pursue knowledge out of a love for it. But Said is vague on the subject of exactly how professional intellectuals might go about turning themselves into amateurs—perhaps in Australia tenure would help. Given his own immense power and authority, not to mention his Chair at Columbia University, Said himself can hardly serve as a model for many of us. After all, nothing Said might do, however amateur, could ever be conceived as frivolous. Few of us share his happy position. Is there no escape?

In the public arena I doubt that there is. In the sort of economic and political system we live in few are likely to have the kind of independence the original Dilettanti had to pursue the serious study of anything from sheer delight. In the private arena, however, there is perhaps still a glimmer of hope. At one level there are the unsupervised reading groups and artists' collectives springing up all over the country, allowing some relief, at least, in those two areas from the professional 'impetus to organise and consciously engage' which Sandy Kirby was so enamoured of. At another level hope entails, I would suggest, a re-evaluation of the concept of consequentiality, of what is of real consequence to us as individuals and what makes us of consequence. It may even entail rejecting all notion of consequence as it is generally understood, at least as a principle to follow in making choices about how to live. And this is almost impossibly difficult.

I tend to think it is particularly difficult for men, at least for real men (in the most thrilling sense) of my generation. Not only are we never truly idle, as women are, but our whole sense of what it means to be masculine is bound up from childhood with ideas about growing, strengthening, producing another generation, doing a good job and leaving a mark, however modest. We must plan, build, discover, forge ahead, change the landscape. Like little statues of Lenin, we all point forwards. That is why I think that the *dilettante* and amateur are both slightly feminised figures in our culture, resisting this onwards-thrusting trajectory to their lives, thinking less about direction than about the pleasures of where they happen to find themselves. They loiter with intent, to see what might eventuate. Sometimes there are momentous consequences, of course, to this excited loitering—a lifelong passion may abruptly flower, for example—but intent is more an eager state of mind than a determination to achieve. It is at the core of the amateur's way of living and learning.

In some ways amateurism is subversive of the culture we've been conditioned by and the determined amateur will find himself or herself constantly advised to give it up—to do something useful, to set goals, to enrol in a course, to apply for a grant—to get back into the system. Perhaps that is what Roland Barthes meant when he cryptically wrote in that note on *L'amateur* that the amateur is 'the counter-bourgeois self'.

Some time ago while I was writing *Night Letters*, in which Dante is a kind of companion to my dilettantish, unscholarly narrator, I gave a talk in which I mentioned, perhaps too airily, that my novel would be in part a commentary on Dante. A questioner rose to her feet and, politely but in some bewilderment, asked me in effect how I could think of doing this when I wasn't an Italian scholar. It was a fair question, although I don't think I answered it very well, anxious as I was not to appear foolish. The honest answer would have been that, as an amateur, it was not my aim to add to the body of knowledge about Dante, nor to write anything of conse-quence about Dante. My aim was to let a love of *The Divine Comedy* give vital meaning to how my narrator experienced the world, to his sense of what it meant to find something *worthwhile*.

The true amateur or *dilettante* will refuse the temptation to have his or her love validated by some authority, refuse to give up that private, ungazed-upon space and continue to nourish a sense of why life is worth living according to other, private rules. It's not much, but it's literally beyond price.

1997

———————————— ✦ ————————————

Maori War

MY FRIEND SPENCER, A NEW ZEALAND MAORI, is what people used to call a good-time Charlie. He is famous, in a small way, for the number of parties he goes to and the way they liven up when he gets there. When I first met him, six years ago, he was running a restaurant near Charing Cross in London. The quick drink he had with his staff after work became a minor legend. People would cross the city at midnight to be there. If they were lucky, they might get away at four in the morning. Not everyone appreciates Spencer's gregarious streak. The Syrian who owned the restaurant, for instance, called in the police when he inspected his depleted cellar. But Spencer believes in the value of a good time. He has faith in the party.

However, when I ran into him in New Zealand, in the summer of 1996, he wore a look of puzzled embarrassment I had not seen before. We were driving around Wellington harbour and he was describing, not for the first time, a trip he had just made to the South Island with his flatmate, Hughie. Fantastic hospitality down south, he assured me. Terrific wines—Cloudy Bay, Moa Ridge— great local beer, seafood, wild pork ... 'the works'.

He paused. 'But things got a bit tricky down there,' he said. 'I was staying with Hughie's family; and we were having a party. There were about a dozen of us; everyone was getting along fine.

'Then I went to the toilet. And while I was in there, there was a knock on the door. And then this voice said: "You fucking Maoris ... get out of our area." '

'What did you do?' I asked.

'I didn't *know* what to do,' he said. 'I was stunned. I just stood there. But I had nowhere else to go, so I went back to the party. I pretended nothing had happened.'

'But who'd done it?'

'It was weird. I went back into the room, and everyone was all smiles. "Cheers, Spence," and all that. I talked to all of them over the next couple of hours. And I still don't know which one of them it was.'

❂

I was eleven years old before I ever saw a Maori. I grew up in Christchurch, a stolid, flat, prosperous town with, historically, only a tiny Maori population. Indeed, the marked absence of natives was one of the factors that inspired the Canterbury pilgrims to settle there 150 years ago. Their intention was to build an Anglican utopia, and in a way they succeeded. Christchurch was 'the cathedral city ... the Garden City of the Plains ... the most English city outside England'.

There was little sign that we were in the South Pacific, and none at all that we were on the edges of Polynesia. English elms and willows bent in the hot summer nor'westers and in winter stood leafless in fogs penetrated by the headlights of Ford Prefects and Morris Oxfords. The tolling of Big Ben for the evening news on the BBC ('This is London') woke us (in a weird twist we barely noticed) every morning. Gilbert Scott's cathedral and the university, the schools, the courts, the clubs, the council chambers had all been built in the proper nineteenth-century Gothic Revival manner, though the Catholics and the banks preferred the classical style. One night in 1868 the great Waimakariri river to the north rose and swept down on the town, leaving the frumpy Gothic buildings up to their bustles in water. But it sank back again, was embanked and channelled and has never since made an appearance in the drawing rooms of Christchurch; even its name, sprawling, like the river itself over a mile-wide shingle bed, was usually reduced to a curt Anglo-Saxon 'Why-Mack'.

And of course there were no Maori. There was one on the shilling, and one on the twopenny stamp—depicted, I think, running through a swamp, carrying a parcel—but his business there, on the stamp and the shilling, and for that matter in the swamp, was unclear to me. There was the occasional article in our school journals on the Ancient Maori, but he meant no more to us than the Roman boy, with his tutor and slave, in our blue-covered *Everyday Life in Rome*.

Then one summer we went to Picton and there on the grass between the hotel and the sea I saw a group of about thirty Maori in traditional costume—a concert party. I can still remember my surprise at the sight of the red lipstick on the women's dark faces and the unfamiliar harmonies of Maori plainsong, and recall how sharply the outlines of the hills seemed to stand against the sky. I was shocked, as children are, by this first incursion of otherness into my life. But there was another feeling. For the first time I realised that even the solid Anglican city of Christchurch, with its fogs and elms, had not risen upon a vacancy. It was a superimposition. There had been something here before us, and—remarkably—it was still here.

When I was fourteen, my family moved to Hawkes Bay on the North Island. Here the question of race was not so remote. The Maori population in and around the twin cities of Napier and Hastings numbered several thousand. Oddly, this had very little effect on the community's self-image. We were, we believed, a little Britain of the south, which just happened to contain two races living side by side. Maori and Pakeha (the Maori term for white people) worked together, played rugby together, intermarried and shared the same rights and interests. It was true that there had once been a war over land and sovereignty, but this was a century ago, and had simply proved our splendid and complementary qualities. The Maori distinguished themselves with their gallantry: their warriors leapt over parapets to take water to dying British soldiers and—in the same battle, or was it a different one?—sent ammunition to the British when they ran out, so that the fight could continue. The whites, in turn, were generous victors, enfranchising the Maori and setting aside seats for them in parliament. The colour bar erected everywhere else in the British Empire was unknown in New Zealand. We were proud of the fact that we, unlike any other white community in the world, called ourselves by the name given us by the indigenous people—Pakeha. No one even troubled to ask what this word meant; today a Maori is likely to tell you it means 'rats' or 'fleas' or some other troublesome pest, but it is probably a contraction of *pakepakeha*, a mythological pale-skinned people in Maori legend, heard singing as they float on driftwood down rivers in flood. We were even proud of the fact that our national rugby team always began their matches with a Maori haka, or war dance. It was another sign that we were, in the official phrase, 'one people'.

The trouble with this ideology was that it did not quite fit the facts. Maori were not quite so carefree and happy-go-lucky as we imagined. On the contrary they seemed, to my newcomer's eyes, to be aloof, tense and ill at ease. And they were poor—you saw them in town and immediately recognised the broken grilles and rusted mudguards of a 'Maori car' (old wrecks were always called that), the back seat crammed with kids. Most of all, they were elusive. Maori boys began secondary school in the third form but by the fifth had vanished; probably into some unknown Maori world of seasonal labour, or into the menacing gangs that had started to form in the state-housing blocks of Hastings.

Nor did we live 'side by side'. Whites lived among Maoris (back then everyone added the English 's' to the word) only in the poorest areas, or if they happened to be in Napier Prison. In any case, most Maori lived in their own settlements—Paki Paki, Bridge Pa or Fernhill—not far away, but just out of sight. Perfectly good roads led to these places, but no one I knew ever went there, and I could not think of a reason that would ever take me there either.

❖

When I was seventeen, I had a summer job in the abattoir at Whakatu, near Hastings, where up to thirty thousand lambs were slaughtered each day. The workers, seven or eight hundred of us, were mostly Maori, though the foremen and the staff in the administration block were white. I was set to work on the 'bung bench' with a gang of five others, all Maori. Our job was to sluice the lamb intestines, which would then be made into sausage skins, or, I was told, condoms—a lowly occupation in this hierarchy of blood and knives and flaying.

I became quite friendly with one of my workmates, Teddy Rau, a boy of about my own age. For four weeks we worked together, and, with our hands full of still-warm intestines, we talked—mostly about sex. He could never tell whether girls liked him or not and was in a state of stifled envy of his cousin, who had several girlfriends at the same time and had even had sex with one of them, on the Gisborne railcar while it was crossing the Mohaka Viaduct.

One night, at the end of summer, some weeks after I had left the abattoir, I went to a dance in Napier with my new girlfriend. We were out on the dance floor, and suddenly there was a terrific blow on my back, just below the shoulder blades. I staggered and nearly fell, but turned to find myself face to face with Teddy Rau. There were two other Maori standing behind him. He stared at me with a blank expression. I looked back, too surprised to speak. I had a momentary notion that the blow started out as a friendly slap on the back, but somewhere in the air between us the open palm changed into a fist. Neither of us knew why; nor did we say a word. Teddy left the dance, and I never saw him again.

A second memory, from that same summer. It was a routine afternoon at Whakatu, but I had missed the bus home after work. The slaughterhouse—a grimy five-storey brick building—stood in a small township of mostly Maori inhabitants, and the narrow horizons of life there, the stench of meat and tallow, and the thought of the surf crashing on the beach at Napier, made the heat oppressive. While I waited, a Maori woman and a young child came past. She had a handsome face, but looked furious, as a sixty-year-old woman well might after a long walk in the hot sun. The child—probably her grandson—was no more than four and was dawdling behind, poking a stick into a ditch. Ignoring my presence, though I was only a foot away, she turned and snapped out three words, like the flick of a whip: 'Come on, Nigger.'

Nigger! A word I no more expected to hear than I thought to see a cross burning on a lawn. I could not tell whether it was a nickname or a casual term of abuse, nor which was worse. Back in the 1850s the word put in a brief appearance, and as tensions rose over land it began to crop up in settlers' diaries and letters. During the wars in the 1860s and 1870s it flourished openly across newspaper columns and in public speeches. But then it edged out of sight, out of the national vocabulary. Despite the casual condescension of whites—every schoolboy had his fake Maori accent and his Maori jokes—I had never heard it used by a white New Zealander.

These two incidents—the blow on the back, the ugly word overheard—were too fleeting and cryptic to cast any shadow over my acceptance of the received version of race relations. We were an example to the rest of the world, right? Two races, one people, hard-working whites, happy-go-lucky Maori, a tapestry of light and shade ... we all believed that. But received versions often have deeper functions—as alibis, perhaps, or spells. As an alibi, this one told us that there were no dark secrets in our past; as a spell, it gave us a pleasant sense of superiority over other white communities—Australians, South Africans, Americans.

In the early 1970s, I went abroad for the first time. Most New Zealanders, leaving school or university, suddenly open their eyes and see where they are—in a small country at the edge of the world. Then they leave as fast as they can. I did the sort of things we all did on this mandatory world trip: helped build a house in Colorado, fell ill in Benares, fell in love in London, where I served gin to glum businessmen in a pub near Victoria, taught French in a riotous and dingy school off the Caledonian Road. After two or three years overseas, most of us return, and so did I. But not for long. Eighteen months later, I was away again, this time to Australia and California. Antipodeans can spend years like this, wavering between hemispheres, unsure where to settle.

During these years away I became aware that racial changes were afoot. Maori protests began, mostly over specific pockets of land that had been seized by the authorities in the recent past or were under threat. Thousands of Maori marched from the far north to the capital, Wellington, five hundred miles away, demanding an end to land appropriation. Later, when I happened to be back in Auckland, I watched in amazement as army trucks rumbled across towns carrying hundreds of police to evict local Maori from a site which seemed not only to be lawfully theirs, but to be the tiny remnant of what had once been promised them in perpetuity.

At the same time, new books appeared that completely rewrote the history of the wars. They argued that Maori had never actually been defeated in battle, but were tricked into surrender, or simply swamped by more and more British soldiers, many sent straight from service in India. After the Indian Mutiny, the attitude throughout the empire towards its subject peoples became much harsher. Even the Maori briefly became 'black vermin'. By the mid-1860s, there were more imperial soldiers in New Zealand than in England or any other British territory.

Suddenly, a hundred years later, the Maori wars began to look very different to us—they became a tale of broken treaties, land invasions, burning churches and tortured prisoners. One settlement of two thousand unarmed, pacifist Maori was attacked and sacked, the men sent into exile, women raped, lands forfeited. The New Zealand ideology of race—our alibi and spell—appeared to be cracking. Even the most hallowed national legends were now embarrassments. At school we had heard of the Maori chief Te Ori Ori who was wounded taking water to a dying British soldier. We were not told that after the battle Te Ori Ori was flung into a prison hulk in Auckland harbour for six months, or that the New Zealand minister of war made a point of forbidding straw mattresses for the wounded.

✦

In 1981 I left again, and this time I did not return for fifteen years, except on occasional flying visits. From the vantage point of a London newsroom, I watched more radical changes unfold. New Zealand became a global byword for the spirit of free enterprise: even more strikingly than Thatcher's Britain or Reagan's America, it grasped the free-market nettle. The welfare state was dismantled, and most state assets—transport, banks, post offices, forestry— were auctioned off. A huge disparity in wealth began to open up.

Not surprisingly, race relations grew worse. National day celebrations of the founding Treaty of Waitangi were disrupted. Huge claims for reparation were put forward by Maori: after all, if national assets were being sold off, why should they be excluded? By 1995 the country was in an interracial uproar. Flags were trampled, buildings occupied, courts disrupted. Children who set fire to a school were described admiringly by their Maori elders as 'warriors of our people'. There were threats of terrorism, of burning forests and bombing dams. The Queen herself was manœuvred into making an unprecedented apology for historic wrongs. New Zealanders I met in London would debate whether the country would turn into another Bosnia or merely an Ulster. A hundred and twenty years after the colonial conflict had ended, the little word 'war' was heard once more in the land.

The Maori demands for reparation and decolonisation and sovereignty were conventional enough; the burning flags and barricades a predictable symptom of unrest. Yet when I read the reports (and even, back home on flying visits, when I wrote them) there always seemed to be something missing. It was as if, after each outburst, a silence fell and people thought: 'That's not what we really meant. That isn't really what we want.'

✦

What we do know—the salient facts—can be marshalled quite easily. New Zealand has a population of 3.4 million people, of whom 400,000 are Maori. They are part of the Polynesian race that emerged from South-east Asia three or four thousand years ago and spread across the Pacific Ocean, reaching their furthest outpost, Aotearoa (the Maori name for New Zealand) between AD1000 and 1350. There they formed about fifty *iwi* (tribes) which were frequently at war with one another.

The first European to sail into view was a Dutchman, Abel Tasman, who departed hastily after a bloody encounter in 1642. The inhabitants, he thought, had 'rough voices and strong bones, the colour of their skin being between brown and yellow, they were full of verve, and wore their hair pulled back in a bun in the Japanese manner'. He called the country Staten Landt, wrongly believing it to be part of a greater southern continent, and it was an Amsterdam map-maker who later named these mountainous islands after a muddy Dutch province in the North Sea.

Then, in 1769, came Captain Cook. And in the following fifty years, shoals of other whites came in his wake—whalers, traders, missionaries and finally settlers. The islands were recognised as an independent nation in 1835, but only five years later, when five hundred or so Maori chiefs signed the Treaty of Waitangi, New Zealand became a British colony.

Under the treaty, the chiefs conceded 'sovereignty' to Britain, and Britain guaranteed something called *tino rangatiratanga* to the chiefs. It seems probable that neither side knew what the other was talking about. To the Maori, 'sovereignty' meant, at best, some remote principle that might protect them from invasion by the French. But to the British, the Maori concept *tino rangatiratanga*— 'the full power of chieftainship'—meant little more than authority within the tribe.

Despite the variety of interpretations—and they pour out today faster than ever—a few fundamentals are clear. One of the purposes of the treaty was to save the Maori from the calamities that had swept over other peoples ruled by Europeans. A humanitarian mood reigned in the Colonial Office in London: it was the heyday of abolition, and the bullying and butchery that had taken place elsewhere were not going to happen in New Zealand. At Waitangi, the British came ashore with promises they meant to keep.

Twenty years later, these promises were all broken. Instead, the British brought invasion, war and the confiscation of land. The treaty was abandoned, remembered only as a curious, romantic frontispiece to the country's history. The idea that anyone should feel bound by it scarcely entered people's heads. It was, said the chief justice in 1877, a 'simple nullity'.

And then, surprisingly, a century later, it came back to life.

At first no one could make it out. It was Waitangi Day 1971, and the usual ceremony was being held in the far north. Naval vessels fired a salute to honour the accession of the Queen; there was a ceremonial Maori challenge and then the usual speech praising the 'tapestry of light and shade', the two races side by side. A bugler sounded Sunset Call, and, in an unconsciously accurate piece of symbolism, the lights on the Treaty House were extinguished, and the naval vessels were lit up in the bay.

At these 131st anniversary celebrations the then finance minister, Robert Muldoon, 'Piggy' to the nation at large, was in the middle of his speech when there was a disturbance. A woman stood up behind him, shouting, waving her arms and repeating a phrase again and again. Muldoon faltered. People craned to see what was happening. Even among the naval guard of honour, standing rigidly to attention around the flag, eyeballs rolled sideways slightly—far enough for the guard to be taken by surprise when a group of young Maori rushed the flagstaff, hauled down the naval ensign and set fire to it. A scrum of police, navy cadets and Maori tussled over the flag, which was eventually rescued and returned, scorched, to its proper place. The young Maori, wearing green wreaths and black clothing, began a slow handclap that drowned out further speeches. Then a squall swept in, and the rest of the ceremony was cancelled.

Nobody really understood what had happened; no one was even sure what the woman was shouting. 'Honour and freedom!' some newspapers reported. 'Honour the treaty!' said others. Apart from that, there was a puzzled silence in the press. It was as if this was the first time anyone had actually shouted in New Zealand: no one knew what to make of it. Only Muldoon got the message. He turned and glowered at the protester. 'That,' he grated, 'is a very dangerous woman.'

Twenty-five years later, there can be no one in the country in doubt as to what was shouted that day ('Honour the Treaty!'). Everything has changed. The dangerous woman has been listened to. A ministry and tribunal have been set up to ensure the Treaty is honoured. Hundreds of millions of dollars have been paid in compensation. Maori now enjoy new rights in property, forestry, fishing, mining, education, broadcasting and culture. And yet the anger has not abated. Maori spokesmen are demanding more than a billion dollars' worth of land reparations. The Treaty of Waitangi has become a weapon in the struggle to turn New Zealand back into Aotearoa—Land of the Long White Cloud.

I felt the full depth of the Maori grievance quite by chance, when I went back to Christchurch last year. I had not been there for twenty-five years, but I wanted to see the country from the flat, stolid, white city of my childhood.

'Twenty-five years?' people said. 'You'll find it terribly changed.'

But when I arrived, late on a rainy Sunday afternoon, it seemed eerily unchanged. A few shiny high-rise buildings had touched down in the centre, but otherwise there was the same deep sabbath calm, the same sense of razor-keen snobbery in the better suburbs—Fendalton and Merivale—and the same magical wood of English oaks and Scots pines near the centre of town. Scenes from childhood are generally supposed to seem smaller when revisited in later life, but this rule does not apply to woodland, for the trees quietly keep pace with the years. The avenues and copses of Hagley

Park and St James Park seemed, if anything, deeper, taller and darker than I remembered.

On my second day there, I went with friends to see an exhibition of late nineteenth-century portraits of Maori. Some of these were rather fine paintings, but the tone was valedictory. The chiefs and the women of rank were depicted as noble, stoic, resigned, the senators of a dying race. It was widely believed at that time that the Maori, whose numbers at one point sank to thirty thousand, were doomed to extinction.

Leaving the gallery I walked across the lawn and found myself in a part of the Botanical Gardens I did not remember. And there I found a circle of standing stones: a cromlech, a henge. It made me laugh at first it was not very impressive, although a circle of black pines added a kind of Caledonian sternness to the concept. But then I wondered how such a monument, twelve thousand miles from Britain, in a country in which such things had never been built, must look to Maori eyes.

We had brought our laws and institutions and planted them in the country. We had introduced our trees, grasses, thrushes, blackbirds; even the English hedgehog snuffled in Christchurch back gardens. But until I saw the hedge of yellowish stones, I had not realised how deeply driven into the turf were the claims of Englishness. Not only had we taken over the present and rewritten the immediate past, we were ready to annex the part of the landscape where imagination and prehistory touch. This circle of stones, no more than a garden folly in one light, seemed also to be another way of telling the Maori absentmindedly and as if without malice, that they were not really there.

From Christchurch I went, on a bright day in midsummer, to Wanganui, a town on the west coast of the North Island. It was late morning—some Maori teenagers were hunkered down on benches in the main street; a few whites drifted from shop to bank and bank to shop. A wide brown river flows through the town, and I went down to a small park on the river bank, between the court-house and the rowing club. Moutoa Gardens is just an acre or two of mown grass shaded with old trees and studded with war mem-orials. So it would be easy to miss the one oddity that it had to offer—a stone pedestal about six feet high inscribed with the word BALLANCE, but supporting the remnants of a pair of marble boots.

John Ballance was an obscure colonial premier, and his broken marble boots were the only sign that for seventy days in 1995 Moutoa Gardens was the centre of New Zealand's growing racial conflict. That May, hundreds of Maori occupied and barricaded the park. The streets nearby echoed to the sound of haka, the Maori war challenge. Cars driven by whites were threatened and some-times attacked. At first, the Maori demanded simply that the park be returned to them; then the demands grew wilder. All public land in the district must be handed over. Whites must pay rates to Maori. Maori sovereignty must be established over the region, indeed over the whole country.

Hundreds of Pakeha cheered outside the courthouse when the eviction order was granted. But on the eve of a massive police oper-ation to break up the demonstration, and breathing defiance till the last, the occupiers slipped away, taking the statue of John Ballance with them. The old colonialist had been visible throughout the siege, a twelve-foot hostage looming above the cooking fires and haka groups. For the first few days the statue remained unharmed, but then it was decapitated; the head was replaced with a pumpkin—not a round orange pumpkin, which might have transformed it into a friendly Hallowe'en ghoul, but one of those grey varieties the same colour as the stone. This gave the figure an air of sinister inanity.

This idiot moonface appeared in all the newspapers, and came to symbolise both this occupation and all the others which sprang up across the North Island at the same time. On the night before they struck camp, the rebels, under the eyes of the police sur-rounding the park, managed to chop Ballance up and cart him away with them.

I wondered what he had done to deserve this special treatment.

Or was he just unlucky to be caught behind enemy lines? Ballance, a Maori leader in Wanganui told me, was a mass murderer. She said he had sent flour laced with arsenic to the tribes living upriver. He had committed genocide.

This was a terrible charge, and I was not inclined to believe it. It did not seem to fit in with even the darkest facts of the country's history.

'How do you know this is true?' I asked.

'We just know.'

'But how?'

'Well,' she said reluctantly, 'it's in the Taylor diaries.'

Taylor was a clergyman in Wanganui in the mid-nineteenth century, and his diaries survive in the town library. But when I read the manuscript that afternoon, there was no mention of Ballance at all.

'What do you think?' I asked a white man sitting on a bench beside the river. 'Ballance and his arsenic—it sounds like a bad business.'

'Oh, no,' he said. 'Ballance was a good man. He did a lot of good for the Maoris.'

This was a phrase guaranteed to make my antennæ twitch. A lot of people—old family doctors, big landowners, magistrates, local policemen—are said to have done 'a lot of good for the Maoris'. It is one of those phrases that is invariably followed by a denunciation of Maori ingratitude, sloth, stupidity ...

I did not have to wait long.

'Oh,' he said artlessly, when I asked what he thought of the occupation. 'We're all racists in Wanganui now. The Maoris are just a pack of lazy, black—well, no, we don't mind the local ones protesting and what-have-you, but the outsiders coming in and stealing, making trouble and giving the town a bad name ...'

He fixed me with a wounded expression: 'Write something good about Wanganui,' he commanded. 'Write about our lovely new velodrome in Cook's Gardens.'

He gazed over at the park and its war memorials.

'We used to get along fine with the Maoris,' he said. 'We never saw any difference between them and us. My boy, he had a Maori pal when he was a kid, and one day his gran said to him: "How's that little black friend of yours?" And he didn't know who she was talking about. That's how colour-blind we were!'

❁

In Auckland I went to a wedding, a Maori–Pakeha wedding. It's worth emphasising that ever since the two races encountered each other, there has been one constant: sexual attraction. Even the war years were marked by alliances and marriages, from the governor and the household of the Maori king downwards.

The wedding was a smart affair. There were a Maori bishop and a knight on the bride's side, and the groom, a middle-class Pakeha, had friends from the art world and advertising. Actresses turned up at the church in racy convertibles; I even glimpsed a top hat or two. The reception was held in rooms at Cheltenham Beach, soft, buttery lighting inside and, outside, the Hauraki Gulf with its necklace of islands and mountains. Just as the champagne corks began popping, a cruise liner emerged from behind the nearest headland, as if part of the general ebullience, and sailed past, filling the windows.

Then the speeches began. After the first, from the bride's side, five or six middle-aged Maori women, dressed in purple and wearing the sort of hats that aunts wear to weddings, were suddenly on their feet in different parts of the room, singing a song, a *waiata*, their hands moving in time. The Pakehas' eyes gleamed: the Maoris were being marvellous!

This is what Maori do, have always done: the women sing after a speech. There is something Attic about Polynesian culture: following a significant action or address, a chorus springs up and comments in song. There is nothing portentous or self-conscious about the performance. On the contrary, it is charmingly perfunctory and usually ends in laughter. Later, I asked one of the women what that first song had said.

'Oh, I don't know what we sang ... I don't remember,' she said.

But a typical wedding *waiata* might praise the speaker or marriage or life in general:

> *Love is not only*
> *a thing of today—*
> *from our ancestors*
> *it has been passed to us, to us!*

Further speeches from both sides followed. One of the speakers, a tall Maori of about forty, with a brilliant, slightly condescending smile, broke into English as he finished: 'For the benefit of our Pakeha guests, I have just greeted this house, those who have lived here before and who are now dead. And I acknowledge that body of water, the Waitemata, and I greet the mountain behind us, Rangitato ...'

This is something that Maori also do, the *mihi*, the tribute to the house, the dead, the landscape. It certainly provided a sharp contrast to the speaker before him, a young Pakeha friend of the groom's. This man's speech went as follows: 'Er, good on ya, mate. You've got yourself a pretty good sheila there. Aw ... I'm no good at this. But, anyway, you know, er ... love ya both [gives the thumbs-up]. Yeah, nice one!'

The speeches continued. A surprising number of the groom's friends wanted to put in a word, but it seemed they had nothing to say. They stumbled for the most part towards the facetious, a sort of boastful inarticulacy. Why, I wondered, did the white New Zealanders, well educated and well travelled, want to prove that they had no store of words to draw on?

It is often said that a sense of inferiority vis-à-vis the Pakeha has fuelled Maori grievances. But so has its opposite—the hauteur of a people who have lived in a country for a thousand years and can overlay every part of the landscape with names in their genealogy; a people who can address mountains. The first time I ever set foot in a Maori household (I was twenty-one, visiting a student friend out in the country), I mentioned a sheer table-topped mountain we had passed a few miles back.

'Does it ever get snow on the summit?' I asked.

'Not often,' my friend's mother said. 'And when it does, the people around here say, "Look, Rangitawaea has put on his cloak."'

I must have looked blank. 'Rangitawaea?'

'Oh, his great-great-great-grandfather,' she said, nodding towards her son.

This seemed to me impossibly grand, a five-thousand-foot mountain becoming, under certain dispositions, one of your fore-fathers, and I assumed that I had stumbled on an unusual shard of family pride embedded in that remote and sandy corner of the country. But most Maori know their past and their surroundings in this way. When I looked out the window from the wedding party across to Rangitato, the low symmetrical volcano beloved of Auckland's tourist brochures, for a moment it looked more solemn and grave than it ever had on the postcards.

On the morning after the wedding I went to the district court in south Auckland, a suburban sprawl of about half a million people, predominantly Maori and Polynesians living in state housing. In the rest of the country, south Auckland is a byword for wickedness and squalor. I had been there before, late one night, riding in the back of a police car cruising the streets of Otara and Otahuhu. Two hours passed before the police radio crackled into life: 'Male Maori teenager wearing Bugs Bunny T-shirt being pursued: has assaulted complainant at Mobil service station and stolen his leather jacket.' That was the sole outrage against law and order committed in south Auckland on a hot Friday night in midsummer.

In the courthouse, I watched the weekend harvest coming in. The nation's coat of arms hung on the wall: a cloaked Maori and a white maiden with a marked resemblance to Britannia gazed at each other across emblems of toil and prosperity—fleeces, anchors and so forth. Below this image sat their modern equivalents: a stout woman, in judge's robes, looking impassively at the stream of young brown faces in the dock.

Their crimes are mundane. X has stolen a packet of chicken breasts from Pak N' Save. Y has kicked over a motorbike parked in Otahuhu's main street. Z has stolen a car from a dealer's yard (his explanation: 'I wanted a car'). The New Zealand police force was established in the land wars in the 1860s as the Armed Constabulary, and its main function was to catch Maori. Looking around Otahuhu District Court today, it seemed it still was.

Yet something was wrong. For a start there was a surprising number of no-shows.

'Call Samson Kerepa.' A pause ...

'No appearance, Ma'am.'

'Charles Putai?'

'No appearance, Ma'am.'

'Ricky Ngatai?'

'No appearance, Ma'am.'

'Aotolo Patolo?'

'No appearance, Ma'am.'

'Jason Bolter?'

'No appearance, Ma'am.'

Even those who have turned up do not seem to be fully present. Some stare rigidly into space; others wave and grin at friends in the gallery. One young man of about twenty with a dark, vulpine face is in a peculiar state which I cannot quite read. He is gazing round from the dock like someone who has just joined a party, but he is also hyperventilating—sucking in air through his teeth and breathing out fast, with a sound like 'faarrrck'.

'I *beg* your pardon!' says the judge.

'Yeah, yeah,' he says, as if to say, if that's what you want.

Trembling on the brink of revelation here is the belief that has penetrated Maoridom, right down to these jobless teenagers—that all of this, from the coat of arms to the majestic operation of the law, is a con-trick. The words hang unsaid in the air: 'OK. I pinched a packet of chicken breasts, or maybe a Ford Fiesta. But you stole our *country*.'

❋

I left Auckland and drove through the Waikato, the heartland, the centre of New Zealand's huge dairy industry. I must have been on this road thirty or forty times in my life, but today, in the light of what I now know happened here, it had taken on a different appearance. This is the place where the worst aggression and confiscations took place, acts for which the Queen herself has apologised—perhaps the first time in a thousand years of English monarchy that a sovereign has signed a document that refers to 'the crimes of the Crown'.

Property known to be stolen looks different from that which has been lawfully acquired. The handsome farmhouses, the endless green paddocks stocked with black-and-white cows are outwardly the same, but they have also now been translated to the uneasy region between right and wrong. They are, in police parlance, 'the proceeds of a robbery'.

The value of these proceeds is still being debated. It was a strange experience to sit in the office of the minister of justice in Wellington and ask what he thought of the main front-page story in the evening paper. This outlined compensation claims by local Maori for the greater part of the capital city itself. Eighty per cent of the suburban areas, where most of the city's 400 000 people live and many important sites in the centre, had, it was said, been wrongfully acquired.

The minister became testy. 'People get excited,' he said, frowning at the phenomenon of public emotion. 'But these claims will be dealt with in the normal way. There's nothing unusual about this at all.'

There did seem to be something unusual to me. Here we were, in the heart of a modern law-based state—beyond the minister's windows rose the pillars of parliament; the Supreme Court was over the way, the US embassy down the road, the Dominion Museum, the stadiums and schools around the capital—and all of it, every stone, stood on shaky ground.

I was driving to Gisborne, to see the replica of Captain Cook's barque, the *Endeavour*, which was circumnavigating the country. In Auckland and the Bay of Islands thousands of people had lined the wharves eager to pay twelve dollars for a tour of the ship, but now a controversy had blown up. Gisborne is a town of about thirty thousand people, half of them Maori. The more radical among them were demanding that the vessel leave the country. It was not welcome, they said. Attempts might be made to sink it. The crew would not be safe if it came ashore.

The grounds of the Maori argument were predictable: Cook was not, in their eyes, the disinterested, stargazing navigator fondly memorialised by whites, but the first robber-colonialist. As soon as he struck land, where Gisborne now stands, he started shooting Maori—a fact overlooked in commemorations of this moment.

'We're sick of you Pakeha jumping for joy every time Cook's name is mentioned,' one activist was quoted as saying in a newspaper.

When I reached Gisborne at about noon, the *Endeavour* had not yet arrived, so I went to the Maori settlement below Kaiti Hill. There I had a friend I had met in Auckland, an economist named Nicky Searancke who had spent years researching her tribe's land and fishing claims and who was about to go to Oxford to do a doctorate. She explained that the situation had grown more complicated. A dispute had broken out between Maori who wanted to welcome the ship and those violently against it. A compromise had been reached. The crew would be welcomed on the *marae*— the traditional Maori meeting place—at Kaiti, but at the same time would be confronted with the Maori perception or memory of Cook's landing.

The *Endeavour* was due to dock at about 1.30 p.m.; while we were waiting, Nicky showed me around the *marae* and led me into the meeting house itself. There are about a thousand of these *wharenui*—'great houses'—scattered across the North Island, some little more than bare halls standing in a paddock, but others immense: carved or darkly painted cathedrals of Maori life. The one at Kaiti is the largest and one of the most famous in the country. Inside, out of the midday glare, there was a meditative gloom. Nicky pointed out the main features, the carved ancestral figures lining the walls, intersected with flax panels woven in a kind of calligraphy that recorded the lives of certain local women and families; the rafters were painted to signify important Maori constellations. We were in a room of words and stars, and, most importantly, of ancestors.

It would be hard to overstate the importance of genealogy in Maori society. The more recent ancestors were gathered in rather reduced circumstances, in oval-framed sepia photographs clustered on the end wall. But the further back they receded, the greater and more glowering the carved figures along the side walls became. This geometry of the past is almost the exact opposite to ours. Our parents and perhaps grandparents may loom over us, but then there is a sharp dwindling into anecdote and anonymity. Maori ancestors, in contrast, grow larger and more important the further back they are, ending up in solid immensities—a range of hills or a constellation of stars. The two geometries never converge, and this is one source of difficulty between the races. Pakeha quite simply do not believe that Maori really care about the past in this way, just as they don't feel responsible for the actions of their own, indistinct forefathers.

Lost among the stars and ancestors, I missed the arrival of the *Endeavour*. This was a pity—I had meant to go to the top of Kaiti Hill and see its sails appear on the horizon, to think of it drifting towards an unknown eighteenth-century coast, or perhaps even succeed in imagining it through Maori eyes—as a great bird that had detached itself from the clouds, or a mobile island manned by goblins. But by the time I reached town, the barque was already on its way up the river, sailing, as it were, past its own consequences— fish factories, car parks, the Millburn cement silo.

There was a big crowd on the wharves, though scarcely a Maori to be seen. The ship docked, and a brief municipal welcome followed. There was a flash of mayoral chain, a town crier in bright blue knee-breeches rang a handbell and shouted 'Oyez', waved his tricorne hat and gave the crew the freedom of the port. Then they were all marched off to the *marae*.

✳

Cook had arrived at almost that exact spot on a Monday afternoon in October 1769. He departed three days later, leaving six or seven Maori dead. He had wanted to load the inhabitants with presents and 'all imaginable kindness' but he could hardly let his crew be attacked or robbed with impunity. The Maori for their part could not allow the newcomers—even if they were goblins—to come ashore and ignore the essential rituals of approach. The result was a strange confusion of uneasy embraces and panicky gunfire.

Two hundred years on, watching those same rituals unfold at the *marae* (and with the memory of the town crier still fresh in mind) it seemed amazing that the two races had ever managed to communicate at all. The twelve thousand miles that once separated them were weirdly compacted in the fifty yards that lay between the sailors off the replica *Endeavour*, held up at the gateway to the *marae*, and their Maori hosts, watching them from in front of the meeting house.

First came the challenge, the *wero*, in which three men chosen for their agility and fearsome appearance advanced towards the gate, uttering hoarse, single cries, their faces contorted. The best description is by Cook himself: 'His gait was singular,' he wrote, 'nor can I compare the manner of his lifting his legs to any thing better than that of a cock sideling to his Antagonist on the Sod.' Then followed a tense business with a green branch and a spear being laid down before the visitors, after which the challengers retreated, with the same gestures and strangely lifted steps, in reverse.

Then came the *karanga*, the call to the visitors to approach, made by an old woman on the porch. This is a call not only from the living to the living, but also between their respective dead. No one I know has ever heard it without the hairs on the back of their neck standing up.

Finally the visitors were ushered forward and seated on one side, and the Maori speeches began. The order of ceremony here, as at the wedding, required that after each speech a song or *waiata* would be sung. But when the second speaker had finished and sat down, a swarm of young men came forward. A frisson went through the crowd.

'It's *Ruaumoko*!' Nicky said in my ear.

'What is *Ruaumoko*?' I asked.

'One of our haka,' she said. 'The big one.' Most people will know the haka, if at all, as the war dance performed by the All Blacks before a rugby international. But that is only fifteen footballers, mostly Pakeha, scattered in a hasty arc over the lush turf of Twickenham or Cardiff Arms Park, performing a manœuvre they've been practising for a week or two in their hotel car parks. A real haka, done by forty or fifty Maori on their home *marae*, as well as being fierce and 'horrid'—the word invariably used by the first European witnesses—is a set of violent and minutely synchronised actions which accompany a chanted poem, perhaps three or four hundred years old, and susceptible to several levels of interpretation, sacred and profane.

Ruaumoko, composed in the eighteenth century, is a classic haka of the East Coast. It invokes the power of the earthquake god— someone never far from one's thoughts in this part of the island. It is performed only on special occasions. As the Maori men advanced, stamping their feet and chanting, the crew of the *Endeavour* looked rather shaken.

'Actually, it's all about sex,' said Nicky. 'Phallic superiority. "We are better men than you. This is our country. Watch how you behave," is what it's saying.' From her tone, I understood that it is both an insult and an honour to have *Ruaumoko* unleashed on you.

It took me some time to find an English text of *Ruaumoko*. It couldn't be translated, I was told; it was not for publication. Eventually I tracked down a translation published in 1943. This turned out to be the sacred—and bowdlerised—version. 'This,' said a prim footnote, 'should satisfy all but deceased Maori elders who held the key to this old masterpiece of the phallic cult.'

> *Hark to the rumble of the earthquake god!*
> *'Tis Ruaumoko who stirs and quakes!*
> *Au! Au! Au e ha! ...*
>
> *It is the rod of Tungawerewere,*
> *The sacred stick given by Tutaua to Uenuku ...*

Cleaving the twin peaks of Hikurangi ...
A gift of the gods! The wonder of men!

I showed the Maori text to a Pakeha scholar of the language. 'Ah,' he said, adjusting his glasses. '*Ruaumoko*! Let me see ... "Over whose hips does the seminal fluid splash?" ... Golly ..."The orgasm like the shudder of the biting dog". Do you know, I really think it might be better to get an elder from the tribe to do this for you ...'

I left it there. I was interested in the words primarily as a contrast with what had happened next on the *marae*, after the haka was finished and it was time for the visitors to reply.

There were various speakers—the Mayor of Gisborne, the captain of the *Endeavour*, a spokesman for the ship's corporate sponsors and so on. Between the second and third of those, something unexpected happened. There was a shuffle of feet and then some of the crew, grinning and elbowing one another, came forward. Some bright spark among them had thought of a riposte. They began to sing:

What shall we do with a drunken sailor?
What shall we do with a drunken sailor?
What shall we do with a drunken sailor,
Early in the morning?

The protocol on a *marae* is strict, and the order of speakers and choice of songs are the subject of endless discussion. That day in Gisborne we were gathered to exorcise a grievance generations old—*Ruaumoko* was a sign of the solemnity of the occasion. And in wandered the Drunken Sailor with his silly grin.

It is easy for Pakeha to make mistakes on a *marae*, especially if they are trying to do things in a Maori way. These solecisms are generally forgiven and, judging from the wintry smiles on the faces of the Maori hosts, 'The Drunken Sailor' would be forgiven, or at least overlooked. Yet I was struck, once again, by the gulf in language and ceremony that yawned between the two races. It is an odd kind of gap: it is not caused by indifference, or contempt or ignorance, although Maori often accuse whites of all three. In the next speech that afternoon, I came closer to understanding its real nature.

The speaker—the corporate spokesman—was nervous, and stumbled over his words: 'Speaking as a New Zealander of, of European distraction,' he said, his voice quavering, 'this afternoon I feel the pain of ... the shocking things ... that happened to your ancestors ...' And in that quaver, I thought I heard the faint, strange, background radiation that hovers through this whole story.

'The fact is,' a lawyer had told me over lunch a week before, 'we *love* the Maoris.' I was startled: this was the sort of thing people used to say thirty years ago but never say today. Not because it is a lie, but because it might be true. And if it *is* true, then it puts us in a worse light than ever. For it is one thing to attack and dispossess a people you dislike or fear—the impenetrable Aborigines, for example, or the Zulu—but quite another to do the same to a race whom you profess to 'love'.

Is it possible even to speak of 'racial love' in the twentieth century? Only with some discomfort, although its opposite, 'racial hatred', makes a sprightly entry into any conversation. Yet in the 1840s it was possible: 'You are the very counterpart of Englishmen,' said Governor Grey to Maori chiefs in 1848. 'In love and mutual trust, the two races will be lost in one.' Most early Pakeha observers concur: the Maori were brave and chivalrous, but also industrious and clever. In the mid-1840s Maori literacy rates were as high as in any country in Europe. In 1842 a missionary wrote: 'Their cry was the same in almost every place we staid at—"Books, books! Give us books, lest we perish!"'

This was the race we entered a treaty with, then attacked and stripped of its heritage.

I was struck by the number of Pakeha, from the minister of justice down, who insisted that they did not feel any guilt for the past. It was like a mantra: 'We don't feel guilt. We won't feel guilt, we mustn't feel guilt.'

That night I slept in a motel a few yards from the beach where Cook and the Maori first encountered each other and I found an image forming briefly in my mind. I saw two figures, a Maori and a Pakeha, locked together in what from one angle was a loving embrace, but from another was a wrestler's grim stalemate. The white's hands covered the Maori's eyes, a Maori hand was thrust across the white's mouth. One was unable to see, the other unable to speak. This ambiguous dream-embrace seemed to sum up much of the past contact between the two races. It has been a long clinch, from which they are only now, with difficulty disengaging.

In Wellington I went to see Doug Graham, the minister of treaty settlements. He is the man in charge of one of the most detested policies towards Maori, the 'billion-dollar cap', a take-it-or-leave-it, full and final settlement for all the wrongs, great and small, that Maori have suffered. A billion dollars, it turns out, is not enough: four days' worth of the Gross National Product cannot erase a century and a half of deep wrong. Oddly enough, among Maori, his standing was higher than that of most white ministers. He is a rare bird among politicians, a Pakeha who has learned his way around a *marae* and can call on rhetoric equal to the occasion. I wanted to see him not so much about compensation but about another issue agitating Maori minds—the second great asset they lost, their own political power, *tino rangatiratanga*.

Nobody today is quite sure what this means. At a gathering of thirty thousand Maori in Rotorua, it seemed to mean picking up litter and taking lost children to the lost children's tent. At the other end, it means wild visions of a separate Maori state—even proposals to disenfranchise all Pakeha, allowing them to stay on, taxed and policed, as guests of Maoridom. Between these extremes are some perfectly sober propositions. Tribal control of expenditure is one—at present, a tribe or *iwi* needs ministerial approval to spend more than two hundred dollars. New constitutional models are being devised, setting up, for example, a separate Maori lower house to propose legislation to a bi-racial upper house. What all the exhortations and plans have in common is a determination for the Maori to regain some control over their lives. New Zealand can no longer remain a little Britain in the south. In some explicit way it must become a Maori nation again.

'We've taken all the power and kept it for a hundred years,' I said to the minister. 'When are you going to give some back?'

'If you mean tribal control of spending—of course, it's absurd they haven't got it. If you mean a national body that can speak for all Maori—excellent. But if you mean an upper house with a power of veto—it's never going to happen.'

'Why call it a power of veto? Why not think of it as a power of approval?'

'We're not even thinking about it.'

'But it's not going to go away, this question. Every Maori I talk to says the same thing. They want their own source of power.'

'It'll never happen.'

I persisted: 'What about the meeting at Hirangi in April? Five thousand Maori chiefs, conservatives, radical separatists. They called it a constitutional convention.'

'Never happen,' the minister said.

A state's first instinct is to preserve itself entire. But there are tricky calculations to be made. Give them too little autonomy, and they will fly off in anger; give them too much, and the game is up.

As it happens, there once was an independent Maori state within white-ruled New Zealand. It was about ten thousand square miles of wild country in the central North Island. Its 'capital' was a place called Te Kuiti—the inverted commas represent the poverty and hopelessness of the people who, defeated and impoverished by Pakeha confiscations, had gathered in Te Kuiti around the Maori king. One of these was a guerrilla leader called Te Kooti. He was not a very successful general—he never won a battle, although he did escape about fifty ambushes and for years led government troops on a ludicrous dance around the country. But he was also a great poet, a prophet and a builder of dozens of *wharenui*, the 'great houses' in which Maori found a redoubt as their old world disappeared under the grass of white farmers.

One evening at sunset, I stopped at Te Kuiti, now a farming town on the main trunk line, and went into the grounds of the first great house he built. An old red van pulled up and the Maori driver watched me with, I thought, some suspicion (over the past few years there have been sporadic arson attacks by Maori and whites on one another's property) but then he drove away. As he left, I saw in the back of the van the same row of little dark heads that I remembered in the rusty old cars of Hastings in the 1960s. While I stood before the locked door, admiring its carved lintel in the dusk, I had a presentiment: that the Maori were going to win their fight to reassert themselves and reshape the country.

I was not sure where this conviction came from: it may have simply been the glimpse of the big family in the old red van. Maori are younger and more fertile than the rest of the population, and as their numbers grow, they will wield more power. On some projections, they will constitute nearly half the population by 2045. As the Maori population climbs, the argument goes, so it will be better represented in the legislature, and the demand for separate chambers—for autonomy—will simply fade away. There have already been a few Maori cabinet ministers; and at present a party dominated by Maori has a powerful but junior role in the coalition government. It has already used its new power in surprising ways: it pushed, for instance, to retain the historic links with Britain, preventing moves to end New Zealand's judicial connection with the Privy Council in London. It is a firm snub to the Pakeha that the Maori should feel that five old men, driving from the House of Lords to Downing Street, should be a better guarantor of their rights than New Zealand's own Court of Appeal.

But Maori power, according to radicals, is not just a matter of counting votes. Some Maori are eager for confrontation on a wider front (witness the assault on the America's Cup, when a Maori student took a hammer to a yachting trophy). One of the most chilling moments of my time in the country was talking to a gently spoken, silver-haired lawyer, Moana Jackson, about Hastings where we had both grown up in the 1960s. He agreed that race relations then were bad.

'What's your definition of good race relations?' I asked.

'When the two races never meet,' he said.

He paused. 'There's no need to be scared,' he said. 'We are not vindictive people. We'll treat you better than you treated us.'

There is undoubtedly a strong tide running in favour of the Maori at the moment, before which the white New Zealanders are strangely acquiescent. But it is full of ambiguous currents, and is driven by goodwill as well as aggression. The old saying—that over time a country assimilates its conquerors—still applies. If violence and death did come, both sides would surely draw back shocked, like swimmers colliding, because many Pakeha want to see the country change, and are drawn to the Maori world for the qualities their own seems to lack. Whites used to boast about a fraction of Maori blood in their veins; now they are learning to speak Maori and proudly recount their visits to a *marae*. Even the most reactionary white will stop in his diatribe and tell you how well he personally gets on with Maori. Not getting on with the Maori suggests you are uptight, stiff, unnatural, and the Maori are seen as the opposite of all that. They are thought to be at home with themselves, and at home in the country.

A friend of mine, an actor called Bruno Lawrence, died not long ago. He was not buried in the local cemetery; the Maori allowed him to be buried in theirs. This was an unheard-of distinction, whispered in tones of awed envy. Bruno Lawrence to lie among the Maori dead! How much better could you get on with Maori than that?

Semi-darkness, an hour before sunrise. A crowd of people, some shivering, are standing in a belt of pine trees. A scythe of rain cuts out the hill across the fields, and a single dark shadow moves along the road towards us and gradually takes shape as a second crowd. The two crowds converge, pause, then come through the gate towards us, one man calling, the others giving the refrain. This is

the opening of a new *marae*, on the wild east coast of the
Coromandel Peninsula.

Perhaps a thousand people have gathered here this morning;
pinpricks of headlights are still coming down the hill towards the
coast. As the procession reaches the new meeting house, the crowd
sheltering under the pines comes forward to watch the proceed-
ings, and I am surprised at how many Pakeha are among them. The
ritual lifting of the *tapu* commences; the house is circled, then ministers lead the way inside, with hundreds pressing in after them,
while hundreds more stand outside listening in the rain to the
prayers, haka, speeches and *waiata* that follow in the usual order.
Most of the Pakeha have no idea what is being said or sung. A
thousand people will soon eat breakfast—cereals, sausage rolls,
club sandwiches, chops, pineapple, melon—in a huge marquee
which billows upwards and outwards in the wind.

Race relations in this area are not especially good. Over the hill
in the town of Coromandel there are two pubs: 'Maoris in the
bottom pub, rednecks in the top pub' was the formula I was given.
Here in the marquee that seems hard to believe. It is now broad
daylight, and a red ensign raps in the wind above the meeting
house, where speeches and singing are starting again. The cooks
are coming outside for a smoke; the teenagers are heading down to
the beach. The opening will last three days, and hundreds of
people will come and go as they please during that time. As we
leave the tent and make our way back to the paddock where the
cars are parked, another question occurs to me. What would be an
equivalent event in my own community? Where would you find
this easy exchange among complete strangers, the palpable sense
of feeling at home in a place you have never seen before? It seems
absurd, but the only thing that comes to mind is a radio talk show.
On Friday evenings there is a nationwide phone-in on a single subject: rugby. Rugby and any topic pertaining thereto. When did
screw-in studs replace nail-on studs? Are the Waikato Chiefs
swinging the ball out wide enough? Why aren't any Super Twelve
games being played in Timaru? Should the national anthem be
played in provincial games against Northern Transvaal?

The switchboard is always lit up. The voices pour in, animated, happy to be together on safe ground. I'm not all that interested in rugby but in the stark farmhouse where I'm staying I tune in too because I like the show's atmosphere of community.

Yet there is something unreal and diminished about the voices coming through the night. This is not really the community, but an escape from it. There is something over-eager and hopeful, something almost childish about them. Something is missing in the Pakeha community: when today's Maori offer visionary models of society, white New Zealanders can no longer point confidently to a superior model. The civic imagery of modern New Zealand is almost comic: here and there across the landscape rise gimcrack images, dopy colossi. At Te Kuiti, opposite the ancient carved meeting house, a huge concrete shearer fleeces a huge concrete sheep. Near the volcanic cone of Mount Ruapehu stands a giant fibreglass vegetable (THE WORLD'S LARGEST CARROT!). Elsewhere you can see a massive cow, a lobster, a salmon and an apple; there is even a four-storey-high kiwi fruit.

By contrast, the new Maori *marae*, with its red gable and figurehead, seems solid, four-square and mature. It is a strange twist in the tale, I think, as we go through the shelter belt of pines, that to such a place as this—in one sense a redoubt against the victorious invaders—so many Pakeha should now be making their way, if only to see what, in winning, they have lost.

1997

————————————⬢————————————

LES MURRAY

On Public Splendour

MORE OF OUR COMMUNITIES need splendour. Public human-made splendour, to lift their morale and give them heart, before a cultural movement of deferring to nature becomes oppressive. In the Old World, outcrops of sublime human achievement are common even in small towns and villages, a glorious medieval church here, a chateau or a worldfamous garden there. These never seem to abash the modern inhabitants, or leave them feeling dwarfed. Here in Australia, apart from one case where a sublime natural site is matched by a world-class building, the dimensions of grandeur and the marvellous are mostly delegated to nature, or hidden away, in the heroic hearts of an outback farming family, say, or a cancer victim, in the biographies of people such as Weary Dunlop or Sister Kenny, locked up like poetry in a book or music between performances. We shy from public monuments now, feeling they will be embarrassing, or that whatever they celebrate will be set upon by some disaffected lobby. We are afraid of architecture itself, for fear that it will be environmentally destructive, stripping away more bushland or bulldozing earlier buildings that were more charming, more humanly proportioned. The value of wilderness suggests, at its extreme, that no faith should be placed on human creation; our dominance of nature is now by implication so complete that we must deny the fact and hide from it. The industrial revolution's belief that we are somehow beyond nature, with a right and duty to reshape it, has been ironically inverted in our time so that we are encouraged to see ourselves as nature's inferiors, a threat to her life and forever incapable of matching her casual marvels. This ideology, promoted to inhibit enterprise, easily shades into a snobbery that allows only the coolest minor creativity in the mainstream, and permits achievement mainly among groups excused from criticism, such as folk artists and indigenes. I wonder: would our culture now allow Sydney Opera House to be started, if it didn't already exist?

Some of our communities—Hobart, Alice Springs, Katoomba, the older parts of Sydney—have natural splendour as part of their very sites, along with interest and charm that may equally be human-created. Lots more have the interest and charm without the natural grandeur: I'm thinking of Beechworth and Fremantle, Launceston and the Adelaide Hills, Newcastle—yes, Newcastle, mostly certainly—and Toowoomba and New Norcia and Broome; the list could go on. Scores of communities live within a wider natural splendour, perhaps mixed with the vast low patternings of agriculture, which may be harder to bring into any single focus. Where is the æsthetic high point of the Kimberley, or the Atherton Tableland? There's none: their grandeur is cumulative and dispersed, inherent in them everywhere. Nature's often like that, and so is the created environment up to a certain point of quality. They're unamenable to the faintly touristy requirements of summation or focus. Human-made splendour, though, can be and must be strongly focused. If it's outdoors at all, it commonly inheres in just one building or a smallish ensemble of them. It is rarely sustained over more than the area of a small city, Venice, say, or the old Moroccan city of Fes. Larger occurrences of it seem to exist only when we see them from a distance great enough to pull them into unity. Manhattan is an utter marvel when seen from the George Washington Bridge, the whole great misty towering island, but down in those streets the wonder vanishes, or tightens into manageable small points such as the top of the Chrysler building or a shop window blazing with cut diamonds. Nothing within the city pulls it into a more powerful shape than the distant view had lent to it. That used to be true of Sydney, too, perhaps less clearly, because the harbour was pervasively marvellous even when not seen whole. The central basin of the harbour, round the bridge and the quay, was a very lovely stage, and people were delighted to play parts of their lives on it—but when the great building of the century made its slow entrance and finally centred the whole theatre on itself, that was when Sydney dared to stop thinking of itself as far-flung and provincial and began to be accepted, and to accept itself, as a world city. Something essential to its self respect had been consummated, and even the belated poppy-felling of public works minister Davis Hughes hadn't managed to prevent it.

All of these thoughts came out of a conversation the other day with a councillor on one of the shires up here. They asked what their municipality needed, and I said immediately: 'Something wonderful: commission something utterly wonderful!' Of course, I know the risk of getting something grandiose and second rate. Canberra is full of such sad failed attempts, below the sublime blue rim of the Brindabella ranges, which are the standard the city has still to match. After we talked, I started thinking about the three qualities which the wonderful thing created in any community, and best of all by that community, would need to have. First might be fixity, being out there unabashedly on view to affect people's spirits at any time, not stored away for exhibit only on arty or festive occasions when people may be admiring mainly themselves. Then might come protection, from vandalism and other dark sides of equality. The essential one, though, which all true grandeur has, would be the quality of being unquestionable. As, of course, nature always is.

1996

DAVID MARR

Windows '97

EIGHTEEN MONTHS AGO, at the back of Surry Hills, a failing pub on roaring Cleveland Street punched two plate glass windows into its walls, and its empty bars were packed with people again. 'It was instantaneous,' says Con Bousgas, the publican. 'I'm absolutely ecstatic.'

Plate glass in pub walls—tough, expensive, Pilkington laminated glass—is an icon of Sydney now. It's not of the order of yellow stone and Marseilles tiles, ferries and avenues of figs, but it's an illuminating, transparent image of this metropolis of seeing and being seen.

Privacy has made way for display. The closed box of the pub has opened its walls and city streets look a little different now. This could be written off, I suppose, as a boring shift in drinking habits: a disturbance registering no more than a couple of points on the Richter scale of fashion, but what's at work here is more peculiar than that. And it's not really—or not only—about pubs. We're falling in love with our streets. Perhaps 'love' is extravagant, a word tossed round too easily at the beginning of a Sydney summer. But there is in the air a new affection for the streets of this city—not as they might be, tidied up by a civilised urban designer, but more or less as they are: crowded, daggy and familiar.

Patrick White once claimed that living in the country meant, for him, death by bush ballads. 'Give me the pavement and the crowd.'

That's exactly what Con Bousgas has given the drinkers at the Bar Cleveland.

For nine years he watched his business drift away. Age and fags and booze cut a swathe through the pensioners. The Police Academy around the corner closed. Breath tests gave Bousgas, more or less, a parish only walking distance across. He thought a lick of paint and smart furniture might bring in young locals but a designer called Emile Carlsson of Blue Dog persuaded him to go further: to open the pub to the street. 'It's gutsy and in your face,' says Carlsson. 'We're not hiding anything from the public: we're not going to be secretive; there is no stigma any more in drinking. This will have an honest, open, atmosphere. It's like flashing: hey man, here it all is.'

On each side of the window are Sydney's great commodity— people. 'People sell people. We could have the best beer in Sydney but you're not going to come in if there are no people. We're all on show: we're looking at them and they're looking at us. We enjoy displaying our pleasure ... I love glass. I just love showing off everything.'

When I set out to track this obsession of mine about plate glass and pubs, I believed the law had once forbidden the sale of booze anywhere that drinking could be seen by minors and passers-by— hence frosted glass, windows painted out with ads of blokes in cricket whites, brown bottle glass, mirror glass, drawn curtains, lowered blinds, planter boxes, pebblecrete and bricks. I hunted for temperance debates on the point, hoping for old-fashioned rhetoric about Sydney and vice but I drew a blank. The Rev. Gar Dillon and I discussed Jesus Christ for a time and he recommended the latest editorial in *Tempo*, the paper he edits for the movement, entitled: 'Look Out Ladies, Liquor Lords Lurking.' At the Liquor Administration Board, there was much the same sense that something must have forced us for all those years to put drinking out of sight, but the walking encyclopædias of the bench conferred and reached the verdict that New South Wales had never had such a law. Only the taboos of the trade turned pubs into closed boxes. This was explained to me by Bill Maloney, who has been in pubs for a million years and now has a perch at the Australian Hoteliers Association. 'No rules or regulations. It was just the way it grew. But the dark days are over now—over with a vengeance in the last six months.'

Old-timers advance a single explanation that doesn't convince: 'Bars were closed shops, a man's world. Blokes didn't want their wives seeing them at the bar and pulling them out.' Perhaps. But there were more windows in pubs once. Many were taken out or boarded up in the fifties and sixties. Why? 'Fear of vandalism,' said the heritage consultant Meredith Walker. She brought into the argument the fact that the breweries owned almost all the pubs once and in those days employed what the trade called 'hotel architects' who set the style of city pubs: 'A couple of doors and a few small windows you couldn't really see through.' It was fashion, of a kind, to drink in the dark.

The Brooklyn in George Street takes the honour for being the first Sydney bar to face the world through sheets of clear glass. The Brooklyn was an old pub in one corner of a fine Edwardian building Harry Seidler wanted to demolish to give Sydney an uninterrupted view of his new Grosvenor tower. Permission was refused. The pub took over the building and opened it to the street in 1991. Customers poured in. The Brooklyn became the pub of the futures traders—that was an omen.

Glass went into the Burdekin in Oxford Street, the Four in Hand in Paddington. When the restaurateur Damien Pignolet and his business partner Ron White bought the Woollahra Hotel, they called in Alex Tzannes whose reputation then rested, for the most part, on a number of exquisite and very sophisticated houses. 'I told them I knew nothing about hotels and they said they knew nothing about hotels, but they'd bought one and wanted me to work on it,' Tzannes says. For the team of Pignolet and White, Tzannes has now worked on the Woollahra, the Sackville in Rozelle and the Clock in Surry Hills. Big windows are part of them all.

What began in the city soon spread to the suburbs. When the owners of the Commodore on Blues Point wanted to rebuild, they called in Kevin Snell who, lately, has been fitting out Armani stores. Snell knows pubs. When he was a kid his parents ran the Imperial, a student pub in Armidale. He learnt then that pubs are meeting places: 'That is the key to all this.' And the view to the street is part of what makes a pub a meeting place. 'Meeting means display. Preening requires to be seen.' Beaches have always been the place for that in Australia, but Snell says we're now willing to admit that the street is a place for promenading too, for flirting and being seen. So pubs need an open view to and from the footpath. This, Snell argues, is an example of a new, more confident way we have of 'meshing' with our own city, a sense of this being where we're staying. 'So we might as well fix it up.'

At heart, Tzannes and Snell are, I suspect, more interested in the street than the pub. 'When you open a window onto a street, suddenly there is a sense of ownership, of responsibility towards the street,' says Tzannes. At Woollahra, the old pub's only civic gesture was a few planter boxes along the wall. Tzannes restored openings bricked up over the last couple of decades and now the pub has become part of the street. 'That's urban and positive. It gives the street a civic dimension. It's not just a place to drive a car. It's a new way of thinking about ourselves and our city, a new sense of what we can do about the city we love.'

What Tzannes calls 'the battle of the last decade' has been to bring civic life back to building projects and to the streets. Pubs are only a small part of this. Big new shopping centres no longer entrap their customers in an interior retail world because shoppers want glimpses through glass of real streets—and the sky—as they wander round those mega-marts. And outside, cars are being allowed back into those dying, car-free precincts in towns and suburbs across Australia. We discover we like traffic in streets. Snell talks passionately about streets and claims that just as we've come to value the 'vernacular' of the bush verandah, so we are confidently coming to accept the vernacular of the street. We don't want to hide the street or build imitation European spaces. 'We're settling down to the idea that it's all right.'

Look around this city now and everywhere you will see people enjoying the street—on the move or behind glass, sitting at an open window or on the footpath. Once we thought Sydney's weather was all wrong for this—too hot, too bright, too windy. Not any more. We have a beer in front of us, or a cup of coffee or something made of smashed bananas and yoghurt. Perhaps we're watching, half-hidden behind a newspaper. There is no view but gutters and awnings and cars and people—but above all people.

The Bar Cleveland looks into a patch of urban Australia that tests this new affection to the limit. Signs are fading. The Golden Pide, shorn of its awning, faces the Tandoori Rasoi across the road. A big gum is lifting the footpath. Mr Stinky's second-hand clothes saloon stands beside an ugly chain pharmacy almost hidden by its own advertising. One sign, in letters metres high, reminds drinkers of the benefits of 'Strong Powerful Panadeine'. Recently threaded through the mad tangle of wires overhead is the Optus intestine bringing cable to Surry Hills.

It's ugly but it's us. Traffic—people, trucks and cars—pours south down Bourke, east–west along Cleveland. At night, all this becomes a pattern of light and dark, of figures moving through the glare of street lights, and pulse of energy that keeps the adrenalin in the bar pumping. The noise, says the designer Carlsson, is part of the package. Inside, the drinkers are on show—and they know they are on show through those big, new sheets of Pilkington glass.

In every suburb—north of Hornsby, south of Sylvania and out to the mountains—the pubs have opened themselves out, except in the heartland of the city, along Oxford Street where drinkers in gay pubs have not wanted to be on show to the street. But the power of plate glass is now being felt here, too: plate glass as a measure, I suppose, of confidence. The Albury put in its glass a little while ago and after Mardi Gras, when chic new furniture arrives, the Oxford will peel off the one-way film from the big windows that have always been there, blind to Taylor Square.

Perhaps plate glass will all turn out to be fashion, another example of Sydney's sheer appetite for change, and we'll wake up one day to see brickies at work again walling up the pubs. I don't think so.

What's going on here seems to have the confident good humour of things that last.

1996

———————— ✹ ————————

INGA CLENDINNEN

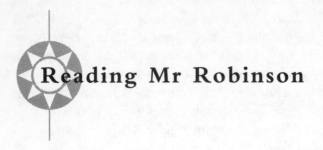

Reading Mr Robinson

I GREW UP IN A ONCE-UPON-A-TIME land when milk and loaves appeared at the door to the jingle of bells and the clopping of hooves, when housewives were wistful Cinderellas in sacking aprons and hair permanently rollered for the ball, when men wore hats, and lifted them to the funerals of strangers passing in the street. That time—the forties, the early fifties—has been mythologised into a Camelot of Anglo-Celtic virtue, or a dark age of tribalism and British cooking. In my recollection, of course, it was neither, but simply the way things were. It is disconcerting to find one's private past, one's little collection of ordinary memories, become a matter of ideological dispute, and to discover, after peaceful decades spent reading historical documents, that you have become a historical document yourself.

The elevation is the more disconcerting because I know almost nothing of the history of which I have now become an artefact, having abandoned Australian History in my heart (the formalities took a little longer) in the fifth grade of primary school. To that point 'Australian History' had comprised a doleful catalogue of self-styled 'explorers' who wandered in what large Mrs O'Loughlin used to call 'dretful desarts', glumly littering names about (Mount Disappointment, Mount Despair, Mount Hopeless) until, thankfully, they 'perished'. (I am happy to report that even in those benighted days and from those benighted texts I noticed that during their wanderings they would occasionally totter past people called Aborigines, and I would think 'at least somebody knows how to manage out there'.) I would look at the wavery little tracks the feckless fellows had left on the school-reader map, and know I wanted nothing to do with them, or any who came after them. That avoidance has been sustained over thirty years as a professional historian living and working in this country. I know the Australia of the past as I know Chekhov's or Tolstoy's or Nabokov's Russia: from novels. Like my Russia, my 'Australia' floats somewhere beyond historical time and geographical actuality: it is a bleached valley, a cluster of tall rooms embraced by a verandah; a suburb; a style, a set of possibilities.

Or so it was. Recently, for no clear reason—the stirring times, perhaps, or fallen victim to that confusion of narcissism and nostalgia which tends to afflict people at the historical document stage—I have wanted to learn more. Another round of novels? Biographies, perhaps? No: I wanted more direct access. I would do what historians always do; I would go to the sources. Or, rather, to one source: this was to be an essay, a Sunday stroll, not a major expedition with elephants and guns. And I wanted at least the illusion of serendipity: I wanted my source somehow to come to me, to appear, like a note in a bottle, a message from another time magically tossed to land at my feet.

And so it happened. Pursuing a quite different matter, I came upon a couple of paragraphs written by a Mr G. A. Robinson. I already knew something of Robinson: that he had been Protector of the Aborigines in Tasmania in the early days, that he had been somehow mixed up with Truganini, that he had brought her to Victoria. That he affected a strange cap, like a pastry-cook gone to sea. And that he was a foolish and arrogant man, or was I mixing him up with someone else? I asked an Australianist who was consulting me as a historical document at the time if he had anything of Robinson's writings. He had: his journal of a six-month-long trip made in the winter of 1841 from Melbourne to Portland and back, with a swing through the Grampians on the home leg. In

1839, after Tasmania, Robinson had been appointed Chief Protector of the Aborigines for Port Phillip District. He was to make over twenty such expeditions, keeping journals throughout. The one my friend handed to me had been edited by a man called Gary Presland, and published by the Victorian Archaeological Survey. Did I want more? Did I want a full bibliography?

I did not. I had my note-in-a-bottle. I would uncork the bottle, and release the Mr Robinson held inside. I would get to know him, and he would be my guide. Of course there were other Mr Robinsons: in the memories of those who had known him; lurking in libraries in the pages of novels and histories. There were the Mr Robinsons of all those other journals; men of the same name and much the same body, but differently freighted by experience and expectation. It was the Mr Robinson revealed between 20 March and 15 August 1841 that I was after.

For an historian it is luxurious indulgence to settle to a single, wilfully circumscribed text. Private journals can be expansive, unbuttoned affairs, and if regularly kept hold at least the promise of revealing not only 'character', but the natural movement of the writer's mind. A couple of hours reading, and I knew I was in luck. Mr Robinson was a most devoted journal-keeper. Almost every night, whatever the hardships of the day, and after he has talked with any 'sable friends' about, he secludes himself to write. The white men travelling with him are convicts or servants: he brooks no intimacy with them; he has his journal for company. The tone slides easily from the practical to something very like the conjugal. He might begin with the weather, and a sharp, analytic account of terrain traversed. There might be housekeeping to do: out-goings of potatoes, blankets, shirts; incomings of natives contacted. He jots down words to add to his lists, of places seen and persons met with, of plants, animals, tools (he dreams of completeness). He relaxes, remembering beguiling things—a flight of blue parrots, a genial dog, geese floating thick as waterlilies on a reedy lake. (He notices animals, and is tender towards them.) And he rehearses the events of the day: confides conversations and encounters, shapes them into narrative, sets them down. His journal will serve as a source for official reports, but it is very much more than that: it is a reviewing, a refreshment, a re-creation of his most private self. He and his journal, in whatever frail light, on those wintry nights, in those comfortless camps.

And we, you and I, reading over his shoulder. Against the odds, the Chief Protector is a natural writer. Occasionally he strikes a conventional attitude, or a too-laconic note stares mutely, but typically he is as direct and crisp as his weather reports: 'Severe frost during the night, ice this morning near thick as a dollar. 10, fine sunny day, tranquil light air.' He wastes little ink on men's appearances (it is character he cares about) but he can toss off the memorable vignette, as of his deplorable convict servant Myatt, negligently negotiating 'the van' through a pass, 'chanting over a doleful ditty peculiar to his class ... his hat over his eyes as he generally wore it ... occasionally run[ning] against stumps and then damning the horses for not taking care'. Arrived at Portland town, Robinson is dined, with metropolitan formality, by Commissioner Tyers. The rest of the company is 'a Mr Primrose, who fills a plurality of offices here as clerk to the bench, sub-collector of customs, and post master. He wears mustaches and rings on each finger, is tall with a morose countenance', and there stands Mr Primrose the rusticated dandy, waiting for Chekhov. The drawings speckling the text are equally vivid: they are as awkward, serious and expressive as a child's. Every cross-hatch of a net, every rail of a fence, is firmly inked in. A girl peacocking in a European frock vibrates with delight; a dancer hooded with grass explodes above spindly legs.

He quickly proves his worth as a guide. He links me back to places long known, but known in the flat, two-dimensional way of places called into being by one's arrival and dissipating on departure: places without a past. On a still autumn day near Port Campbell I watch my young sons dive for sea treasure. Crusts of blue pottery glint in their hands. More sea treasure: in the April of 1841 'a large quantity of wax candles' drifts ashore on a nearby beach. Local blacks tie the candles in their hair; local whites trade in them. (The price rockets: Mr Robinson is gratified to be given 'three or four'.) For years I have felt a subliminal twitch of irritation when I cross a bridge on the way to the beach house. 'Merrijig Creek', it says, sweetly. Mr Robinson tells me 'Merrijig' means 'good' or 'fine' in the local tongue ('They asked me if I was pleased, saying Merrigic Elengermat, Merrigic Warr Nerbul, of course I say merrigic, and they were pleased'), and now I hear a soft babble of happy voices when I pass. Trivial things, but they render time transparent. A small new fact, and a landscape dulled by familiarity is suddenly sharp and clear; the details quietly disaggregate, as quietly rearrange themselves; perspectives steady—and open like flowers. The past is present again: contingent, heavy with promise.

Or with shame. Robinson encounters a wandering family: a man, his wife, an infant, two very young girls. They are Wol-lore-ret, or what is left of them; the tribe, they say, is 'plenty all gone' ('plenty shoot him white man'). Robinson suspects that the little family is allowed to survive because the girls are kept at the 'nefarious disposal of white men'. His suspicions are confirmed when he hears them saying over their few words of English: 'Well done fuckumoll, go it fuckmoll, good night fuckmoll'. 'Wol-lore-rer'. A flinch of recognition: I know a place called Willaura. I used to spend school holidays in that territory. There were no people around then; just the scatter of big sheds and the little weatherboard house, with the Harbells somewhere across the railroad track and over the rise. No-one else. Just sheep, a few crows, the usual rabbits. Now there will always be people there: a man, his wife, an infant, and two little girls telling over the white man's litany: 'Well done fuckumoll. Go it fuckmoll. Good night fuckmoll.' And behind them, others. How many others?

Mr Robinson is a fine guide, to things unknown, or unacknowledged. He is also, it must be admitted, a rather foolish man. He lacks political sense, inflaming resentment in men on whom he must depend; he bullies and badgers subordinates, and bores and irritates superiors. Easily flattered, he is even more easily offended. He is impatient: he is always 'going on ahead' and getting lost, and when he does he blames someone else. He is humourless, priggish, jealous, and vain.

He is also brave, independent, and tough. He is making this journey, like most of his journeys, by choice. As Chief Protector he could have left the 'fieldwork'—the noting of past traces and present signs of Aboriginal presence, the listing of Aboriginal names of persons and places, the 'protection' of Aboriginal survivors—to his four assistants in the field, who would have much preferred him to stay at home. But off he jogs in his fifty-first year, a portly, high-coloured person (he rides with a leaf between his lips to protect them from sunburn), ranging twenty and more miles a day with the van dawdling along somewhere behind, subsisting largely on flour and tea and mutton—when he can get it, when Myatt hasn't lent the tinder box to a crony or forgotten to make the damper; when he hasn't got himself lost and spent the night huddled under a tree. Physically tough, his moral toughness is almost excessive: he advances on homesteads where he knows he will be less than welcome, where he must depend on the settler's hospitality; we tremble; in he stalks, stiff-necked, looking for trouble.

These are desperate times. Violence among blacks is increasing, between and within tribes, even within families, but it is violence between blacks and whites that he dreads. Rumours flicker ahead like marsh-fire: they must be tracked down and scotched, or many blacks might die. He can seem absurdly partisan. Whatever the fall of the evidence, he favours the natives. If sheep are missing, wild dogs did it, or the shepherds let them stray, or exchanged them for access to a black woman. A shepherd speared through the walls of his hut as he sleeps must have provoked the attack. He believes such men, 'the sweepings of NSW and VDL [Van Diemen's Land]', to be capable of anything, and if their gentlemen employers might have little stomach for casual killings, they know the value of sheep hauled stiff and seasick from the bowels of ships, or walked overland from Sydney. They are too valuable to fetch up filling a native's shrunken belly. It is difficult to identify the shadows fleeing from the sheepfolds, difficult to identify them among the stringy figures down at the river camp. Best be rid of the lot: clear them off and keep them off, and if you have to use a few bullets to do it—well, so be it. Robinson can see, in the silence of deserted habitations, in the faces of the frightened survivors, how close the settlers are to success. The signs are everywhere. At one of the few stations where blacks are still tolerated, a large swivel gun stands mounted at the homestead. Travelling through a specially tense region he makes only one entry for the day, but that is enough: 'All the shepherds I saw today have double barrel guns. The natives say, "by and by no good"'.

The facts of white violence are easily discovered: the natives tell him. Their stories have the surreal authenticity of a silent film. At a camp near the Wannon the people are weeping. A man and two women have been shot. 'The men had told them to come and they would give them damper. When they went, they shot them.' The little figures run, jerk, throw up their hands, fall. Who are the killers? 'Purbrick's men.' Their names? 'Jem, Barry and Bill or Paddy Jem and Bill or Bob and Larry ...' The names are fluid as water. Robinson perseveres: he tracks the men down, and takes their statements. But he knows that nothing can come of it: with native testimony inadmissible in the courts, 'the whole matter falls to the ground, and the white ruffian may with impunity deny his black victim'. Even when the killings are admitted, there is no redress. Pyrenees natives give him the names of seven blacks shot by a leaseholder called Francis. Robinson records the names. Some days later he visits Francis at his homestead. The settler tells his story: he was riding down by the creek, natives attacked him, he shot four. He also caught a black at his fold, and shot him, too. He had reported the incidents to the government. That, he assumes, will be the end of the matter.

As it proves. Robinson steps aside ('I told [Francis] I did not intend to enquire, it was in [Assistant Protector] Parker's hands and was his duty'). Then he seems to forget the whole miserable business. Later that night he is deep in his domestic war with Myatt: the dolt has failed to shield the van against the weather, failed to make up his bed; he has had to do it himself; the rain beats in on him all night. But the killings are not quite forgotten. Francis had offered him a bed—a warm, dry bed, with 'clean sheets and pillowcases'. He had been pressing: he had even promised to play his fiddle (Francis is a lonely man). Robinson refuses: he will not sleep in the proximity of such a man. For the first time we hear what is to become a little refrain: 'He acknowledged to five. The natives say seven.' Instead, he goes back to his camp and his rain-wet bed, to write it down. Even if the law—the law whose agent he is—averts its face, he will keep the record. 'He acknowledged to five. The natives say seven.'

The evidence for some black crimes cannot be talked away. He meets Governor La Trobe in Portland. La Trobe warns him not to take a newly contacted band of 'wild' natives too near the town. There has been a 'horrible murder' by Glenelg natives of a Mr Morton, a 'kind and humane gentleman', and his man Larry. The servant had been stretched on his back with spears driven through the palms of his hands, and 'they had cut the flesh off his bone when alive and eaten it'. They had also eaten of Morton's dead flesh. Robinson is shaken: he typically dismisses tales of cannibalism as hysterical fantasy ('all fudge!'), but he cannot impeach this source. Later the same morning he is shepherding his 'shy and savage' flock to a more secure camping ground when they are hallooed after by a mob of predatory whalers, promising blankets, tomahawks, handkerchiefs, avid to get their hands on the women. He chivvies his people along, gets them settled. At midday Mr Blair, Police Magistrate of Portland, and Mr Henty, its leading citizen, seek him out at the camp. He records the ensuing conversation energetically, and at length. (They being too mistrustful of the blacks to dismount, he must have had to look up at them throughout, which would not have helped his temper.) They show him the letter telling the gruesome details of the Morton killings. The two men 'were under great excitement—thought the natives of this [Glenelg] tribe should be exterminated'. Robinson admits his own dejection of spirit, but pleads the necessity of more knowledge, and more understanding. The discussion becomes warm. 'Mr Blair said he knew what he would do if he was Governor. He would send down soldiers and if they did not deliver up the murderer he would shoot the whole tribe. I said it would not perhaps be so easy. Mr Henty said there would be no difficulty on the Glenelg as they had only the river to fly to and they could soon flush them out from among the rocks.' And so, heatedly, on. Two days earlier Robinson had been desperate for these gentlemen's approbation, but when they finally turn their horses' heads for town he is heartily glad to be rid of them.

It is a taxing night. Both his own and the 'wild' people are in an excitable state. In a squabble over a piece of bread one of his men hurls a spear. It whizzes close by his head. More blacks arrive, strangers, 'the most turbulent and noisy natives' he had ever encountered, and settle themselves close by his tent. Nonetheless, the old energy is back, and he is himself again. Alienated from his own people, surrounded by unknown, possibly dangerous natives, he is where he chooses to be.

It is that steady preference which makes him remarkable. Irascible with whites, he is preternaturally patient with Aborigines. He is, in fact, a most earnest anthropologist. The entry for Saturday 17th April, from Assistant Protector Sievewright's camp: '8 a.m. Heavy rain and a westerly wind ... Busy collecting vocabulary. My tent, as usual, since day dawn thronged with natives.' This could be an extract from Malinowski's diary—except that Malinowski would never tolerate 'savages' in his tent. Robinson aims to record the name and affiliations of every Aborigine he encounters. They yield their whitefellow names readily enough, but are reticent about their own. He coaxes them, carefully records the strings of unfamiliar syllables (the driving, eye-baffling hand slows to careful legibility here). Talking with one group, he suspects a connection with a tribe to the east. He begins to sound out the easterners' names. No response. He perseveres. 'Ning.cal.ler.bel.' The natives begin to sing. It is a long song, and 'at the end of each stanza Ning.caller.bel was mentioned by name'. Bravo, Mr Robinson! Yet he has the grace to acknowledge that even hard-won 'knowledge' can be wrong: he tirelessly checks his information. He is alert to the rhetorical element in native violence. When a mêlée erupts at Sievewright's camp, the men 'in single combat and then all together clubbing and wrestling,' the women 'vociferating at the top of their breath', all is ferocity and pandemonium. Yet with interesting intermissions: 'at intervals the fighting would cease and the combatants would stop and taunt. A boomerang or spear would be thrown to provoke the combat and the battle renewed'. 'It reminded me,' Robinson writes, with uncharacteristic dryness, 'of a Hibernian fracas.' He accepts close physical contact, and its penalties. 'Wild' Aborigines 'paw ... me about,' one in particular 'rubbing his hand about me ... feeling my limbs and soliciting my clothes'. Vigorous investigation of his person escalates to what looks like a collective attempt at a shakedown: hands tug at his clothes, pull at his reins, slap at his horse; he retains his physical and moral poise. And when he contracts a painful and obstinate 'pustulence [sic] irruption' (scabies?) from those patting, poking hands he continues to offer up his person, saying: 'I could not rightfully be cross or unkind to these people. It was their custom and, as the old saying is, when in Rome do as Rome does.'

There is vanity in this. He enjoys the accoutrements of office: travelling heroically light, he nevertheless carts his uniform with him, and wears it on grand occasions. And he loves being recognised. Riding ahead of his party, he comes upon women and children gathering yams. Normally they would scatter at the sight of a white man. 'When they saw me they ran to where I was standing. Joy was in their countenances.' He is even more delighted when the recognition scene is witnessed. Proceeding with his natives, a convict, and, by most happy chance, a 'Mr Adams', a local settler, they see a long file of 'wild' natives, most of them armed ('the spears ... newly sharpened', he says with relish, and we wonder how he knows) advancing towards them. Undaunted, alone, he goes forward to meet them. 'I held up my hands.' They halt. Working his way down the line, 'I shook each of them by the hand and patted them on the head.' Their submission is immediate, total, glorious: 'They repeated every word I spoke to them ... I distributed to each a medal which I suspended to their neck ...'. Gifts cascade from his hands: headbands, handkerchiefs, necklaces to the children. Then, the punchline: 'Mr Adams said he never saw natives so obedient to anyone as those natives were to me.' Mr Robinson's cup runneth over: that night he has a sack of Mr Adams's potatoes sent to the

natives, and throws in a piece of pork for VDL Jack and the repro-
bate Myatt. On the evening before a planned rendezvous with all
the blacks of the Port Fairy region he is blissful: 'My mind is now
at ease and I feel satisfied. Providence has crowned my endeavours
with success.' The next day he crows, 'Such a meeting has never
been held with these people, either within or out of their district ...
What has been done in 7 weeks.' There are equally lyrical accounts
of the trust he inspires in individuals. One example: 'I started from
Synnott's with the Barcondeet native to give me information but as
it was raining hard I cantered on at a brisk pace and my Aboriginal
friend ran and kept pace with me. He was armed with spears. He
kept chatting about his country and calling out the names of different locations and said his country was good country. I answered
in the affirmation [sic] which afforded him satisfaction. I am certain the poor fellow would have run the whole way, 12 miles, had
I not stopped him and desired him to wait for the van and come
with it.'

It is an affecting picture: the young black rendered immune to
rain and natural fatigue by affection, chattering freely in the benign
presence of his Protector. Who, taking thought for his charge,
gently puts an end to this enchanted run at the stirrup. We splutter
and choke: Robinson glows. On that day of triumph near Port
Fairy he had gone to the assembly point early, and had addressed
no more than a few words to the nervous crowd when his
entourage rolled in. Immediately, one old man 'thrust his arm in
mine as if apprehensive of danger ... and walked with me whilst I
gave the necessary directions to my people'. Later, distributing gifts,
'I became most popular with the juveniles, even the little children
came and clung onto my knees like children do a papa.'

Clearly, Mr Robinson is getting a lot in return for those potatoes
and headbands and handerkerchiefs. Can a balance be drawn? To
begin at the material level: it is painfully clear that the natives are
hungry; that food is the most urgent necessity. (Robinson keeps an
anxious watch on the depletion of native game, but the vestigial
groups he and we encounter could not hunt anyway, and their
vegetable foods are being ravaged by imported flocks.) He does

what he can, coaxing and bullying flour or sugar or the occasional wether out of grudging settlers, but it is never enough: even the feeding of his immediate entourage reads like a continuous loaves-and-fishes miracle. Knowing the bitter cold of southern nights, he hands out blankets when he has them, but blankets are in chronically short supply. For the rest, he might barter a knife for a spear, or reward a special courtesy with a tomahawk, but what he mainly gives are small, cheap, easily transportable things: caps, handkerchiefs, beads, medals, headbands, and lots of cards, or 'letters', as he sometimes calls them, magnificently inscribed with his own or the Governor's name.

At a casual glance this looks to be the familiar swindle: the European trash deployed in a thousand shameful encounters to bamboozle and diddle the locals. Certainly Robinson seems blind to the gulf in utility between the objects he offers for those he covets for his 'collection': a cap for a cherished spear or a woman's indispensable bark bucket is no exchange. Perhaps there can be no equitable exchange between a people with an abundance of mass-produced items, some of them purely decorative, and another whose economy is so dour that bodies are rendered sacred by the application of mud. But the flow of small, highly visible objects has less to do with exchange than with power. To Mr Robinson, they signify personal authority. To other whites they offer reassurance: a warrior sporting a cap and clutching the Governor's card seems no longer a warrior. There is, however, another effect. A native in a cap holding out his card or his medal can be less easily classified as a natural but undesirable infestation of the land: he is marked, however feebly, as human, and so potentially within the protection of the law.

There is a kind of reciprocity here, if a skewed and fragile one. But the limits are firmly drawn. Coming upon some shelters, Robinson and his party prowl about, and pry into the baskets they find hidden in a couple of hollow trees. Robinson acknowledges some feelings of delicacy—he looks, he says, only because 'the customs and manners of these people were new to me'—but he looks nonetheless. He finds a jumble of objects: bone awls; bits of broken glass, of lava, of scoria; lumps of ochre and pipe-clay and iron; a stick for stripping bark; an amulet; a few items of European dress. It is an odd and oddly poignant collection, this survival kit for difficult times, and we can only guess at its meaning. Robinson takes two of the awls, leaving 'a new cotton handkerchief' in return. He takes something else, and for this he leaves no payment: 'I found a lead pencil whole in their basket and as I needed it, I took it away.' He does not wonder how they got the pencil, or why they treasure it. The instruments of literacy belong to him.

On the emotional plane the scales tilt differently. Robinson is as good an anthropologist as he is because he is attentive to his subjects' behaviour, and he is attentive because they charm him. For a time I was puzzled by his coolness towards his most constant native companion, 'VDL Jack'. He brought Jack—alias 'Tunerminnerwait' or 'Napoleon', and soon, beyond these pages, to become suddenly, shockingly famous—from Tasmania. Jack is indispensable: he guards the camp, finds lost wagons and horses, informs on black and white alike, and when Robinson wearies of the all-too-carnal investigations of curious 'friends', he hands Jack over to them like an amiable long-limbed doll. Yet Robinson's references to him are few, and coolly instrumental. I suspect it is Jack's 'sophistication', his learnt amenability, which renders him uninteresting in his master's eyes. Robinson is quickly wearied by excessively 'wild' natives, with whom he can have no 'intelligent conversation'. He is bored by docile ones, save as stock figures for the tableaux-vivant of his private theatre of vanity. What he likes are people sufficiently knowledgeable of white men's ways to be attentive, yet retaining their exuberance and spontaneity. Consider his attitude to 'Eurodap', alias 'big' Tom Brown, who makes his entry into the journal on April 6th. Initially he is allocated three characteristics: 'This was an intelligent man', 'he had on a jacket and trousers', '[he] was quite delighted to see me'. Thenceforth Eurodap slips constantly in and out of the pages. He is useful: he knows the country, he supplies names for places and things, and when strange natives are sighted it is Eurodap who is sent out to fetch them in. But Eurodap is primarily valued not for his usefulness, but for his personality: his vivacity, his expressivity, his gaiety. When new groups must be entertained with song, Eurodap excels. He takes joyful liberties. Robinson famously detests obscenities, especially in native mouths. ('Fudge!' is his own most violent epithet.) So Eurodap gleefully plays Grandmother's Steps: 'Eurodap said white shepherd too much no good talk to black fellow and then gave me a specimen of his proficiency etc. g-d d-m, you bl-y lyer; you old bug-ger; be off; d-mn you, etc., etc. He was going on with these blasphemous epithets when I told him to desist and that they were very bad.' Then comes the journal entry for June 25th. It comprises two sentences: 'Tom Brown killed. Went from McRae's to Winter's.' The entry immediately following briefly describes Eurodap's death: he has been speared in some fracas, seemingly while trying to mediate. It is impossible to establish clear detail or sequence, because the journal's sturdy march through the days collapses at this point: there are seven separate entries, all of them, confusingly, dated, for the four days following the death. Only on the 29th of June does the steady progression re-establish itself.

Am I making too much of this? Perhaps. Were this fiction, I would know that all things said and left unsaid, all disruptions, were intended to signify. But this is not fiction, and I cannot be sure. I do know that Robinson, among whites a stiff, awkward fellow, and tensely competitive, is with Eurodap and others like him relaxed and genial, because he need fear no challenge. With them he believes he finds the security of uncontested—because uncontestable—inequality. In their company, and possibly only in their company, can his human affections be fully liberated.

If this is 'condescension' in the old sense, affability towards one's (putative) inferiors, it is also something very like love. While most whites view the exuberance of black sociability with distaste shading into revulsion, Robinson basks in it. Blacks swarm in and out of his tent without let or hindrance. Information sessions are informal to unruliness: he grumpily complains of the impossiblity of getting everything down on paper while two or three people are roaring out the names of the creatures they have collected for him. He attends corroborrees devotedly, and stays to the end. When the going is hard he walks so that blacks may ride, 'to encourage them', he says. He persuades nervous novices to climb on his horse, and laughs at the result. And he responds with expeditious tenderness to individual distress. An old chief he had talked with through a long evening is embroiled in what becomes 'a general fight with clubs and Mulgas' at Sievewright's camp (a fight which Robinson implies he quells, 'I went among them'). The old man, lightly wounded but heavily excited, frantically urges the whites to get their guns and shoot the opposition. Robinson coaxes him into the Assistant Protector's hut, and soothes him with tea and damper. (Later he orders a general feast of 'mutton, potatoes and tea' for all combatants.) He actively enjoys physical contact with bodies other whites see as diseased, verminous, loathsome: 'pustulent irritations' notwithstanding; if he is hugged, he hugs back. (I have become very fond of Mr Robinson.) On no direct evidence whatsoever I am confident that he shares his blanket from time to time with one of the 'fine, sprightly girls' he admires so frankly. He accepts other gifts freely offered; he is susceptible to women; so why not? ('when in Rome ...') It is the brutal sexual politics of most black/white couplings which appal him, not the act.

Of course he does not really 'do as in Rome': the assumption of special status is always there. He records the native protocols governing encounters between strangers—the period of silent watchfulness; identification through the painting of faces and bodies; the formal exchange first of words, then of song and dance—but he does not follow them. On the contrary, 'when natives appear I break through all Aboriginal ceremony ... and go forth and meet them'. Once again we hear that biblical reverberation. But I doubt his physical tolerance and ready emotional intimacy finds its ground in some bloated messianic fantasy. His relaxation and warmth of spirit before Aboriginal otherness is a private, secular grace.

Nor is the traffic entirely one way. A recurrent anguish in the study of cross-cultural communications is to watch questions being asked which can make no sense at all to their audience: across the gulfs of time we hear the silence of perfect incomprehension. Mr Robinson asks the right questions. This is an accident.

His purpose is to collect things: above all names, of individuals, clans, places. He is eager to get the affiliations right. Fortuitously, he is mapping the Aboriginal world of meanings and imagination, and that makes him a man worth talking to—a man to whom it is possible to talk. Just west of Mount Cole he falls in with several families. 'I repeated a string of names of tribes and localities all of which they knew, and were astonished at the extent of my information.' He so impresses another woman with his knowledge of 'tribes and persons and localities' that she is persuaded that he must have been a native of those parts come back as a white, and grills him until she has constructed a plausible genealogy. An old woman wandering with the remnants of her family over their usurped land 'enacted a variety of events connected with the history of her country', and then, 'in a dejected and altered tone', deplored its loss. Robinson interprets all such eagerness to talk with him as naïve tributes to his personal charisma. He does not ask why the magic works best on blacks already experienced in white depredations. We must remember that Robinson presents himself as a man of authority, and claims access to remote powers. He enquires into serious matters. And he writes such matters down (remember the pencil). I suspect it is this rather than his personal allure which makes Aborigines ready, even eager, to talk with him.

He is also a man capable of astonishing, painful opacities. A few days before the end of his journey a handful of natives, survivors from two tribes, attach themselves to him. He notes that they are 'very communicative'. They give him a new name, 'meaning in their own tongue "great" or "big" chief'. They beg his protection against the whites who 'drove them away and said "be off"'. ('Too much "be off" all about', they say.) He tells them he would help them, but that he has no time now. They weep, and ask him for a 'letter'. When he leaves, their leader pursues him to offer a last-minute gift: a particularly fine emu-feather belt. Surely they are desperate for his intervention? Surely he can smell their fear? We can: the pages reek with it. But it seems that he cannot. He remarks on the intelligence of one of the young men ('a promising youth if attended to') as if we were still at the dawn of the world. Then, charmed with his name, delighted with his gift—flattered by the tears—he rides cheerfully on. He finds the day 'beautiful', the country 'uncommonly good and pleasant'. He concludes the entry with a casual observation: 'These plains must ultimately be made use of for sheep grazing. The government must lease them.'

❂

Sir Thomas More summed up the human agony attending the great land-grabs of sixteenth-century England in a masterly image: 'Your sheep, that were wont to be so meek and tame, and so small eaters, now ... become so great devourers, and so wild ... that they eat up and swallow down the very men themselves.' Three centuries later, we watch that perversion in nature being re-enacted in an English colony. Two peoples whose interests are perfectly inimical are in contention for the land. The Aborigines are the weaker; they will go to the wall. Astonishingly, no clear provision is made for them: they are cast out of their territories to die. That much is cruelly apparent from Robinson's own writings. So how to explain that casual, shocking comment? What is wrong with this man? Is he a fool, a hypocrite, a moral imbecile; another thick-skinned imperialist playing bumpo with a wincing world?

I think he is none of those things. Rather, he (like so many others) has contrived ways to live with the appalling, immutable fact of Aboriginal death. Initially, his brisk tone, his lack of intro-spection, his radiant vanity, had led me to think him a straight-forward sort of chap. That was, as it always is, hubris: 'simplicity' in humans is a reflex of distance. How many of us dare to pretend to understand those to whom we stand closest? (How terrible the punishment of those who do.) I have come to think Robinson lives in the stretch of a terrible contradiction, the tension of the stretch being betrayed in persistent patterns of conduct—for example, that compulsive 'going on ahead'—and equally persistently, if more subtly, in certain oddities of style. As I read, I was more and more struck by disjunctions not adequately explained by appeal to the 'journal format': too-abrupt transitions between subjects, irritable

returns to matters done with, radical switches of mood. An
unmoored sentence recalls some past contretemps—the affair bites
at him still; he rails for a sentence or a paragraph against 'the condition of the original inhabitants of this land'—then pivots
abruptly back into busy work. These disjunctions thicken (this is
impossible to demonstrate in a narrow space; I can only assert it)
at times of tension. It is as if his mind suddenly lurches, and
swerves from some unseen impediment. I have come to think that
these judderings, along with his irritable, urgent energy, are indicators of what we used to call 'cognitive dissonance': an uncomfortable condition in which a mind veers and twists as it strives to
navigate between essential but mutually incompatible beliefs.
Time and again he approaches overt acknowledgment of the
incorrigibility of black/white relations; time and again he pulls
away to the refuge of the trivial and merely vexing. He 'believes' in
his work: that is transparently clear. But he also knows, at some
level, and only intermittently, that his naggings about the law and
his handing out of blankets and 'letters' are futile; that he can do
nothing to slow the avalanche. His treasured 'authority' gives him
power to coerce only the victims, not their oppressors: 'I sent for
this native but the man said he would not come. I said he was
under my protection and I would soon make him.' The equations
are bleak. The law is the blacks' only protection: the law grants
away their lands, and fails to protect them from wanton, most
deliberate murder. The 'Chief Protector', for all his posturings and
protestations, can effect nothing. The Chief Protector is a sham.

These are unendurable truths. So he keeps himself busy: he
quibbles and quarrels and shifts the blame, lectures stiff-faced
settlers, pats the patting black hands, hands out his blankets and his
cards. He is hopelessly divided: scanning the land for kangaroos,
he is simultaneously assessing its potential as pasture. He indulges
in the fantasy of missionaries everywhere: somehow, the natives
must be quarantined from the contagion of evil. 'White men of
respectable character', men like himself, should 'attach themselves
to the native tribes and control their movements'. But even if that
were to happen (he knows it will never happen) where could they

go? He strives to gather up his wandering people like some Old Testament prophet in flight from catastrophe. But the catastrophe is all around him, and there is no Promised Land.

So on he rides, watching for a curl of smoke, or boughs bent to shelter shivering bodies. He is searching for ghosts, and the shadows of ghosts. He sees crumbling mounds of shells, the long depressions which mark communal ovens, and hears the silent hubbub of a vanished encampment. He gathers the survivors, distributes his little gifts, lights his illusory flares of hope. He counts them, scrupulously. He records their names. Absurdly, he gives them new ones, but these are not real names. Real names differentiate and connect; they have social meaning. These names, like his medals and his letters and his blankets, are tokens merely: amulets against death. These people are ghosts already, they have no substance. At a station one day, begging flour, they are gone the next: they can be made to vanish at a word: 'He said he would have none of them about his station.' 'Be off!' These Joes and Jacks and Mollys have entered the numbered anonymity of death: 'He said he killed four of them. The natives say seven.'

Every night this burdened, driven man steals time from sleep to assemble his information, to fix the flux of experience, to construct his self-protective, self-exposing account of things. He is an addicted writer. Some entries—those triumphalist narratives and tableaux, with their preposterous biblical resonances—must have been long in the writing. He has taken pleasure in their crafting. And occasionally, just occasionally, especially when he has been forced to stare for a moment into the abyss between rhetoric and action, he stumbles upon images of haunting power. From the first days of his journey he makes frequent reference to a place called 'Boloke'. There is a great lake there, and an abundance of fish and fowl which still draws natives from all over the region. So rich is the abundance that this is a traditional meeting place for the ceremonial resolution of conflict, a place of feasting, and of celebration. Through the slow drudge of days 'Boloke' shimmers on the edge of awareness as a vision of peace and plenty. Then he goes there—to find desolation. The lake waters have been sucked up by drought. There are signs of many natives: 'a vast number' of old shelters, abandoned tools, and everywhere on the beach their tracks, 'thick as sheep tracks'. But he sees none. Instead, there are dead eels everywhere, on the sand, on the banks, strewed along the beach. At the deserted camps 'dead eels lay in mounds; thousands of dead eels, and very large ones too'. Crows feast upon them. There are also 'numerous tracks of cattle, sheep and horses'. Robinson lingers: he looks, wonders, notes down what he sees. Then he moves on to more practical matters—but not before he has fixed an image which murmurs awareness of another, more terrible destruction. Later, at the Francis homestead, he flounders shamefully, making his only protest against the settler's slaughter of blacks by his refusal of a bed for the night. (An Aboriginal eyewitness confirms his suspicion that Francis and his men had killed the people at the river camp without provocation, but he keeps his miserable peace.) Then, as he mounts his horse to leave the following day, he sees a human skull. He has seen skulls on display before, in particularly troubled areas, but this one is lying on open ground within yards from the woolshed, and hard by the road, 'on a small bare hill where sheep had been folded'. Robinson realises that it must be the skull of the man Francis had shot at the sheepfold, that the body had been left—had been ordered to be left—to lie where it fell. (Kurtz stirs in his corner, lifts his gaunt head.) 'I showed it to the natives and they said "Mr Francis killed him, Mr Francis shot plenty blackfellows, all gone black fellows." I asked the youth where the other remains were, he said taken away by the dogs.' Robinson picks up the skull, puts it in his van. And then he continues with his travels and his general observations: 'Francis is fencing in a paddock; he has a woolshed and several huts. The soil in this part of the country is of an inferior quality, red sandy loam from 2 to 3 inches deep ...'. From horror to banality in a breath. Nonetheless, the horror is preserved; it is in the record now, for any of us to read.

❂

Across a landscape transformed by our meeting I look back to Mr Robinson. He is riding through a cold rain. A figure runs beside him, running easily over the land. He is young, and strong, but he is already a ghost. Perhaps he knows that, because as he runs he names the places of this, his country. Measuring his breath to his stride, he sings its names and its beauty. It is possible that this white man will hear, and hearing, write. It is possible that someone, some day, will read and remember.

1995

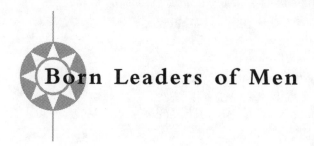

Born Leaders of Men

The Hon. John Howard, Prime Minister of Australia

In which we see how grace and intelligence are good qualities in a leader.

Mr Howard, thanks for coming in.
Hang on, I'm not quite ready.
I'd just like to talk to you about the Wik decision.
Hang on. I'll be with you in a minute.
You're going to extinguish Native Title, aren't you?
Whoops, good grief. Hang on, I'm sitting on something. What's this thing?
Oh I'm sorry, that's my pen.
It's yours?
Yes. I must have left it there.
I think this is mine, isn't it?
Can I have a look? No, that's mine.
I just sat on it.
Yes, but it's my pen.
It's yours?
Yes.
Why aren't you using it, if it's yours?

What do you mean 'using it'? It's my pen.
Yes, well you're not using it.
I don't need it at the moment, Mr Howard. I'm talking to you.
Well, you don't need it then. I'll have it.
I'll need it later.
OK, I need it now. I'll have it.
Look, you can use it.
You want me to use it?
Yes, that's OK. You can use it. We can both use it.
We can both use it?
Yes.
OK. It'll be mine then.
Why is it yours because we both want to use it? You're not using it now.
Yes I am, look at this. (He writes) 'This is my pen. It is nice.' I'm writing, look at this. There's writing coming out the end of it.
That's not what it's for.
Not what it's for? Of course it's what it's for. What else can you do with the pen?
Do drawings.
You do drawings with it?
Yes.
Writing's more important than drawing. I'll keep it.
No, it's not. I've always done drawings with it.
Yes it is. Writing's more important than drawing. I'll keep the pen. That's settled. What was your question? Wik? Native Title?
What if I want to do drawings?
Well, you don't, do you? You've just said you wanted to talk to me.
Why can't we share the pen?
No. Too much uncertainty.
What do you mean 'uncertainty'?
Well, I wouldn't own it that way, would I?
Why should you own it? It's my pen.
We've just been through that. I want to use it, you're not using it at the moment. I'll have it, thank you. Let's get on with it.

Why can't we both use it?

Why do you want it at all? You're not using it.

It belonged to my grandfather.

All right, I'll give you a couple of bucks for it.

Hang on. My Howard, I'm not interested in the money. Surely we can both use a pen. You want to write with it, I want to do drawings. What's the problem?

Too much uncertainty.

Why do you keep saying there's uncertainty?

Listen, I don't want to hear a lot of drivel about some mystical semi-religious historical connection with the pen. I need to use the thing.

I need it too, Mr Howard.

To do drawings?

Yes.

What do you do for a living, son?

I do drawings.

Well, you can get another job, can't you?

Where? What other job?

Can't you get a job writing?

No. Why should everybody have to get a job writing?

Why can't you get a job writing? What's the matter with you? Is there something wrong with you?

Mr Howard, what I do is drawings.

You're bloody hopeless I reckon, you people. You're bloody hopeless.

Mr Howard, it would be quite easy to share the pen.

No, it wouldn't.

Why not?

Because I'm not going to bloody do it, that's why.

On what legal basis can you make that claim?

Do you speak Latin?

Yes.

Finders keepers.

Mr Howard, that pen is important to me. It's part of my heritage.

It's part of mine too.

It belonged to my grandfather.
I'm going to give it to my grandson.
I don't see why we can't share it.
Too much uncertainty. We've been through all that. What did you want to ask me about?
I was going to ask you about extinguishing Native Title.
Oh shut up, I'm sick of you.
Mr Howard, thank you for coming in.

1997

❂

The Hon. Paul Keating, Treasurer of Australia

Mr Keating, you said the other day you had made some pretty bad mistakes with the economy, that the indicators point to a disaster and that you were trying to do something about it.
As I said at the time, it's actually far too late for that. We're embarked upon a policy of damage control.
How's it been going?
It's going pretty well at the moment. We've spoken to a lot of industrial heads, corporate leaders and so on.
Have you been speaking to any of the ordinary people?
Yes. As I say, we've spoken to a lot of industrial heads, corporate leaders and so on. They don't come much more ordinary than that. We're talking very basic motor skills here. They're not very high up the food chain, some of these people.
Do they understand your position?
I think so. Some of these people have made very big mistakes themselves, and I think there is a recognition that, as with any other gamble, it could just as easily have come off.
Could it?
Well, no, not in this case, but I think that's the way they see it.
How did the Premiers' Conference on Housing go today?
It didn't happen.

No?
No. We have a snooker tournament in March every year, and this time it was a housing summit.
Have you got anything to say to the average Australian?
Yes. I would say to the average Australian Bloke ... after all, we've put him through some hoops lately ... I would just say to him, very sincerely, 'Thanks very much, hang in there, and stick with us'.

Incidentally, when I speak of the average Australian bloke, I mean women too. The Australian Labor Party has a very strong commitment to women and policies on women. In fact, the Prime Minister on this very programme the other night mentioned the education of girls, which is obviously paramount among them. So I would say to any Australian women watching, when I say 'Australian blokes', obviously I mean them too.
And what is your platform on women?
I don't actually have at the present moment a copy of the full policy on women. I'll tell you what, though, ring my secretary, tell her you've been speaking to me, and she'll get you one.

Gallipoli
The Hon. Bob Hawke, Prime Minister of Australia

(This interview took place in flight on the return trip to Australia from the 75th anniversary of the landing at Anzac Cove on 25 April 1915.)

Mr Hawke, it's been quite something this week, hasn't it?
It's been fantastic. It's been one of the great things you could ever go through as an Australian. I wouldn't have missed it for the world.
What do you think is the significance of the Gallipoli experience?
It's a unique experience in Australian history. A lot of lessons. I think the main lesson is that we as Australians have got to control our own destiny. We must never again allow ourselves to be put in the position of being ordered to do things by other people—not our idea, we don't control it, and frequently we're

not even told the full story. It's a unique experience and that's a very valuable lesson.

Is the experience unique, though?

Totally unique in Australian history.

What about Bullecourt?

Aside from Bullecourt. Bullecourt was very like it.

Fromelles?

And Fromelles, yes. Aside from Bullecourt and Fromelles, totally unique.

And what about the Somme?

And the Somme. Take those three out and it's unique.

Passchendæle?

Well, take the First War out, then. It's completely unique aside from the First War.

But what about Singapore?

And Singapore. First War and Singapore—take them out and it's a totally unique experience.

Cassino?

And Cassino. Well, take the Second War out as well, take both Wars out. Outside war, it is a totally unique experience.

What about Maralinga?

Outside war and Maralinga, obviously, but the lesson's the same at all times. We as Australians have got to control our own destiny. We must never again get in the position of being ordered to do things by a lot of other people.

On another subject, why is the consumption tax debate back on the agenda?

The OECD wants us to introduce one.

Why don't we export more wheat?

The Americans won't allow it.

Why don't we sell more beef?

The Japanese don't want us to.

What's happening at Nurrungar?

I don't know, I haven't seen the forecast.

North-west Cape?

Nobody knows what's happening there.

Finally, Mr Hawke, what about the boys who never came back, the Diggers who never returned? What do you think they would think of Australia's position now?

I don't know. It's difficult to say. I'd be speculating.

Well speculate. Would they be for it or against it?

Dead against it, I would think.

Yes. (looks out porthole) *What's that big thing out there?*

That? That's a wing. There's another one out the other side.

Where?

(both look) Well, there was earlier.

The 1989 Ashes Series
Mr David Gower, Captain of the England Cricket Team

(Mr Gower's face appears at the dressing room door—he does not open the door very far and seems somewhat reticent about being interviewed.)

David Gower, thanks for your time. How is the series going in your view?

He's not here at the moment.

Come on, David. How is the series going?

It's going very well at the moment. Things are looking pretty good. The lads are all pumped up. There's a good spirit. It should be a good game down there in Edgbaston. We're looking forward to it.

Did you expect to be two-down after two Tests?

He's not here at the moment.

David, come on. Did you expect to be two-down after two Tests?

Things are going pretty well at the moment. The weather report looks good and we're hoping for a pretty good tussle down there at Edgbaston.

Can I ask you about the English captaincy?

He's not here just at the moment.

David, the English captaincy ...

He'll be back in a moment.

Do you think you'll win at Edgbaston?
It should be a good game down there. The lads are very pumped up and really looking forward to it.
David, do you think you'll win?
No, probably not. No, I wouldn't think so.
If you're not going to win, what are your expectations?
We've got an expectation, we've got an agenda, we've got an aim for Edgbaston and we hope to work towards it and achieve it.
And what is that aim?
We'd like to get Stephen Waugh out.
During the match?
No, probably not at Edgbaston, but certainly some time before August. We'd like to get him out before he goes home.
Any other problems.
Yes, we do have another couple of minor problems.
What are they?
Batting.
Yes.
And bowling.
Anything else?
Fielding.
What are your batting problems, David?
Probably the main problems we have at the moment would be Boon, Border, Taylor, Jones, and of course the Big Two.
Lawson and ...
Lawson and Hughes.
What about your bowling attack?
We do have a couple of bowling problems, yes.
What are they?
Alderman, Lawson, Hughes, Rackemann, Healey.
David, will you retain the captaincy?
He's not here just at the moment.
David, come on, I can see you. Don't be silly.
Actually, we have had a meeting about the captaincy and unfortunately at this stage it does look as if I will retain it.
Really? Why is that?

We can't get anyone else to take it on. Unfortunately, the prime candidate is apparently unavailable.

Who is that?

Stephen Waugh. He plays for the other side.

How are your preparations going?

We are planning to field a team of ten fast bowlers for the Edgbaston test.

Do you think you'll get who you want?

We hope so. We've got a hit list of all the ones we want. We're working our way through them and we hope to get as many as possible.

And who are they?

Alderman, Rackemann, Hughes, Lawson.

David, thanks very much.

He's not here at the moment.

1990

DENIS BYRNE

Intramuros's Return

THE FORTIFIED TOWN WHICH THE SPANISH began building on the edge of Manila Bay in the late sixteenth century came to be known as Intramuros, literally, 'within the walls'. If the name suggests a certain insularity, a certain comfort to be taken from being inside rather than outside the walls, then this is hardly surprising: as a Spanish colonial enclave Manila was so fabulously remote that galleon-delivered mail from the court in Madrid took two years to be delivered there. The very idea of holding such a distant possession was, you might think, so preposterous, so presumptuous, that the native population might simply have been unwilling or unable to believe it had been colonised until it was too late to do anything about it. The Spanish residents of Intramuros for hundreds of years prohibited the native population, together with the Chinese and the *mestizos*, from dwelling inside the walls or from even being present there after nightfall when the gates were shut and the drawbridges drawn. Perhaps the Spanish were made nervous by the daring of the venture which had brought them to this place; perhaps after dark, lying in their beds, they retraced in their minds the long, tenuous route back home. If, as Susan Sontag says in *The Volcano Lover*, a collection needs an island, then the Spanish, who collected islands, needed Intramuros.

I had gone to Manila in 1989 to examine the problem of conserving pre-hispanic archæological sites. Intramuros was thus outside my brief and I only gradually became conscious of its existence and history. Standing at the window of the second-floor room at the National Museum where I was reading through piles of old reports and site records, looking across a stream of traffic and a dusty park, I could see a corner of the Spanish wall and the confusion of rooftops and low façades which lay beyond it. There in 1571 Miguel Lopez de Legazpi laid out a gridiron of seventeen streets on the site of what had been the palisaded fort of Rajah Suleiman who was driven out—the Spanish were derisory about his small brass cannons. Intramuros's defences were elaborated and modified over time to produce a system of massive stone walls complete with moat, seven gates, several bastions and ravelins, and a large fort in the northwest corner guarding the river mouth.

By the seventeenth century Intramuros housed six monasteries, fifteen churches, two universities, several schools, two palaces, and numerous warehouses for the galleon trade. Fountains played in courtyards and plazas, windows 'glazed' with pearlshell blocked the glare of the sun. This seemingly sleepy town at the edge of Spain's colonial empire seethed with political machinations and intrigues, with commercial rivalries, ecclesiastical fervours and schemings, to say nothing of the torments and ecstasies of the heart and flesh. The islands never really made any money for Spain. For hundreds of years the colonial government depended upon the annual galleon from Mexico and the cases of silver pieces it brought. The bells of Intramuros rang to greet it when it sailed into the bay, *te deums* were sung and masses of thanksgiving were said. People slept more soundly at night.

Then into the bay in May 1898 steamed Admiral Dewey's modern armoured squadron which sank the pathetically ill-prepared Spanish fleet: three months later the Spanish ceded the Philippines to the United States in exchange for twenty million dollars, and an army of occupation was landed to scuttle the nationalist revolution which had destabilised the Spanish in the first place. To the American newcomers the resources of the archipelago were scandalously underdeveloped, crying out for enterprise and modern principles. While in some ways Intramuros stood for everything they rejected in the Philippines, they were not incapable of enjoying its Old World flavour, the exotic nature of the religious fervour concentrated there and the slightly disreputable air of the back streets, the cafés and bars. They located their own business premises and homes outside the walls, across the river and in the bayside suburbs.

The terms 'Americanisation' and 'modernisation' were interchangeable and were used with equivalent zeal. The American administration set about providing water and sewerage facilities, repairing and widening streets, installing streetcars and giving the city a 'modern cleaning' every day.[1] It planned to demolish the obsolete stone walls around Intramuros in the interests of modernisation—it was as if they felt the place needed a good airing—but a report commissioned from an eminent American landscape architect recommended they be retained and the old Spanish city be preserved. In Southern California in the 1890s the Arroyo Set was creating the mock-Mediterranean 'mission look' from the ground up; in Intramuros the Spanish look was already in place, all that was missing were the palm trees and lawns, and these could easily be arranged. So it was that Intramuros stayed largely unchanged and modern Manila grew up around it.

I had already been in Manila for two weeks when I first went to Intramuros. The sun beat down out of a clear sky as I made my way purposefully across the Luneta, that strip of public gardens which separated Intramuros from the once fashionable, now run-down, area to the south. The dry lawns of the Luneta were where people who came into the city on Sundays lay and slept when the sun slid down into Manila Bay: they slept, whole families of them, and if you strolled through there in the evening you felt strangely intrusive. The Spanish wall was almost as wide at the base as it was high, the opening in it which I approached was not one of the original gateways but a breach punched through in 1904 to allow traffic to pass more easily. What must originally have been the jagged edges of this breach had been dressed back and the stone had healed to its old colour. I stood for a while in the shade, inside the wall's thirteen-metre thickness. A little further along towards the bay the wall had been breached by British artillery during the Napoleonic Wars, when the Spanish had been temporarily relieved of the archipelago. The Japanese had entered Intramuros unopposed in 1941 but three years later the returning Americans blew gaping holes in the wall over on the river side and through them had poured tanks and troops to flush out the Japanese whose fortunes had so dramatically turned. The only people the wall had ever really kept out were Filipinos and that perhaps was its true significance: a line drawn between coloniser and colonised, white and brown, We and Other. Passing a knot of school girls going the other way, I passed through to the We side.

I walked along below the three-storey façade of a high school, past some godowns and shophouses, none of which looked more than a few decades old, and then turned into a smaller street. Islands of smooth cobbles were surfacing through the worn bitumen overlay of the road. On either side were the roofless shells of what had evidently been large pre-war buildings; separating them were open, weed-grown expanses. I stopped in front of one of the stucco-covered shells, peered through a large arched window-opening and saw remnants of a tiled floor just visible through the weeds, its decorative design difficult to make out through the leaves, the bits of rusted wire, and the scraps of yellowed newspaper. My eye caught a movement over by the opposite wall—a woman had been sitting on a wooden box, holding a baby, and now she was reaching up to where a towel was hanging on a nail which had been driven into the faded yellow surface of the plastered masonry. She looked about my own age but was probably younger and she had her back to me, oblivious of my presence. There was no one but me on the pavement: back where I'd come from I could see traffic and a few pedestrians passing by the opening of this ruined street but the sound barely reached me in what seemed to be a vacuum lodged between the lines of an otherwise overcrowded city.

A bit further along I came to an open area strewn with stone rubble and crossed by a line of telegraph poles festooned with blue-flowering lianas. On the other side of this space, perhaps 200 metres away, was Intramuros's bayside wall, angling up the side of which was a stone stairway. I began to make my way over to it, following a walking track worn through the grass—the street had simply faded away. Still I saw no people but when I came to the edge of a terrace and was about to jump down I noticed the slight figure of a man asleep on the grass below. I went around him and he didn't wake. A skinny white cat with a bent tail stood in the grass, eyeing me.

Given the decay which flourished elsewhere in that quarter it was strange to find that the brickwork of the stairs, when I reached them, had been recently restored. Up on the rampart, opposite the top of the stairs and projecting several metres out into the former moat, was a roughly semi-circular brick and stone bastion. Whatever superstructure the bastion may originally have had there was nothing there now, just the semi-circular wall a couple of metres thick which you could easily walk out along. The bastion's hollow, well-like interior was choked with a luxuriant and unruly shrub, long curved arms of which reached up into the still air.

Beyond and below the bastion was the manicured lawn of the golf links which had occupied the moat since early in the century when it had been drained of its brackish water as part of a sanitation drive. I looked down at a putting green, its surface mown into broad stripes, and a painted bamboo stick with a flag on the end standing in a neat round hole. The disjunction between this vision of smoothness and the scene of ruin I had just walked through was extreme. The smooth green tide of the golf links lapped against the outside of the wall with an air of intent, an implied threat that the future was recreational.

When I turned and looked back over Intramuros, the almost complete absence of anything intact dating from the Spanish colonial period came as a surprise even though I'd been warned what to expect. The panorama of broken walls and weed-infested spaces, relieved only by the squared-off concrete shapes of more recent structures, was an artefact not so much of the three hundred years of Spanish and the fifty years of American colonialism but of the week in February 1945 when Intramuros was caught up in one of the main actions of what we refer to oxymoronically as the Pacific War. What had happened in February 1945 had begun with a failure of communication in the Japanese military command. Admiral Iwabuchi Sanji neglected to follow the plan General Yamashita Tomoyuki had formulated to pull all his forces out of Manila once it became clear that the American advance on the city was unstoppable. After tenaciously defending key installations around the city during the first weeks of February a substantial part of the Japanese force of some 20 000 troops withdrew into Intramuros and the major public buildings which stood in the parklike space around it. These buildings had been erected by the Americans in the 1920s and thirties using earthquake-resistant reinforced concrete and the Japanese now fortified them with heavy-calibre guns salvaged from their naval ships lying sunk or damaged in the bay. In the ensuing battle the buildings had to be taken by 'hand-to-hand combat' (which in fact included the use of bazookas, hand grenades and flame throwers), the fighting proceeding corridor by corridor, room by room, through build-ings—City Hall, the Executive Building, the Treasury—whose white-pillared classical forms emulated Washington. After the war the Executive Building became home to the National Museum and it took a bit of imagination for me to visualise Japanese machine-gun positions at the corners of those parquet-floored corridors where teenage security guards now sat quietly at their desks.

Despite their militarily hopeless position the Japanese declined either to surrender Intramuros or release the thousands of civilians trapped in it. For a week, commencing 17 February, MacArthur deployed his entire artillery against the Walled City, firing mostly from the other side of the river in a bombardment which destroyed or badly damaged almost every structure inside it, killed most of the civilians, and finally breached the walls in the northeast corner. American assault troops entered there but still had to take Fort Santiago and other heavily defended positions inside. The Japanese fought virtually to the last man. In what is known as the Battle of Manila they lost 16 665 dead as against 710 American dead. Most estimates put the total of civilian dead at about 100 000, many of them killed by the Japanese in reprisal or sheer anger, but most of them falling victim to the bombardment. The American command was itself shocked at the extent of the devastation when it toured central Manila after fighting ceased on 3 March: 'Manila in effect has ceased to exist,' commented General Eichelberger.[2] Of Intramuros he said, 'it is all just graveyard'.[3]

A graveyard. Yes, you could imagine that easily enough. The vacant lots and the empty shells of buildings which I gazed at from up on the wall were sites where thousands died under fallen roofs and walls, trapped in raging fires, cut down by crossfire in the streets, or run through by Japanese bayonets. In the weeks after Intramuros fell, American bulldozers cleared rubble and pulled down parts of structures deemed to be unsafe; the last of the accessible dead were pulled out and taken away to be buried.

I came down from the wall and walked back the way I had come. It was forty-four years after the events of that February, events which nobody in Manila now seemed to speak of. In the streets of Intramuros there were no monuments to them. If you hadn't known better you might have concluded that the Spanish churches and convents, the fountains and the rows of pearlshell-windowed townhouses had simply fallen victim to the non-military attrition of termites and tropical weather.

The heat was draining me. I worked my way over towards the outline of the rebuilt cathedral and stood at the counter of a corner store, slowly drinking a bottle of Sprite. Across the counter three boys were sitting on boxes playing a game of cards. They were interrupted by a woman who came to buy matches, sliding her thin silver coins across the scratched lime-green Formica. The radio played a Pet Shop Boys dance song, the repetitive, disembodied voice from London strangely in harmony with the torpid, pre-monsoonal afternoon. A little further up the street were the walls of the cathedral, the baroque version which rose in the 1950s from the rubble of its predecessor destroyed in the war. The blocks of grey volcanic stone looked too mean to be left exposed—it looked like a cake waiting to be iced. A few bicycle rickshaws rattled along the street. I was lingering over the Sprite, putting off the moment when I would have to make a move, kidding myself that I was blending into the scenery. On the opposite corner, in the yard of a warehouse, two boys without shirts were prancing around in front of a pink radio perched on top of a petrol drum. You wouldn't even notice them in a nightclub but here, in the open air, on their dance floor of oil-stained dirt, poised and ritualistic, they looked significant. One of them left and the other sat down on a stool in front of a mirror nailed to a fence, gazing critically at himself and touching his hair. Along the street a woman was in a phone booth, her free arm extending out through a broken window, her hand idly tearing strips off a poster pasted onto the outside of the glass. Her hand stopped, motionless, in response to some point in the invisible conversation and then slowly tore another strip off the poster and let it flutter to the ground.

Accounts of March 1945 mention that even after the fighting ceased it was a few days before the haunted-looking people began to come out onto the streets from the places where they had been hiding or trapped. What was left of Intramuros was still smoking; even with jeeps running around the silence following the bombardment must have been extraordinary. There are photographs of Intramuros landmarks like Letran College showing them still standing but totally pockmarked, charred, windowless, and frayed at the edges.

A Carl Mydans photograph shows three young women walking down what appears to be a residential street outside Intramuros. A street which a typhoon appears to have passed through: flattened houses, shredded, leafless trees. The women are holding their noses as they pass the corpse of a boy sprawled face-down across a tramline. Another photograph by Mydans must have been taken from the hood of a jeep—there is the young bespectacled soldier driver, a woman with frizzy hair in the passenger seat next to him and, on a split-bamboo platform laid across the back of the jeep, a woman with a gaping leg wound lying stretched out (her eyes are closed but she must be alive because her hand is gripping the bamboo). The woman in the front has blood on the hand she is using to hold the front of her dress together and she has a numb, far-away look in her eyes. The driver by contrast is looking straight at the camera with his mouth open.

When Douglas MacArthur arrived in Manila in 1935 he was charged with preparing the defence of the Philippines in the eventuality of armed conflict with Japan. Clouds of war were gathering over the South China Sea. MacArthur had been army Chief of Staff in Washington and came with the reputation of being a brilliant strategist, earned in Europe during the First World War, of being an outspoken proponent of right-wing politics, and of being amazingly arrogant. Bataan, Australia, New Guinea, Japan, Korea all lay ahead of him and he would barely set foot in mainland America again in the next sixteen years. The quest for wide open spaces and new resources, or whatever it was that made the frontier a necessary part of the American world view, pushed that frontier westward to America's Pacific coast and then further west across the sea to the Philippines (only stopping, you might argue, in Vietnam). It was a preoccupation which saw MacArthur's father, Arthur MacArthur Jr, fighting Indians on the frontier in the 1860s and fighting republican Filipinos on Luzon in 1899. An irony of going West was that you eventually and inevitably found yourself in the East.

MacArthur took his task seriously, but the defence of 7083 islands against a modern naval power was never going to be easy; it didn't help that Washington was reluctant to provide the necessary money or arms. Still, the feeling in Manila was not one of panic. A popular racial chauvinism, shared by MacArthur, derided the idea of the Japanese being tough opponents for white soldiers. Japanese soldiers, among their other liabilities, were believed to be chronically myopic (cartoon caricatures of the Japanese at this time often showed them with thick-lensed spectacles)—they wouldn't be able to shoot straight When the attack came in 1941, MacArthur had a force of 80 000 poorly trained and equipped Filipinos and 22 000 US soldiers, 207 military planes and a small number of torpedo boats. The airforce was destroyed on the ground and the ground forces were withdrawn onto the Bataan Peninsula; Manila was declared an open city in order to spare it from attack.

Accompanied by his wife and young son, MacArthur withdrew to Corregidor, the island fortress at the tip of Bataan. Before they took Manila the Japanese bombed part of the north side of Intramuros, destroying a church and damaging several other buildings. Even as the hundreds of American civilians still resident in the city were being interned the majority of the governing élite, their erstwhile 'brown brothers' were enlisting in the Japanese collaborationist government. Bataan and Corregidor held out for five months but before it fell the MacArthurs, under orders from Washington, escaped by boat to Mindanao and then on by plane to Australia. It was in Melbourne in March 1942, outside Spencer Street railway station that MacArthur uttered the famous words, 'I came through and I shall return,' having scripted them into a speech on the back of an envelope. His office had to run the script past the Office of War Information in Washington which pleaded for the 'I' to be changed to 'we'.[4] MacArthur stuck with the 'I' and the rest, as they say, is history. It is here that the Return appears to have begun its career but in fact, if fact can be brought to bear at all on so slippery a phenomenon, it traces back to the besieged Corregidor where General Sutherland and the Filipino journalist Carlos Romulo coined the phrase as a slogan to boost morale in the occupied archipelago (Manchester, 271). They had presented it to MacArthur who assimilated it and, promising he would be back, boarded the PT boat for the hazardous and uncomfortable journey south.

The idea of the Return was so personalised, so mythologised, and so powerful that it is difficult to know how to draw lines around it. Those who still believe that history consists of a linear narrative might do well to consider the Return because it refracts, it occurs before and after itself, it multiplies and even, in a sense, it never happens at all. Following its first public appearance, in Melbourne, the idea of the Return began to proliferate. William Manchester describes how:

> *Throughout the war American submarines provided Filipino guerrillas with cartons of buttons, gum, playing cards, and matchboxes bearing the message, and they were widely circulated. Scraps of paper with 'I shall return' written on them were found in Japanese files. There was even a story—which made effective propaganda even if it was apocryphal—that a Japanese artillery battery opening a case of artillery shells in the middle of a battle, found the sentence neatly stencilled on each of them. (272)*

The centrepoint of the Return occurred on 19 October 1944 at Red Beach on the island of Leyte, when MacArthur waded ashore from a landing craft but even that was a highly unstable moment. The US Third Fleet and Seventh Fleet stood off the coast of Leyte near Tacloban and at daybreak they opened fire on the beach; waves of infantry were sent in and MacArthur himself headed shoreward in a landing craft with his staff, journalists, and the president of the Philippine government in exile, Sergio Osmena. The landing craft ran aground fifty metres out from shore and MacArthur and his party were forced to disembark and walk in through the water, an army photographer taking a picture of them in the process. MacArthur was evidently annoyed. He had long anticipated this moment and if he had visualised striding up the beach immaculate and heroic—he had a reputation for neatness—he now found himself up to his knees in water. But later he saw a print of the photograph and realised it captured the very essence of the Return. I see him looking at it in the wardroom of his flagship over breakfast the next morning, sipping coffee from a thick china mug, thoughtfully stroking his chin: in a flash of postmodern insight he sees that the Return will go on and on. The scowl on his face which the photograph captured was actually intended for the person responsible for running him aground but it would be seen by the world as being addressed to the Japanese.

The following day for the benefit of other cameramen he organised a repeat performance at nearby White Beach, complete with landing craft, wet trousers, and defiant expression. He repeated it during the Luzon landing in Lingayen Gulf, noting in his memoirs that his error in choosing a boat which took too much draft had become a habit with him (see Manchester, 409). There was nothing accidental about it: at Lingayen he refused to alight on the landing pier which had been erected especially for him, insisting that the door of the craft go down in the waves so that he could wade ashore just as he had at Leyte. Mydans' famous picture of this rerun is almost identical to the 'original' Leyte enactment. The photographs of the Return—that is to say, one or other of its enactments—spread across the world, a copy of one of the Leyte pictures even reaching the desk of General Yamashita. But Yamashita refused to believe MacArthur had really been there—the photograph, he suspected, was of a fake landing staged in Australia. Actually, it was probably of the fake landing staged on Leyte.

The replicability of the Return, both by graphic reproduction and live performance, its instantaneous transition into myth, lent it omnipresence. It is always with us now, pulsing away in the space of pure representation.

One Saturday night during the time I was writing this piece in Bali I went to have dinner with some friends at a semi-open-air disco on the edge of the beach a kilometre or so down the coast from the bungalow I was living in. It was eight o'clock and the dance floor lay empty beneath its vast thatched roof; we had a table on the terrace, directly above the deserted beach. At a certain point during the meal, as clearly as if it were tapping me on the shoulder, I had a vision of MacArthur wading in to the beach behind me. The image was crystal clear: the faded cloth general's hat, the Ray Bans, the imperious set of the jaw, the other officers beside him and behind him and, fanning out further back, the soldiers in steel helmets and battle dress. I turned and cast a furtive look at the empty beach. The conversation at the dinner table continued but so did MacArthur: the Legian beach dogs stood staring, then ran yapping back up the beach as the moonlit phalanx advanced through the shallows and then up over the dry sand, across the terrace and onto the dance floor, still in formation, where they broke into a 1940s dance step under the dark, lustrous eyes of the waiters whose unmoved, beautiful faces insisted they had already seen everything. There was a thin drift of sand on the dance floor's polished concrete surface.

✵

I may seem to have strayed a long way from Intramuros but I am moving towards it much as MacArthur moved towards it in late 1944 and early 1945: circuitously but with speed. In his book, *Speed and Politics*, Paul Virilio charts the accumulating role of speed in the history of warfare, a sequence that leads from the medieval fortress whose power lay in its immobile, static resistance through to the 'lightning warfare' of the Third Reich in which 'stasis is death'.[5] It seems MacArthur had not grasped the full implications of this in 1941 when the Pacific War began. Upon the unexpected arrival of the East in the space of the West with the Japanese attack on Pearl Harbor (Hawaii being quasi-West) MacArthur appears to have fallen into a semi-catatonic state of indecision which allowed the Japanese, to their own astonishment, to destroy his air force on the tarmac at Clark airfield fully nine hours after word of the disaster at Pearl had been radioed to Manila. Other feats of Japanese speed followed, notable among them the extraordinarily fast transit of the Malay Peninsula which led to the fall of Singapore. The West's previous apparent monopoly on rapidity was broken.

Three years later, in the closing months of 1944, MacArthur demonstrated a rejuvenated facility with time and motion, surprising the Japanese by bypassing the Talauds and Mindanao to strike directly at Leyte, and swiftly proceeding from there to the invasion of Luzon. The landing at Lingayen Gulf, some 180 kilometres north of Manila, took place on 10 January. MacArthur was hoping he would be able to celebrate his sixty-fifth birthday in Manila on 26 January. He ordered a fast-moving force to make a dash behind Japanese lines to free the American internees at the University of Santo Thomas and Bilibid Prison and meanwhile moved his main forces rapidly down the central plain of Luzon, encouraging a situation in which the three US divisions competed to be the first to enter the city. On 6 February MacArthur sent out a communiqué to the effect that US troops were rapidly clearing the Japanese from Manila and that 'their complete destruction is imminent'. Congratulations poured in from Roosevelt and the Allied leaders and by 10 February the General was planning a great victory parade through the city. *Newsweek* announced MacArthur's victory in a headline which read: 'Prize of the Pacific War: Manila Fell to MacArthur Like Ripened Plum'.

The reality as it emerged in the days following was that the Japanese were still firmly entrenched in Manila south of the Pasig River. Americans tanks and artillery were being brought to bear on Japanese positions and, while US troop losses remained comparatively light, civilian casualties and damage to the city were beginning to escalate. The irony of the Japanese position was that after the speed and modernity they had shown early in the war the remnant of their force in Manila was now stationary, entrenched in heavily defended key buildings and holed up in Intramuros, an ancient fortress and precisely the class of object which gunpowder and speed, Virilio notes, had made obsolete. The original logic of the ancient fortress, that Time 'was beaten by the static resistance of the construction materials—by duration', no longer applied. In Manila in early 1945 time was already ahead of itself—or should one say that victory having already been announced, MacArthur's troops were 'behind time'.

One of MacArthur's lieutenants of the time reported that the General was shattered by the holocaust in Manila.[6] Be that as it may, he clearly intended to control the way the outside world saw the battle. He censored the heading 'Manila is Dying' from an outgoing press report and regulated against any future use of that particular phrase. Not in this one stroke of the censor's pen, but definitely, methodically, and even as it was happening, the destruction of Manila began to be edited out of history. I came to see the current restoration of Intramuros to its eighteenth-century Spanishness as a further step in this general line of finesse.

If there was a single main reason for Manila's destruction it was the perceived necessity of minimising American combat casualties. In Honolulu in 1944 MacArthur had given Roosevelt an assurance that the Philippines could be taken without a high casualty rate, an understanding which was crucial to his being allowed to proceed with the invasion in the face of opposition from those like Nimitz who wanted a direct strike at Formosa, that island then to serve as a springboard for an invasion of Japan itself. MacArthur refused to allow aerial bombardment of Manila but it is generally conceded that the massive use of artillery had much the same effect. Most of the approximately 100 000 civilian casualties were the result of artillery fire and it is difficult not to conclude that the very low American casualty rate was obtained at the expense of the very high civilian one.

The deadliness of the Return was eclipsed, for the world, by the glamour of the idea of the poor Filipinos being delivered from the sons of Nippon. The destruction of Manila was somehow, has somehow, been lost in the momentum of a myth which had assumed unstoppable proportions even before the liberation hit the city. Thereafter the mythology of the Return rolled on and the attendant destruction faded away.

In the library of the War Memorial Museum in Canberra is a photograph, dated February 1945, of a US soldier half-sitting, half-leaning, on a sea wall at the edge of Manila Bay. He is looking through a pair of field glasses across the bay to where, in the distance, an immense plume of smoke rises; he appears to be observing the bombardment of the city. The picture is clearly about distance: the luxury of distance, the closing of distance effected by field glasses, the reduction of space by modern artillery which enables destruction from a safe distance. When I read the daily press coverage of the Pacific War for February 1945 in the *The New York Times* I felt I could understand how distance affected reporting of the impact on civilians: the correspondents were always, obviously, behind the artillery barrage and would not have witnessed its immediate effect; by the time they had the opportunity to move freely around Intramuros and nearby areas the centre of 'public' attention had moved to the assault on Corregidor and then to the battle for Iwo Jima. The war rolled on. Also, though, it seems to have been a matter of policy either to not gather or not to release figures for civilian casualties; consistently, casualty figures were given for Japanese and American soldiers but not civilians.

One of the last acts of the Return was the trip MacArthur made in March 1945 from Manila to Corregidor for a flag-raising ceremony with the troops who had retaken the island fortress from the Japanese. His party travelled in four PT boats, the same number used when he had fled the island in the same month three years before. It was almost as if he was reversing the film, effecting a restoration of things back to the way they had been and, in the process, erasing the loss of face he had suffered when the Japanese invaded. In his *Reminiscences* MacArthur devoted a page of text to his return visit to Corregidor and was similarly expansive about the visit he made to the ruins of his former penthouse apartment on top of the Manila Hotel and the emotional scenes which greeted him at the internment and prisoner-of-war camps. But he had nothing at all to say about the bombardment of Manila and the destruction of Intramuros and he made no mention of the civilian casualties. He had distanced himself from that side of things. Filipinos, for their part, had no choice but to deal with what had happened to Manila and they did so in very different ways. Carlos Romulo blamed it all on the Japanese whom he saw as engaged in a kind of religious war.

> To me, perhaps Manila was more terrible because it was my city that lay black and gutted and reeking, mile on mile, where once had been beauty and modernity and progress, a mingling of the romantic past with the future that was a delight to all who knew Manila.
> These were my neighbours and my friends whose tortured

bodies I saw pushed into heaps on the Manila streets, their heads shaved, their hands tied behind their backs, and bayonet stabs running them through and through. This girl who looked up at me wordlessly, her breasts crisscrossed with bayonet strokes, had been in school with my son.

Beginning with the first week in February, the Japanese Army in retreat had participated in three weeks of unprecedented sadism.

In those twenty-one days they had succeeded, under imperial orders, in blotting out the greatest Christian city in the Orient and wiping out the symbols of Christianity in the Philippines. Only the broken walls of our beautiful, centuries-old churches were left standing in the rubble that had been Manila ...

Now in retreat, this February, they tried to wipe out all Christian evidence in our land, for it was this they hated most in the Filipino race. To them our faith was the mark of our trust in the white race to whom we were united in religion and ideology.

To the Japanese Christianity and democracy were twin evils and the Filipinos in Manila paid for holding to both beliefs.[7]

Absent from Romulo's account is any mention of the fact that many or most of those in the class to which he belonged had collaborated with the Japanese; absent also is any acknowledgment of the toll taken on civilians and churches by MacArthur's bombardment. The 'handsome' US Army which Romulo identified with so closely was seen differently through the eyes of the writer Carmen Nakpil:

I spat on the very first American soldier I saw that unspeakable day in February 1945. A few seconds before, he had shouted at me from behind a tree in the Malate street—'Hey you wanna get yourself killed?'

I crossed over from the middle of the street where I had been walking and saw that his features were flushed with fright as he hunched behind a tree, rifle and steel helmet, dusty uniform and large wooden rosary beads which he wore like an amulet round his neck. Damn you: I thought. There's nobody here but us Filipino civilians, and you did your best to kill us.

I spat, but I was dry throated and he was not aware of my scorn. I had not eaten or slept for more than a week. My husband had been tortured by Japanese soldiers in my presence, and then led out to be shot. Our home had been ransacked, put to the torch, its ruins shelled again and again. I had seen the head of the aunt who had taught me to read and write roll under the kitchen stove ...

I had seen all the unforgettable, indescribable carnage caused by the detonation of bombs and land mines on the barricaded streets of Ermita and the carpet-shelling by the Americans which went relentlessly on, long after the last Japanese sniper was a carcass on the rubble. I had nothing in all the world except the dress on my back, an unborn child in my belly and in my arms, a little daughter, burning and whimpering with the fever of starvation ...

So this was Liberation. I was no longer sure what was worse, the inhumanity of the Japanese or the helpfulness of the Americans. It had turned out to be a macabre sort of friendship.[8]

Nakpil's account is not anti-American, to my mind. Rather, it expresses a civilian predicament: the distinction between being killed or wounded up close and in a spirit of anger or hatred by the Japanese was not so different from being killed or wounded from a distance, unintentionally (collaterally, as we now say), by the Americans.

In the months after 'Liberation', as MacArthur was overseeing the reinstallation of the pre-war government prior to his departure for Tokyo, homeless people began to reinhabit the ruins of Intramuros. Some of them may have lived there previously, some gravitated from other destroyed parts of the city or drifted in from a poverty-stricken countryside looking to try their luck in Manila. They erected shanties out of salvaged bricks and broken beams, sheets of roofing iron and odd blocks of stone: the genius of necessity, architecture without architects. In clearings amid the rubble, in the shadow of the partly destroyed walls, and even in holes gouged out by shellfire in the very body of the walls themselves, the squatters became a familiar aspect of post-war Manila.

There are accounts which tell of former residents begging the US Army Corp of Engineers in March 1945 not to pull down what remained of their Intramuros houses; they wanted to stay and rebuild, but the bulldozers continued their work. As the Intramuros shanties sprouted out of the ashes there arose elsewhere, on the edge of town, new élite suburbs like Makati and Forbes Park. A conservation architect I spoke to said he could remember quite substantial fragments of some of the Intramuros churches still standing when he was a boy in the late 1950s. But when they began to build Makati the ruins were literally mined for old stone. Now, he said, you could find the fine old granite of Intramuros on the bathroom and living-room floors of those suburban mansions.

In a country like the Philippines where the affluent few are proportionately so very few, enclaves like Makati stand not just for luxury, cleanliness, and modernity—they stand for security. This was especially so in the late fifties and early sixties when lawlessness was increasing in Manila and when Intramuros, that former island of Spanish privilege, turned into a slum and a place to be avoided at night. The great walls which had once kept out the rest of the city now served to shield the rest of the city from the sight of the squalor within. It was considered by the élite to be a pool of disease and crime—it was 'a dangerous place to tread' and a 'haven for the underworld'.

The Filipino élite looked askance at what had happened to Intramuros, but if it had vacated the place it certainly hadn't relinquished it. Intramuros was simply in extended purgatory awaiting restoration. The waiting lasted through the 1950s. Fort Santiago was declared a Shrine of Freedom in 1950 in honour of the nationalist hero, Jose Rizal, and of those tortured and killed in the dungeons there by the Japanese, but it wasn't till 1961 that a programme to restore the Fort was inaugurated. Five years later Ferdinand Marcos, in his second year of office, established a restoration committee to oversee the reconstruction and maintenance of the walls, gates, and bastions of Intramuros and its surviving 'historical edifices'. Gradually there developed the idea of a restoration programme which would recreate the Walled City as it had been under the Spanish, and to achieve this they began moving out the riff-raff: 4000 squatter families were trucked to small settlements forty kilometres north of the city in 1963. The slate was being cleaned.

The restorationists and administrators were installed somewhat to their own embarrassment in a newly built office tower in the heart of Intramuros, on the site of what had been the Spanish governor's palace. The building was a very model of the sort of structure they considered unsympathetic to historic Intramuros but in it they enjoyed excellent working conditions on the spacious, well-lit, air-conditioned floors which they occupied. It was the sort of place you could stay clean in a white shirt, the sort of place that made you feel purposeful and efficient the moment you walked through the glass doors. In the National Museum, by contrast, based in the run-down 1930s Executive Building where rainwater came in through broken windows during storms and ran down the stairs, my hands were always grimy and sticky from a combination of my sweat and the dust which had settled on the old files. The plumbing had failed and there was nowhere to wash. I could live with the irritation but I enjoyed the few days I spent in the office of the restorationists, asking questions and looking through the archive of pictures they kept there which showed Intramuros at various times in its history. My hands didn't stick to the pages of my notebook but I felt a twinge of disloyalty to my friends sweltering away over at the museum—they resented the gulf in size between the funding which poured into the restoration and the trickle of money they were given to protect and manage the thousands of pre-hispanic archæological sites in the country.

The afternoon I finished with the picture archive I took the lift down into the pungent reality of the street below and set off walking back to my guesthouse on the other side of the Luneta. Still familiarising myself with the streets, I took a meandering course which took me past a restored section of the main wall and then past vacant lots where cars and trucks were being repaired. Old tyres and rusting springs, engine blocks and chassis littered the ground there instead of potsherds, eighteenth-century roof tiles, broken stone flagging or anything else which might have suggested colonial Spain. Through the open door of a wooden shack a small girl was asleep on a seat taken from an old car; above her, pasted onto the bare wood, were coloured pictures cut from magazines. Film stars and volcanoes. Then I was in a street which had a row of shops and houses built, probably, in the 1950s. Weeds grew from ledges on the façades and there were shirts and a little Superman suit, complete with cape, hung out to dry on a balcony. The building was the colour of the light-brown concrete blocks it was constructed of, but one of the house fronts on the ground floor was painted pastel yellow—it had a light blue picket fence outside it, a pink-and-white striped plastic awning above it, and two plants growing in pink pots on either side of the gate. It stood out like a Samoan postage stamp stuck onto a coarse brown envelope. Taped to the inside of the single window was a poster of a singer, a young man with light brown skin and black spiked hair, wearing a faded denim jacket. The hand he held out in front of him looked like it was about to snap its fingers. I had to stop walking in order to take this scene in, and as I was standing there, savouring it, a youth came out of the door and behind him, her hand on his shoulder, a woman in an apron. She was saying something to him and he was looking at the pavement, silently nodding his head. He walked off up the street and she was about to turn back inside when she saw me looking. She seemed puzzled for a moment, screwing up her eyes, but then laughed, pleasantly. She must have decided I was just some species of tourist. I moved off, thinking about how nice this was: uncontrived, not a hint of the mock-Spanish about it. There was probably a law against it. Later, when I immersed myself in the events of 1945, I couldn't look at a scene like that without thinking of the fire-gutted shells of houses and the people who might have been inside them when they were hit. Mothers and sons, for instance.

The last thing that caught my attention as I passed out of Intramuros was a black-and-white sign: 'You Are Within A Historical Zone. Vehicular Gates And Pedestrian Gates Are Open 5.00 a.m. To 10.30 p.m.' It was part of the restorationist effort to stop container trucks and the families of their drivers using the Walled City as a camping ground, conveniently handy to the docks. Squatters, those opportunists who would insert themselves and their squalor into any available opening, were now thought to number about two and a half million people in Manila, or about a third of the city's population. They were not enemies of heritage, it was just that heritage wasn't a priority for them; if they weren't kind to the ruins perhaps it was because they were too close to ruin themselves, poverty being just ruin without the romance.

The National Library building stood on the edge of the Luneta. It had the light, optimistic lines of the 1960s but it had a ventilation problem—it was as if it had been designed to be air-conditioned and then, at the last minute, the architects left the air-conditioning out. On the steamy Saturday morning I went there to work I lasted only an hour or so in the reading room, battling drowsiness, and then packed up my notes and left.

The sky had clouded over and a light rain had begun to fall, only to evaporate instantly on the pavement. I bought a drink at a kiosk in the park and then walked along a path to where a relief model of the Philippines had been constructed in a large shallow pool. It was one of Imelda Marcos's more successful ventures into the field of public art and was a personal favourite of mine. I had a general weakness for that sort of thing: the fake rocks and boulders of cement grottoes, the blue-and-white ferro-cement ice caves and cliffs which you find in the polar bear enclosures of the better class of zoo. I probably had a weakness for the idea that this was a less sinister form of duplicity than that going on in Intramuros. The rain began to fall more heavily, wetting the miniature archipelago—streams began to flow down the green painted valleys of Luzon's Cordillera and the islands of Mindoro and Palawan stretched away through the rain-ringed waters of the pool, pointing the way beyond the park to the bars of Ermita.

With my notes dry inside their plastic wallet there seemed no reason not to get wet. The rainwater trickled down my face and there was the sudden cold of my wet shirt sticking to my skin. I made my way slowly back to the guesthouse and had gotten as far as the Midtown Hotel when I heard the sound of running feet approaching me rapidly from behind. I spun around warily, the way one does, preparing myself for God knows what, and found myself face to face with Aniceto. I'd met Aniceto during my first week in the city and had gone with him to a beach on Mindoro for the weekend. Some years previously his family had been relocated from an inner-city squatter's enclave to a distant shanty town in order to make way for one of Imelda's urban redevelopment projects. He came into the city every couple of days to earn a bit of money here and there; he worked as a waiter occasionally, he cruised the Luneta. On the boat over to Mindoro he'd told me he believed in mermaids and when we were drinking Tanduay rum in the evening, listening to the waves on the beach, he'd enchanted me with stories about his childhood on Negros, about the house built on poles out over the water and about waking in the morning to jump out the window straight into the sea. I'd briefly cherished the idea of retaining him as a guide through the madness of Manila's public transport system but I could never depend on him to turn up at the right hour or even on the right day.

Now he stood there panting and grinning, his hair plastered over his forehead by the rain. He told me I looked like a drowned rat.

'Where have you come from?' I asked, impressed by his ability to materialise like this. In the back of my mind stirred the knowledge that another version of this street must exist, one which was quite opaque and closed to me, one which Aniceto walked in and out of at will. The world of local knowledge.

'Up there,' he gestured vaguely with his thumb towards an old grey block of apartments behind some dripping broads leaved trees. 'I was visiting my friend and we were standing out on the balcony when I saw you walking past without an umbrella.'

'You are really very wet,' he said, looking me up and down.

'Well, yes,' I replied absently, looking up at the balconies of the apartment block, looking for a way into Aniceto's version of Manila, but seeing only wet concrete and dusty pot plants.

'No,' he stated with conviction. 'You hardly ever see foreigners get wet—they are always in cars or they have umbrellas. They don't get wet.' It was as if the white race, in addition to its other advantages, was innately waterproof.

'You should have been an anthropologist,' I said.

'Thanks,' he replied. 'There is still time.'

I suggested we go to Intramuros, to visit Fort Santiago, and an hour or so later we were sitting in the back of a jeepney, the sun now shining as we edged our way through the traffic.

Fort Santiago occupied a wedge of land in the northeastern corner of Intramuros which projected out into the mouth of the Pasig River. We arrived outside the fort's monumental gateway, built by the Spanish in 1741, and paused to admire its stonework and the large wooden relief carving of St James on horseback set into a space above the arch. The gateway had been badly damaged in 1945 when American tanks had blasted their way through it and what we were now looking at was the restored version, circa 1982. 'We are good at fixing things, no?' Aniceto offered, as if some expert comment might be expected from him—but he then took the opportunity to tell me he had never been to Fort Santiago before.

Beyond the gate was a large lawned space which tapered toward the river and was crossed by pathways bordered with low clipped hedges. The only really substantial structure was an old-looking white building of two storeys which housed the museum dedicated to Jose Rizal; there, in what was now known as the Rizal

Shrine, he was held prisoner by the Spanish for nearly two months before being taken out and shot by a firing squad in Bagumbayan Field, now the Luneta, on 30 December 1896. Aniceto and I stood at the entrance to the cell on the ground floor where Rizal had secretly penned his farewell to the Philippines, *Me Ultimo Adios*. Like the tens of thousands of school children and family groups who filed through every year, we cast our eyes over the simple wooden desk in the middle of the small windowless room.

Upstairs was a large gallery housing Rizal memorabilia. Moments of his life were caught in dark oil paintings which lined the walls. He was a fifth-generation Chinese *mestizo* from a wealthy family—the paintings showed a refined, intelligent young man. We peered into a cabinet containing books which had been owned by his family, one of them open at an engraving of the Inquisition, showing a man hanging from a ceiling by his hands. A glass case contained some of Rizal's clothes: a white shirt with fragile lace, a pair of his black pants, a pair of white silk socks. I was astonished at how small the clothes were, almost like those of a child, and pointed this out to Aniceto in the sort of hushed voice that everyone else in the room was communicating in. 'We *are* small,' he murmured back.

As we were going back downstairs Aniceto remarked on how well preserved the building was.

'Oh, this is all reconstructed,' I said. 'Fort Santiago was an absolute ruin by the time the Americans captured it from the Japanese in 1945. The US Army used it as a depot for a while and then squatters moved in—it wasn't till the early fifties that some members of the Lions Club came here and discovered that the ruins of this building, where Rizal had been imprisoned, were being used as a toilet.'

'Really? They were shitting here?'

'Yes. At that time all that was left there were some falling-down walls with grass and weeds growing inside them. Anyway, the Lions Club said it was "disgraceful", the government moved the squatters out and provided the money to rebuild. And so here it is.'

Aniceto said, 'They should have a notice somewhere explaining all that—I feel like I've been tricked.'

Near the exit there was a big painting of the moment prior to Rizal's execution in which he looked out at us from the canvas, his back turned to the line of soldiers. I thought, momentarily, of the clothes upstairs and this small man's body torn by the fusillade of nineteenth-century bullets. Back outside we walked around the compound of the fort for a while before climbing up onto the rampart from where there was a clear view over towards the docks on the edge of the bay. Below us two golfers in Panama hats were walking along the grassed bottom of the broad moat, their heads inclined in conversation, each holding a club and swinging it slowly and decoratively.

'Aniceto, did I tell you the restorationists are planning to fill the moat with water again?'

'No, I didn't know,' he said, drawing closer, almost conspiratorially. The golfers were passing directly below.

'Yes, they feel the golf course spoils the historical feeling of the moat. It's what they call an unsympathetic use.'

'Unsympathetic?' he said.

'Yes, like being disrespectful.'

'I was just thinking about the squatters who were down there in the fort. I don't think Jose Rizal would have minded the squatters—it was only a prison for him, right? He would have hated it. He might have been pleased it was destroyed and that Filipinos later came to shit there.'

As we left the fort I told Aniceto of my recent visit to Santa Ana Church; how after I left I had gone down a narrow back street where, in the very shadow of the church's back wall, I'd come upon an open-air workshop where plaster statues were being mended. Several were standing together with arms and legs missing, most of them more or less life-size. They were all of Jose Rizal. The man working on them had told me all the schools had statues of Rizal and when they were broken they brought them to him. There was a sense, I thought, in which the cult of Rizal had been used to promote a commonality between different social classes, an illusion of common history and common experience to paper over such matters as the upper class collaborating with the Japanese during the war while ordinary people starved. There was a sense in which heritage stood for amnesia. As when President Carlos Garcia in 1961 made a speech in Fort Santiago to initiate the restoration programme and said, 'these mute stones shall always be eloquent witnesses that while there has been tyranny in this country, we as a people have never bent our knees before the tyrants.' He said they were restoring the place so that it could be 'a shrine to which our people may repair in times of national stress, to draw the inspiration and moral strength needed in solving the serious problems of the nation'. In other words, if you were one of the poor whom national independence had only made poorer, don't go to the mountains and join the NPA, instead go to Intramuros and reflect upon your national heritage.[9]

We walked in a circuit which took us past Letran College where boys in white shirts and ties, children of the middle class, looked down into the street from the upstairs windows. You could almost smell the chalk dust and the dog-eared text books. No sign of 1945 there: the pockmarked walls had been replastered, the windows had been reglazed. Outside the seventeenth-century church of St Augustin, one of the only buildings spared by the shelling—miraculously, so it was said—a wedding party had just arrived. The bride stepped gingerly out of a cream coloured Mercedes Benz and stood like a dried arrangement on the old stone flagging while her attendants adjusted the folds of her veil and train. There were video cameras, well-dressed children running about, and a priest talking to a couple of fair-skinned altar boys in the shade of the doorway. I suggested we go in for a few minutes but Aniceto declined. 'Look at the way I am dressed,' he said, as if I should know better. He was dressed the way he was usually dressed.

Instead, we followed a lane behind the church down towards the bayside wall, quite close to where, on my first visit to Intramuros, I had climbed the rampart and stood on the bastion. Something I hadn't known at that time, nor on this visit with Aniceto, was that it was upon this bastion, the Bastion de San Jose, that MacArthur's pre-war office in Manila (1935–41) had been located. Known as the House on the Wall, it had windows on all sides and looked a little like a control tower at an airport. In a room furnished with flag standards and a Chinese screen, MacArthur had sat behind a large Chippendale desk where he struck visitors as being immaculate and fresh-looking despite the heat (he maintained a wardrobe of thirty-five uniforms and changed three times a day).

Up in his office MacArthur dominated Spanish Intramuros. The defence of the Philippines against the Japanese was planned there and during the tense weeks of December 1941, following Pearl Harbor and the destruction of America's Philippine air force at Clark Field, MacArthur continued to work in the office as Japanese Mitsubishis and Zeros flew freely overhead. The humiliation must have been difficult to bear. He ostentatiously insisted the Stars and Stripes continue to be flown over the office, disregarding warnings that this made it an obvious target.

There we stood, Aniceto and I, at that time of the afternoon when the air was so still, looking across at the House on the Wall but not seeing it. Aniceto had his hands in the back pockets of his jeans and his feet well apart; squinting in the sunlight, he looked both sensitive and tough. He looked composed: in his way, he was every bit as immaculate as the General. He had other things to think about. For my part, I probably looked a little perplexed and tired. My research project seemed to be going nowhere and I wasn't sleeping well. It was very hot. Neither of us said anything. We looked across at the absent office as if it had never existed, as if certain decisions hadn't been made there in 1941 and as if our lives were untouched by them; as if the chain of events which ended by producing the state of ruin around our feet had not begun up on that wall. Not knowing any of this, we turned around and walked off to find somewhere to eat.

On the side of the river opposite Intramuros sprawls Binondo, Manila's Chinatown, the congested heart of the old commercial district where dim sum vendors and noodle bars rub shoulders with Catholic churches. Attached to the side of a building near the Binondo end of the MacArthur Bridge at the time I was in Manila was a giant handpainted billboard of Bruce Lee, 'The Legend', in cut-out style. Naked to the waist and a few shades browner than he might have been in real life, he surveyed the streets of Binondo with his disciplined gaze, his pumped-up preparedness contrasting with the disorder in the streets below.

In 1945 the district had been badly damaged by demolition charges set by the retreating Japanese and by the ensuing fires. But even while the shelling of the south side of the river was still in progress the Binondo area came to life in a frenzy of haphazard Liberation commerce. Manuel Buenafe, in *Wartime Philippines*, describes how, as southbound shells whispered and roared over-head, people set up tables on the footpaths selling fountain pens, wooden shoes, cigarettes and shellfish. Barber shops and shoeshine boys appeared.

> *And there were cafes—the Victory, the American, the Mabuhay, Uncle Sam's, Sloppy Joe's, all hole-in-the-wall places—selling coffee at 15 centavos (20 with sugar), egg sandwiches at a peso-fifty, and liquor at a peso a shot. While GIs surged through their doors, the owners hammered and pounded and sawed enlarging their establishments.*[10]

Life has a way of going on. It went on again, too, in Intramuros when the tanks moved out and the squatters moved in. But whereas in Binondo people opportunistically hammered and sawed their way to a new future, in Intramuros this was only per-mitted to happen until the authorities had marshalled their resources to stop it. And when they stopped it they did so in the interests of restoring the place to its colonial Spanishness. As well as the lean-to huts of the squatters a whole raft of other urban facil-ities and activities were outlawed. They included gasoline stations, bus terminals, mortuaries, lumber yards, junk yards, cock pits, race tracks, massage and sauna parlours, burlesque theatres, juke boxes, overly loud transistor radios and fun machines, bull rings, and neon signs. Not just a class of people but a part of the city's ordinary life was to be declared undesirable and sanctioned against. It went without saying that Aniceto and most of the things he might have cared to do would have no place in this environment of rarefied, historical wholesomeness.

This litany of exclusion apparently included any mention of the 100 000 dead civilians: MacArthur's Return would be commemorated not where it ended, in the smoking ruins of Intramuros, but where it began, on the beach at Leyte. A larger than life-size sculpture of the General's unscheduled wading now stands in a pool at Red Beach— an almost perfect realisation in bronze of the photographic image of the event, the formation of metal men in uniform wades forever towards the shore. Also in Leyte, in 1974, Imelda Marcos spent several million dollars constructing what purported to be her ancestral home, as a venue for a party celebrating the thirtieth anniversary of MacArthur's landing. One drama queen, you might say, deserves another.

I was sitting at a café in Bali one morning reading the *International Herald Tribune* when I came upon a mention of how, on that day fifty years ago, American carrier-based planes had destroyed Japanese airfields in the vicinity of New Guinea. MacArthur, I realised, was returning again. From now until 19 October 1994, the fiftieth anniversary of the landing at Leyte, there would be numerous references to his progress through the southwest Pacific on his way back to the Philippines. Three thousand kilometres away to the east of Bali, MacArthur was on the move again, island by island, battle by battle. It almost made me nervous.

A few weeks later while looking at some photographs of war damage in Manila I came upon a picture of one of the 1930s neo-classical administration buildings which looked strangely familiar. The front portion of this four-storey building, with its row of columns and its sculpted pediment, had evidently been so heavily shelled that most of it had collapsed into a hillslope of rubble. It looked like the Legislative Building, now the National Museum. But it couldn't have been, I told myself, as I knelt on the plywood floor of the bungalow holding the picture up to the light. I had been based at the Museum during my time in Manila, had sat in its rooms and walked its corridors confident in the belief that I was in a pre-war building. Which, of course, I was. It was just that it had been largely destroyed and rebuilt in the meantime, it was just that nobody had thought it worth telling me this. I spent a confused half-hour carefully comparing the 1945 picture with recent pictures of the building before this really sank in. There was no mistake: the room where I'd spent weeks working on the old files simply didn't exist in the 1945 picture. It had disintegrated and fallen into the tangled mass of rubble and twisted steel reinforcing. Once I was convinced, confusion was replaced by an odd sense of lightness.

1995

[1] See the *Fourth Annual Report of the Philippine Commission* (Washington: Government Printing Office, 1903), p. 88.

[2] See D. Clayton James, *The Years of MacArthur*, vol. 11 (Boston: Houghton Mifflin, 1975), p. 644.

[3] See Michael Schaller, *Douglas MacArthur: The Far Eastern War* (New York: Oxford University Press, 1989), p. 97.

[4] See William Manchester, *American Caesar: Douglas MacArthur* (Hutchinson: Melbourne, 1978), p. 271.

[5] Paul Virilio, *Speed and Politics*, trans. by Mark Polizzotti (New York: Semiotext[e], 1986), pp. 10, 67–8.

[6] See Paul P. Rogers, *The Bitter Years. MacArthur and Sutherland* (New York: Praeger, 1991), p. 263.

[7] Carlos P. Romulo, *I See the Philippines Rise* (New York: Doubleday, 1946), pp. 223–24.

[8] 'Consensus of One', *Sunday Times Magazine*, 23 April 1967.

[9] For a review of the post-war restoration work in Fort Santiago, see Carlos E. Da Silva, 'Discovery of Rizal's Improvised Chapel-cell at Fort Santiago', *Journal of the Philippine National Historical Society*, 9, nos 2 & 3, 1961.

[10] Manuel E. Buenafe, *Wartime Philippines* (Manila: Philippine Education Foundation, Inc., 1950), p. 256.

Comfort in Arrears

> *... I felt his hand*
> *heavily on my shoulder, and knew what coil*
> *binds life to life through bodies, and soul to soil.*
> —R. D. FITZGERALD, *'The Wind at Your Door'*

THE CEMETERY IN THE SMALL South Australian coastal town of Port Vincent is directly across the road from the white beach where I learned to swim, in the hot December of 1961. On a long and narrow patch of land, the cemetery runs along the roadside parallel to the shore; for a little way it's sheltered from the wind by a line of big old black-looking pine trees, untidy but comforting. One of the oldest monuments stands over a grave that seems too big for just one coffin; the slab over the grave is lichened and cracked, but the lettering on the granite headstone is all too clear. 'SACRED', it says,

> To the memory of Augustus Craigie
> Aged 43 years,
> and of his eldest Son, Augustus Craigie,
> Aged 10 years.

> Who were burnt to death in the scrub at Surveyors Point,
> Yorke Peninsula, on Monday 20th Decr. 1869, whilst
> endeavouring to save a flock of sheep in their charge,
> the property of Mr. Goldsworthy.

> Leaving a widow and four children
> to mourn their loss.

Summer after summer I swam unknowing in the clear water across the road from this story. The Mr Goldsworthy in question, my great-great-grandfather Stephen, came to Australia from Cornwall at twenty-one, an age which suggests the possibility of disagreement with his parents about the advisability of emigrating. But there would have seemed no future at all in Britain for a Cornish farmer's son; he had clearly had enough of the Hungry Forties, and arrived in Australia in March 1847, the worst year of the Irish Potato Famine, the year that Emily, Anne and Charlotte changed the face of literature forever, the year before Europe erupted into revolution.

On the day of the bushfire Stephen Goldsworthy was forty-three, the same age as his shepherd, Augustus Craigie. With his own eldest son, John, Stephen was on his way to help the shepherd, coming in a horse and cart from thirty miles away, through uncleared scrub and bushfire smoke. Just up the coast from where the Craigies died, the fire closed round Stephen and John and forced them over the twenty-foot cliff and into the sea; the cart caught fire and had almost burned away before the horse came crashing down behind them. As red-hot leaves and branches rained down from the top of the cliff they ducked under the water and came up for air amid burning debris, helpless to do anything about what was happening further down the coast. The horse, miraculously, did not die; but there was no saving the 1800 pregnant ewes, and there was no saving the Craigies.

The shepherd lived, conscious and lucid, for two hours after he was found. They bathed his burns with the remedy of the times— kerosene—and chunks of cooked flesh came away with the cloth. The roasted body of the child was discovered, among hundreds of blackened sheep carcases smelling horribly of mutton, by his mother.

The story puts out untidy narrative tendrils that disappear off the edges of Page Two of the *South Australian Register* for December 23rd 1869. Stephen, it seems, got out of the water, looked at the dead, surveyed the blasted landscape and the wasted livestock, looked in on his wife Elizabeth, and set off alone on foot back into

the bush to find the nearest magistrate, someone who could officially record the deaths and perform the inquest. What was he
thinking? Later there was a move in the community to get up a collection for Mrs Craigie so that she could travel with her remaining
children to America, where she had 'friends', a word which in its
Victorian usage means connections, relatives, somebody who'll
look after you. But there's no indication of whether that ever happened. Where did she go? How, five days after the deaths of her
husband and her son, did she and her remaining children spend
the Christmas Day of 1869?

The Craigies died a little way inland from the cemetery. Looking
at the surrounding countryside it's hard to imagine how a fire this
murderous could start or grow, hard to imagine what would feed
it; for that wheat-and-barley district now, though gold in
December and green in June, is largely a treeless and denuded
moonscape, and for its part in this also, my family must put up its
hand. On a day in winter when the town is very quiet, when the
yachts and visitors have gone and the beachfront kiosk is closed
and the playground empty, when no car passes and no dog barks,
you can almost, if you stand there at the graveside for long enough,
hear the screaming of the terrified horse. You can't hear the
Craigies above the noise of the fire and for that you are thankful.
But on the stone the Craigies speak and do not cease to speak.

My grandfather, typing carefully at his desk in 1955 in the isolated
farmhouse where my father was born, a few miles northwest of the
Craigies' grave and a few miles north of Stephen's, wrote out this
story for my father, as part of a painstaking document he titled
'Old Pioneers'. His main concern in compiling this record seems to
have been to remember and honour the dead, and to ensure that
his descendants did the same; his main source seems to have been
the *South Australian Register*, the nineteenth-century Adelaide newspaper, whose archives he must have taken considerable trouble to
consult and from which he must have copied large patient tracts in

his late-Victorian, post-copperplate hand. The document contains not just the story of the Craigies but a number of other things, including a list of carefully preserved words from the language of the Aboriginal tribe of the area, and a list of the diseases which, by the time my family first arrived in 1847, had already all but wiped out the tribe, courtesy of whalers and sealers and sailors, seaborne and unresisted.

His tone about everyone—the Craigies, the Aborigines, his own grandfather—is the same: respectful and a little bit sad. He was a farmer and an RSL stalwart and a true-blue Liberal voter and it was 1955, but he seems to have had no trouble acknowledging the ambiguous nature of the family's history, and was, indeed, at pains to write it down. It is quite clear, partly from the contents of the document but mostly from the fact that he felt moved to write it, that he understood precisely the degree to which his own very modest prosperity was grounded in the deaths he was recording.

❊

It was fortunate for him that he wasn't trying to do this now. The current debates in Australia around history, race, responsibility and sorrow have made it almost impossible for me to find a way to tell this story. One particular kind of self-righteous urban historian would demand of me that I turn it into a mythic tale of martyred worker heroes and rich pastoralist villains, but apart from the ludicrous inaccuracy of such a picture, Stephen Goldsworthy seems to me guilty only of not getting there in time to die with the Craigies, and anyway, one demonises ancestors at one's peril.

On the other hand, and worse, the conservative triumphalist view would involve impatience at my dwelling on unpleasantness, sacrifice, danger, loss and the responsibility of employers, and would scorn the notion that I am, 130 years later, somehow implicated in the story of the Craigies. That side of the debate would accuse me of metaphorical black-armband-wearing, as though taking it for granted that remembering the dead is somehow despicable; in that respect, the use of the phrase 'black-armband historian' as derisory, much less as having anything to do with the idea of guilt, is one of the weirdest scraps of conservative rhetoric that ever found its way into public discourse. Like a black armband, this essay is indeed intended as a sign of the remembrance and mourning, but I don't feel guilty about the Craigies. What I feel for the Craigies is gratitude and grief, and an obligation to remember the connection between my life and the manner of their death.

If anything, I've got off lightly. Numberless contemporary Australians have more sinister and problematic family stories from the past than mine. No doubt at least one of the many Robinsons in the Melbourne phone book is descended from the George Robinson—his name ironically identical with that of the Protector of the Aborigines who recorded this story in his diary—who, on 27th June 1841 in Western Victoria, roasted an Aboriginal child alive at the campfire and kicked another one to death. And R. D. Fitzgerald's poem 'The Wind at Your Door' wrestles with an ancestor who earned his living and his grant of Crown land as an army doctor presiding over convict floggings:

> That wind blows to your door down all these years.
> Have you not known it when some breath you drew
> tasted of blood? Your comfort is in arrears
> of just thanks to a savagery tamed in you
> only as subtler fears may serve in lieu
> of thong and noose—old savagery which has built
> your world and laws out of the lives it spilt.

Fitzgerald would no doubt be retroactively accused now of being a black-armband poet. But at the time, like my grandfather, he was writing into an imaginative space that was not yet being ideologically struggled over and divided up; each was free, in his way, to work out his own relationship to the story he was telling. If my conservative grandfather had thought that in telling the story of the Craigies he might be accused of going over to the other side, he would have stopped like a shot. I think.

Since I began to write this I've spent an afternoon in Adelaide's

Mortlock Library. I wanted to look at the *South Australian Register* for December 23rd 1869, to check my grandfather's source and see if he left out anything I would have put in. All he left out was the atmospherics—the *Register* tells of the blistering heat that day, and the northerly gale ripping up trees by the roots—but then he wasn't really the atmospheric type. What does seem to have struck him is the dramatic intersection of individual ordinary lives with the forces of history and nature; maybe this was something he'd already learned about in 1917, fighting in the trenches.

Sitting in the library peering at the tiny print on the screen of the microfilm reader, I felt closer to him than I ever did while he was alive, wondering if anyone else but me had looked at those pages since he did in 1955. I'm curious about what he thought he was doing, and about whether he dwelt—as surely he must have done—on the day of the fire and the things that happened in it, and about what drove him to write it all down. And I'm wondering what that thoroughly decent, hard-working, hat-wearing, easily-shocked old digger would think about being derided as a black-armband historian, forty years later, by the people whose side he thought he was on.

1997

Auto/biography

I SHALL BEGIN QUITE CATEGORICALLY by stating that unlike some writers, I come from a family whose main export is storytelling but whose main obsession is with truth.

My father's side hailed from Macau, a little Portuguese enclave on the China coast with a certain languid reputation for casinos and sultry prostitutes. Compared to its thriving and energetic neighbour Hong Kong, it just didn't do so well. It is full of churches with garish statues and on a good weekend people will drive to the churches because churches always occupy the most picturesque spots, in order to wash their cars. This is a ritual which combines religious superstition with the Grand Prix, which is Macau's only claim to fame. But Macau produced great fabulists as well. After all, Latin culture has always believed that life is an invention. You make it or you fake it. One of the greatest, my uncle Umberto Rosa de Castro, claimed to have been a Jesuit priest and to have founded the monastery on the western side of Coloane island.

Why did you leave the priesthood? I asked him once, having encountered him dressed rather shabbily in a plush hotel lobby.

There wasn't any money in it, he claimed.

It transpired that he had built a fake monastery with fake saints' bones, plastic stained glass windows and was charging a huge entrance fee when the authorities and the Catholic church caught up with him. Hyper-reality was the business of my Uncle Umberto. Fake history and theme parks, false roses and real names. He left the church, he said, because he believed the Catholics were as humourless as the Communists.

1999, he kept saying, will be a bad year. That will be the year China resumes the enclave.

What will you do in the meantime? I asked.

Run a car-wash, he said.

I can count at least three uncles who are going to be in trouble when one truth replaces another in 1999. They have faked their lives so many times they'll simply have to go to the United States. Unfortunately autobiography will be closed to them there. In the US it is only allowed to the rich and famous. Iaccoca, Trump, O. J. Simpson. Would you trust those names? You see how one of the enduring things about autobiography still stands: truth is what fame postulates; the name of the game is the game of the name.

And the game of authenticity is, of course, a power game, substantiated in large part by the notion of genre.

You can begin to see what terrible things genres are; they imprison every situation within the expected. Genre categorisation exerts a disproportionate power over books. Just ask any judge of a literary prize how they classify fiction, non-fiction, poetry, drama and history.

Let me give you some examples of the power of genre and categorisation. My novels *Birds of Passage* and *Double-Wolf* are frequently found in certain bookshops under the category of 'Wildlife' and 'Nature'. They are never sold there. My novel *After China* once appeared on the 'Travel' shelves, and did quite well. My second novel *Pomeroy*, which was written cold-bloodedly and deliberately to parody all the genres it could possibly accommodate—the thriller, the crime novel, the romance—had at its heart a postmodern puzzle and a thinly disguised autobiography. It scored this for a review: In *Pomeroy*, Castro is simply trying to get onto the crime shelves.

Well, nothing could have been further from the truth. In that novel, I was really trying to get on the 'Deconstruction' and 'Literary Theory' shelves.

I suppose I'd been fighting against genre classification all my writing life, and the generic function I've used most of all to do this is a form which is not only unstable in itself and which has undergone intense transformation, but which has the potential to transgress the furthest. This is the auto/biographical form. The slash is already an implosion of multiple forms, dividing the conjunction of prefixes and yet allowing the crossing over between self, life and writing. But while all this should be pretty well accepted and expected in postmodern times, in practice there are still problems. Arts funding, for instance, cannot be made efficient without classification. Classification, as Michel Foucault showed us in *The Order of Things*, persists as an enlightenment project well beyond the era of representation, when a new episteme or system of knowledge requires a breakdown of such classifications.

One of the problems we had at the Australia Council, for instance, was that in order to obtain a certain grant you have to have had at least one book published. We came across a snag, however, in the tribal Aboriginal situation. The so-called autobiographies that were being classified were mostly written by Aboriginal women, and were no doubt valuable contributions to a communal writing and history, but official opinion was that they were oral histories, and could only be one-offs as well as first-time books, therefore we would need a special category in the guidelines allowing for this. In truth this was entirely incorrect. These were not autobiographies in the European sense. They were communally accepted truths which were identifications with tribal rules. They were, in the Western sense, inventions and re-inventions. They were not one-offs in that they could be written again and again with different narrators. Tribal law required that the secrets not be revealed to outsiders, so the notion of a historical document incorporating knowledge of an Aboriginal community was again incorrect. The self in a community such as this is not the self as we know it. It stands part-way between singularity and collectivity. That is, the self achieves its identity as an extension of the collective, the self as part of the group, but this doesn't exclude any of the motives for bringing such a document into existence. There may be a parodying element or joking element in the work which we take too seriously. There may be the impersonal documenting of a lived testimonial as part of a strategy to win political ground. Whatever the case, the argument over Aboriginal autobiography was blind to the fact that we in the West tend to conflate human culture and history with the lives of extraordinary individuals, and thus to extract a 'confession' and an authority from the singularity of these individuals.

The identity principle is a difficult one to shuck off—the habit of identifying an author with his/her character or narrator, of legitimising fact through organising a criterion for validity, of conflating truth with logic. But, as Nietzsche has said, language cannot absolutely affirm anything since it is based on the collective lie of subjective empirical laws and grammatical structures. He argued that the difference between truth and fiction, philosophy and literature, verification and the rhetoric of performance, philosophical persuasion and literary troping is finally undecidable. That is why in recent controversies over literary hoaxes, arguments conducted using the category or genre of 'faction' are so ineffectual in dealing with the prickly separation of fact and fiction. 'Faction' is a genre invented to give legitimacy to the person of the author and not to the text. It is the truth claims made outside of the novel that represent any possible arena for these arguments. But the novel itself must be debated purely on literary grounds within the confines of the text. As Tennessee Williams liked to suggest, a writer shouldn't let a few facts get in the way of a good story. This is why I fear for the attrition and deterioration of the word 'literature'. If 'literature' were politics and history as so much contemporary theory wants to make it, then we would have had no Tolstoys or Shakespeares, no Patrick Whites or David Maloufs, because, as others have noted, writers are astoundingly bad at politics and history ... in the way that we normally read them. The facts are bent and there is no compensation. Higher truths are at stake, made available to those who share the passion, but this is possible only through the advocacy of a 'morality' of style, the intimation of a moral authority. But it is the way that we have structured these genres which causes this perceived 'necessity' to delineate and rank, when it is really our own inability to come up with any absolutes. The space of 'literature' has justifiably been violated for its claims of sanctity, but new privileges cannot easily be conferred on strictures which have been proven to be equally inauthentic in accounting for multiplicity and complexity.

It is necessary to follow a little of the history of autobiography in order to assess the tortuous restrictions placed on it by the notion of genre.[1]

The most obvious set of oppositions occurred around about the beginning of the nineteenth century. This was in response to a new kind of writing known as the 'self-biography', postulated by Isaac D'Israeli, which contained already a kind of hybrid instability. Critics began therefore, a campaign to restrict the form according to whether it was fact or fiction, literature or history, private or public, whether it dealt with the self or with identity and whether it was subjective or objective. The thrust was coming from a tradition which basically saw as a breakdown in civilisation the separation of the individual from what was known as a 'public wholeness' or the socius. The ancient Greeks, for example, were seen not to have had the interiority which separated the ordinary citizen from his society. Any aberration could conceivably be linked to the voices of the gods. But the nineteenth-century conservative attempt to rein in autobiography from these schisms and paranoias took the form of restricting the parameters of autobiography to the upper classes, where 'career', breeding and morality could be vigorously monitored. In this way too, was individualism safeguarded from alienation. This agenda immediately appropriated what can now be seen as key concepts and models according to the 'great men' theory. This latter canonised the 'seminal' autobiographies of St Augustine, Rousseau and Goethe and the concept of 'genius' was vigorously separated from that of the 'common'. Women, of course, were restricted to the 'memoir', a lower form which supposedly catered for the domestic and the personal, whence introspective unhealthiness like vanity and morbidity emanated. Individual introspection was particularly denigrated, without regard for any multiplicity of the self, a restriction of reading which led to Rimbaud's cry of anguish: *Je est un autre*. The I is an Other, he wrote, not only positing a multiplicity of selves but selves that are, as George Steiner said, 'parodistic, nihilistic anti-matter, radically subversive of order and creation'.[2] Selves, in other words, that are provocatively anti-classificatory, anti-theological and very much a counter to what Simcox, Carlyle and Arnold proclaimed as pressing for some sort of holistic, 'objective' presentation of the self.

In the twentieth century, T. S. Eliot, that harbinger of modern alienation, felt it necessary to invent an 'objective correlative', a need for a connection between feeling and reality in order to counter any critique of pure introspection. His notes to his poetry were often an assertion of the authority of definition which testified to both a labyrinthine dissimulation and an 'explicable' objectivity. The interesting thing was that the writing could not be controlled by such 'theoretically studied' processes. It overflowed the shelving. But in generic terms, autobiography itself became a devalued form existing in the spaces which fell outside both fiction and history. Either because it wasn't objective enough or because it relied too much on facts to be taken as art. The hostility towards introspection went hand in hand with an elevation of an aesthetic which functioned as a kind of gate-keeper between art and text, especially when autobiography began to decline in critical estimation. In other words, a text could be delegitimated as being an 'autobiographical novel' or elevated as 'not merely autobiographical' but 'epic', as in the case with Dante. As biographers have pointed out, his life was extremely sketchy, a fact which nevertheless did not prevent nineteenth-century critics from referring to it constantly in order to link Beatrice with a Florentine banker's wife. This kind of process is just as untrustworthy a critical tool as the postmodern attempt to delegitimise the author. Postmodernism has exacted a price in that while 'truth' is interrogated and deconstructed and made a variant of language (see Derrida's demolition of Rousseau's claim to 'autobiography' as truth and personal experience), it has neglected its own reliance on rhetorical manipulation ... its own lack of immunity. This is most evident in the sterility of style I find in most 'postmodernist' works. I would say that most Modernist works have been postmodern before the term was invented, because from the moment that language registered an instability and a conscious awareness, multiple meanings were immediately generated. Deconstruction merely took the credit of regeneration away from the author.

The nineteenth century made the definition of autobiography an exclusivity linked by certain commonly used words. The words genius, gender, genre and eugenics are all engendered from the ancient Greek word γιγνεσθαι (geniothaï), which means 'to be born' or 'to beget'. But in the restricted terms of autobiography, women, foreigners, hybrids of all kinds, and certainly the common people, were excluded from its canon. Autobiography was the birthright of some people, but not of some others. Thus Havelock Ellis could use autobiography as a 'scientific investigation', linking it with generic purity, claiming that social environment and classification could determine one's character. Edward Paxton Hood and J. Lionel Taylor both speculated on human types within autobiographical discourse and voiced a rising concern with 'national decadence'.

The idea of national decadence and forms of cultural pessimism such as perceptions of literacy rates have always been at the forefront of a conservative backlash to other issues like immigration and alleged social engineering. The cry 'civilisation as we know it is about to end' is a repressive hypothesis which serves to resurrect a formerly dominant critical form, and really says nothing about the perceived decline of canons. Shakespeare will always be Shakespeare, but this does not exclude reading elements of his plays in the way Granville-Barker did, nor interpreting them from a New Critical stance, nor theorising about them in a deconstructive fashion. Yet it seems that from the nineteenth century we have inherited a necessity to imperialise interpretation, to link it with the cultural history of the nation-state. What was in or out depended on its perceived truth-value in mytho-historical terms. Dilthey and Misch both saw autobiography as having a significance grounded in history and self-awareness. Roy Pascal believed modernity had produced a 'malaise' in contrast to the awareness of history in the classical age ... thus leading him to make the very strange statement that autobiography should only be written in later life, from which sense can be made of the past, as though there was a static standpoint from which everything could be viewed.

One can see, I think, even from this potted history of the criticism of autobiography that the genre itself, through rigid interpretation, had an incipient 'use-by' date.[3] The setting up of genres has an implicit seed of decline because genres enforce boundaries that writing is *obliged to cross*. Consequently, the shift that necessarily took place from the spiritual and moral concerns of autobiographical criticism to psychological, narratological and sociological concerns, occurred precisely because writing will always transgress genre and will always use genre to exercise its own coming into being. I write precisely because I want to write myself out of an artificially imposed corner. The autobiographical element leads the way because it is the most direct form of transgression. The 'I' deliberately invokes multiplicity. Declares itself against authority. Places itself at the very juncture of risk. I see the critic as a challenge. I use critical theory to subvert genres. Mainly because hybridity, a mixture of forms, a mixture of character types and ethnicities, is what I bring to writing. It is what the 'I' is. A proliferation of selves. A juxtapositioning of differences. I am not only Portuguese, English, Chinese and French, but I am writing myself out of crippling essentialist categorisations, out of the control exerted over multiplicities.

Hybridity is a powerfully transgressive property and it has an ability to destabilise genres. Challenging critical boundaries, it seems to me, is the very crux of writing as a vocation. And not only because sclerotic cultural myths have, in a sense, created border posts whereby your personal history determines whether you can enter or not, but because like the Oedipal epigone, the offspring of strong literary traditions must necessarily kill one's literary father in order to establish one's own strength as a writer, paradoxically feeding off and destroying in the same way as deconstruction does.

So one is constantly overturning not only one's own education, but inventing one's personal history in order to counterfeit time and destabilise traditional genres. And it is that destabilisation which makes writing interesting as deliberate miscegenation. As Jacques Derrida has said, generic boundaries have also been used as racial boundaries.[4]

Authority, of course, is re-asserted over the creative product. Everyone's first novel is automatically claimed by critics to be autobiographical in some way. Mine wasn't. My first novel *Birds of Passage* was described by one critic as a *confessional* novel, which immediately begged the question about truth-claims which in turn controlled and structured what could be said about the novel. Did those things really happen to Chinamen in Australia in the 1830s? Can the novel be anything more than a confessional bit of interiority fashioned with little historical fact? History, regarded as stable and static, was being used here to delegitimise my novel. Little regard was taken of what the Chinese themselves may have written. But surely even that too is beside the point? The point is that truth is available only in the telling and has no privileged existence in real life beyond human language. As Raymond Williams has said, there is a negative definition of fiction placed against a pseudo-positive definition of fact. Both these definitions omit the spectrum of propositions and modulations involved in any understanding of reality.[5] Three different people will see three different kinds of truths in any ordinary situation. When it comes to a distinction between the written life and the lived life, fact and fiction become meaningless categories. A poignant conceit was inserted in my novel as well. Roland Barthes, the French writer, makes an appearance. His deferred death is hinted at and glossed. The death of the author is the life of the work. Once narration takes place, the truth is in the telling. It cannot exist without the telling. 'How many children had Roland Barthes?' is neither a real question nor a rhetorical one. Barthes is a body of work, and not a live or dead body.

The truth-claims of science, literature, history, myth and fiction continued to interest and disturb me. In Sigmund Freud I suddenly found someone who didn't give a damn about crossing all these forms. Freud was imposing, impressive, brilliant and authoritative. He was everything the nineteenth century needed for autobiography to recuperate its greatness and to police its rigid boundaries. But he did nothing of the sort. He was very much the subject of my third novel. Freud declared, without cringing, that the novelist had always preceded the scientist. He made so-called 'discoveries' from his own dreams. He wrote about autobiographies without placing them on any literary or social scale. He found that 'lies' could be turned to advantage, that the unconscious is only visible through fictions which the patient invents to represent the unconscious. The unconscious, therefore, could be substituted for that problematic word 'truth'. Freud also manipulated and structured his case histories to create his theories. Thus *Double-Wolf* was my attempt to place the slash between *auto* and *biography* in the way that Freud had done. I assumed the identity of one of his patients, the Wolfman, who had a recurring dream of wolves and who wanted to be a writer. In my taking on of a dead figure in order to re-vivify the unconscious of the 'I', I was transgressing and trying to find new dimensions to ego-psychology and psycho-biography by disburdening myself of the restrictions of positivism. I had seen how that particular brand of British philosophy had dried out the style of its writers. By subsuming case history to literary theory and intermixing this with a transcendent personal vulnerability, I and my characters were attempting to adopt a self-narration in the Nietzschean sense as well as announcing the death of the unified subject. This was the double enterprise.

It was in writing *Double-Wolf* that I began to read Nietzsche seriously. In writing *Ecce Homo*, Nietzsche, as Jacques Derrida has said, 'told his life to himself' as it were.[6] According to Derrida, Nietzsche sent the text out into the world to be signed and returned:

> *The ear of the other says me to me and constitutes the* autos *of my autobiography. When, much later, the other will have*

perceived with a keen-enough ear what I will have addressed or destined to him or her, then my signature will have taken place.[7]

A sort of detour via the other and then returned back to a dead sender. Derrida describes this as a form of *thanatography*. Nietzsche speaks about his own illness and the death of his father at the same age as his at the time of writing—forty-four—presenting himself as 'already dead'.

Well, at the age of forty-four, I was writing my novel *Drift*. In it, I wanted to 'hear myself speak' as it were, casting a dead author in my voice in order to lament the literal death of a culture, the Tasmanian Aborigines. In B. S. Johnson I was able to use the auto/biographical trope to the full, crossing the borders at will, because I found the detour via the Other ... that is, I became accustomed and confident enough now to write in a form which precluded the assumption of a 'unified subject'. I was no longer intimidated by reviewers who tried to 'seek me out' as it were, questioning my usage of dead, but no longer real, people in my fictions. In *Drift* I have an Aboriginal Other, Tom McGann, who is able to return B. S. Johnson's textual corpus, bringing it back to be heard again, in a kind of eternal return.

The critic Paul De Man has probably written on this most succinctly. In his essay 'Autobiography as De-facement' De Man outlines two tropes which he suggests as the mainstays of the auto-biographical form.[8] Although he was speaking about Wordsworth, the same applies equally to fiction as well as to poetry. The *epitaphic* trope he suggests as 'the fiction of an apostrophe to an absent, deceased or voiceless entity, which posits a possibility of the latter's reply and confers upon it the power of speech'.[9] This is carried out by my character Tom McGann. The *prosopopœic* trope confers a mask on a person, the feigning of a person when we bring in the dead. It is a fictional address from and to the dead, or as De Man has it, a *voice-from-beyond-the-grave*. This was my engraving or *graphein*, embodied by my character B. S. Johnson, an English writer who committed suicide in 1973.

While I approached the auto/biographical project with perhaps the by now wholly internalised and subconscious intention of exploding autobiography as an outmoded and meaningless genre, De Man systematically deconstructed autobiography as an impossible genre. He argued that the assumed referential status of autobiography reveals the fictionality of all referentiality, remarking that it is equally possible that the autobiographical project produces and determines the life. In other words, generic criticism, theoretical critique, literary theory, the imposition of rigid forms do have important inputs into the production of writing itself. What generated many of my novels was exactly this consideration and escape from expected form. But this signature, this return to me of an auto/biographical project in which I am no longer present is exactly that morality of style I hinted at above. Freed from politicisation, it encapsulated a complete vulnerability.

Reading practices, thus, tend to influence writing practices. This is the postmodern project, one that many writers are trying to avoid because it involves too much reading. But certainly discovering that I was writing in the prosopopoeic mode gave me the necessary confidence to go on, realising there were intellectual underpinnings beneath my fiction and not merely generic re-establishments of sensibility and story. Critical theory thus enables a certain *confirmation* of the writer's project. The prosopopoeic encapsulates that project of hybridity which is so dear to me ... the crossing of two worlds and two genres; two worlds in terms of that of the mask's and that of the author's; two genres in terms of the autobiographical and biographical. This deconstructs the 'person' of the author, although I fully realise it leaves me completely vulnerable to constructions of inauthenticity. And yet I would prefer it to the kinds of restrictions a critic like Philippe Lejeune would apply, when he says:

> An autobiography is a retrospective prose narrative produced by a real person concerning his own existence, focusing on his individual life, in particular on the development of his personality.[10]

Finally, auto/biography demonstrates the impossibility of totalisation and closure of any written text. 'Mongrel' forms such as this and collaborative authorships provide problems for the traditional critic and bookseller. Maxine Hong Kingston's *The Woman Warrior*, in its interweaving of fact, fiction, myth and memory crossed many of the boundaries. As did Germaine Greer's *Daddy we hardly knew you*. The reviews of the latter will show how some people couldn't cope with cross-genres at all. My thesis is that cross-genres relieve the schizophrenic pressures upon the dichotomy of authenticity and inauthenticity. In a way, they re-establish the bicameral forms of mental life excised from today's positivist and repressive consciousness. If you cross borders regularly you do not really have to defend them.

❂

Well, back to my family. My ex-Jesuit uncle is now having a ball in the US, writing his autobiography. He's already made two television appearances to promote what is as yet a non-existent book. On my mother's side, the side obsessed with truth, nothing has been said. I asked her once why she won't write anything down about her life. After all, her mother was from Liverpool and had sailed to China in the early twenties to convert the Chinese to Christianity. Her uncle was killed by a shadowy political group in Nanking just prior to the war. Why don't you write it down? I asked.

What for? she replied. It's all in my head.

I mean for others. Maybe I should write it, I carped.

She shook her head. It's better in here, she said, touching her temple. Nobody would believe the things I have to tell. And besides, why would you want others to know?

I thought that this was probably the Chinese way of passing on history. It certainly is the Aboriginal way. Why do we all have to go writing things down all the time? I went for a pen. My mother called me back.

When, she asked, are you going to take over your uncle's car-wash and make some real money?

1995

[1] I have drawn on Laura Marcus's invaluable *Auto/biographical Discourses* (Manchester: Manchester University Press, 1994) for much of this.

[2] *Real Presences* (Chicago: University of Chicago Press, 1989), p. 99.

[3] See also Elizabeth Bruss, *Autobiographical Acts: The Changing Situation of a Literary Genre* (Baltimore: Johns Hopkins UP, 1976), and Ashley, Gilmore & Peters (eds), *Autobiography & Postmodernism* (Boston: University of Massachusetts Press, 1994).

[4] 'The Law Of Genre', in *On Narrative*, W.J.T. Mitchell (ed.) (Chicago: University of Chicago Press, 1981), pp. 51–77.

[5] *Marxism and Literature* (Oxford: Oxford University Press, 1985), pp. 146–9.

[6] *The Ear of the Other: Otobiography, Transference, Translation: texts and discussions with Jacques Derrida*, Peggy Kamuf and Avita Ronell (trans.), Christie McDonald (ed.) (Lincoln and London: University of Nebraska Press, 1988), p. 12.

[7] *Op. cit.*, p. 51.

[8] Paul De Man, *The Rhetoric of Romanticism* (Columbia University Press, 1984), pp. 67–83.

[9] *Ibid.*

[10] 'The Autobiographical Pact', in P.J. Eakin (ed.), *On Autobiography* (Minneapolis: University of Minnesota Press, 1989), p. 4.

CHRIS WALLACE-CRABBE

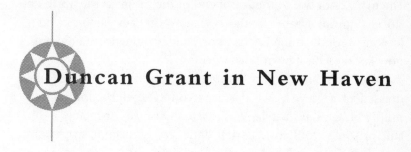

Duncan Grant in New Haven

WHERE IS THE PAST? WHAT HAS become of it? In what fashion have
some parts of it remained comparatively vivid, others more or less
extant, but in far vaguer outlines, while most of it has gone
entirely, 'gone even from the meaning of a name'?

Seemingly, we recall past events only in so far as they recompose
themselves in one of two ways: as an anecdote or as an image. The
latter is more likely to be the case when the memory has been
highly dramatic, or traumatic. Thus, I recall as an intense image the
moment, years ago, when I was riding a horse over an awkward
little gully among blackberry clumps and a stout bramble suddenly caught me across the forehead, tearing my skin and drawing
blood. This image has the feel of immediate physicality. My mental
body passes through it once again.

Let me go further back. In 1966 I had my only direct contact
with the Bloomsbury group, having the good fortune to dine with
Duncan Grant. It would be delightful to reconstruct that evening
in depth; I have tried to do so for weeks now, on and off, coming
up with a cluster of imprecise images, temporal sequences and—
far more clearly—spatial alignments. They can be drawn together
as follows.

It was a buffet dinner, given by the Master of Yale's quasi-gothic
Jonathan Edwards College. The first room we entered was

dominated by a large table, around which the guests circulated, drinking wine, chatting and then loading their plates with dinner. The main door was at the south end of the room: at the north end stood Duncan Grant, in the company of Paul Roche, a good-looking, blond, young English poet, and a young woman, whom I now know to have been Roche's wife.

Grant was small, very suntanned, smilingly wrinkled, and dressed in a greyish tweed suit, at once expensive-looking and mildly bohemian in style. Was it actually tweed, or merely a thick suit of some woollen material, dark grey with faint stripes, and rumpled? Do *tweed* and *rumpled* have more or less the same cultural connotations?

The first room seems to have been lighter than the second: was it natural light, coming in through the diamond-paned windows? Did we move into the second room with our plates? I think so, and the second room strikes me as greenish in its dominant tone.

What was talked about has largely gone, except that I discussed poetry and poets with Roche, who was to read some of his mediocre poems after dinner. Also my sense of Grant was more limited than it was to become later on. At that stage I had not even begun Leonard Woolf's autobiography, the first volume of which I was to read in January 1967. Surely I already knew that Grant had been Keynes' lover; but I was entirely ignorant of his relations with Vanessa Bell, except that I'd already have associated their colour-fully post-impressionist painting styles. Perhaps—probably—we talked about painting.

He looked like a gnome, if gnomes can generate an instanta-neous charm: brown, creased, humorous and almost handsome. He must have asked me something about Australia, expressing his sorrow that he had never been to that continent. No doubt I told him that a prominent Australian painter, Len French, was currently at Yale. Perhaps we spoke at some point about one or other of my current obsessions, Piero della Francesca and Matisse, both emblems of a post-impressionist taste which had in some sense reached me by way of Bloomsbury. But today I cannot recall a single word that we said.

At some stage I spoke to Roche about English and Australian poetry. Robert Graves was mentioned, that much I recall. And events must have come to an end with Roche's reading—unless we had coffee and port afterwards.

What surprises me about this, as about so many other memories, is how far the human content has leached away. The furniture, the windows and above all the alignments of those two rooms stay with me far more strongly than any sharp image of Grant. Or do they? Are any of these images really sharp? Memory's slides hardly ever are.

Yet it is curious to think of that antithetical and in some ways extremely British figure holding court, or at, least providing interest, at a university where painting had for so long been dessicated by Joseph Albers. Or one in which the black-on-black painter, Ad Reinhardt, the big man from Buffalo, had told a perplexed audience that 'interest is of no interest in art'. We were in the heart of that territory which has been characterised by Lucy Lippard in these words:

> Progress is supported by morality, in this case a morality outside
> of religious or theoretical confines, but distinctly rooted in
> puritanism, native or philosophical. It involves a dislike, or
> fear, of abdicating to the pleasure principle and was first based
> on a standard of self-denial.

On the fact of it, Bloomsbury was many a long mile from New Haven, but one of the tricks played by Yale and Harvard is to be museums of the world, gathering everything in as it passes by, hence Duncan Grant and Jonathan Edwards.

Even the strongest physical memories can be subject to perceptual ambiguity. For example, I have a powerful memory of breaking my wrist when I was seven. I can see myself falling over on the tiny front lawn in Canterbury Road while playing chasey around an ornamental cypress. The trouble is, I can see the event both from inside and outside my then self. And it is brought up a shade more vivid by a dream I had long afterwards about that same block of flats.

All which suddenly reminds me, for no reason, that when I met Duncan Grant I was wearing a speckledy light brown suit of Donegal tweed. And there's something, merely the ghost of a memory, about the attractive timbre of his voice. But at that point memory has become utterly attenuated, since my recollection of his speaking could not possibly be described as aural; not any more, even if it ever was after the evening of our meeting, the evening on which I touched the mysterious hem of Bloomsbury.

1996

Depth Soundings

IT'S A PRETTY FAIR ASSUMPTION to say that today music is the most popular of the arts. Constant Lambert's thirties' scorn of 'the appalling popularity of music' seems now merely a Jeremiah-like clearing of the throat before the deluge to come.

Immediately, one must enter the reservation that music's popularity is of several orders, some of them decidedly low-lying. If Andrew Lloyd-Webber has made more money than all the composers of the past combined, that may be a measure of the delta-like spreading of electronic networks rather than an indication of a complete decline in taste. It's also important to stress that much of what music does nowadays is a species of self-effacement and corporate underlining. Even serious films which would not stoop to kitsch scripts have to fill their soundtracks and reinforce their action with musical scores of various degrees of hyperbole. Where once a Walton or a Prokofieff provided film music, today even such a film as *The English Patient*, a work of a certain level of seriousness, is saddled with an inflated and undistinguished score.

An amusing side-issue of this habit of the movies of never doing without melodramatic musical backing became noticeable in the sixties and seventies. Many serious classical composers in those decades had embraced the full avant-garde fig: the only place you were likely to hear new music of a diatonic order, or, as Darmstadt would have said, reactionary sort, was on soundtracks. Though Schönberg, Berg and even Xenakis could have accompanied motion pictures as effectively as more conventional composers, the movie moguls insisted on Rachmaninov-cum-Copland. Like Diaghilev refusing to embrace an entirely homosexual world and insisting that theatre would lose its glamour and its economic viability if female beauty were excluded, Hollywood maintained the Romantic convention—it knew what audiences were used to and would continue to expect. Commercialism will always have this bias. In opulent societies the highbrow and the avant-garde can prove successful and guarantee their leading figures a prominent profile and reasonable riches, but for fame on a world scale and for fabulous wealth, the coordinates of art must stay within unadventurous limits.

Worse than what happens in the cinema is the habit of employing music as upholstery. From snatches of 'Greensleeves' and 'Rule, Britannia' on answer phones to muzak tape-loops in every sort of outlet from supermarkets to crematoria, music keeps the unmercantile anxieties of silence at bay. Music or muzak has become the accepted equivalent of the radio engineer's signal of human existence, the call-sign of immediacy. And musical 'wallpaper' will do this better than 'white noise'. Music is not actually wrapped round purchases, but it frames the point of sale. It has become an essential adjunct of twentieth-century popular commerce. All this is the decadence of a once-famous doctrine, that of 'The Music of the Spheres,' a Paracelsian notion that every human or natural action has its equivalent vibration in the sympathetic world of sound. *Live? Our background music will do that for us!* It is an uncomfortable paradox that we can weaken what we love by overusing it. And by misusing it. The despoilers of musical significance don't so much overvalue music as prostitute it. They are not innocent music-lovers whose habit of diminishing the art is simply to have it playing continuously. Theirs are the actions of malign wizards, a consequence of applying sympathetic magic cynically. Unfortunately, there is something of real value there for them to be cynical about.

Those of us who love music and admit to the charge of relying on it too much, of wallowing in it even, feel a self-justifying need to explain not just how necessary it is to us but also the source of its power. This necessity strikes us as a metabolic as well as psychological need. To speak for myself, I experience music as a whole world—not just an alternative universe to the visible and tactile one around me, but as a different and confirming grid in which the bewilderments of existence are straightened out. Music is like Cleopatra as Shakespeare recorded her: everything becomes itself therein. It is more than art and much more than commentary; a sort of second existence.

But if this essay is to be of any use, it must come down from its unprovable high horse and make more feasible assumptions. I propose therefore to examine just one central concern of music as an art—its relations with meaning.

There is an instinct about, even an easy-to-understand intellectual basis to, what moves us in literature and painting. Emotion first, then meaning, and perhaps technical mastery are all perceptible in poetry, prose, painting and sculpture. Even the most dedicated nihilist, the most devoted follower of *non sequitur*, finds it impossible to escape entirely from meaning in literature. A scrambled piece of novelist's 'free association', a page of *Finnegan's Wake* (the modern version of a medieval illuminated manuscript), a minimalist's foray at tail-chasing, a volume of 'language poetry' with few clues as to which parts of speech its constituent words are—all these literary artefacts exist within a force field of meaning. If a poem, a painting or an installation approaches meaninglessness, this is likely to be a matter of conflicting meanings cancelling themselves out rather than of pure chaos.

Meaning is not the be-all and end-all of the literary and plastic arts, but it is an inescapable concomitant. Being a product of the human mind, music, of course, has meaning too, equally inescapably.

But what is meaning in music? How does it work and what is its language, its system of signs, its discrimination among sounds? Must we approach it always by analogy? Are we forever condemned to use the method of metaphor, of speaking of music's effect on us by indicating states of mind aroused which are familiar from literature, drama, and theology, or directly from personal experience?

I have no doubt that I will be using just such analogous devices as those deplored above. But I hope also to bring some major dilemmas into the open. There is bound to be a contrast between the laboured process of reasoning in words and the natural experience of listening to music. But you cannot use music to explain music.

Hans Keller attempted musical analysis employing only freshly composed music of his own as comment on the piece he was examining. He chose the first movement of Mozart's Piano Concerto in C, K. 503, and indeed did manage to reveal that everything which its sonata form structure required to make it a masterpiece of logic and sensuous sound has been ordained by Mozart and set in place by him. But it hardly helps us understand how Mozart's composition was made. What is the listener to do thereafter beyond jettisoning Keller's analytical supplement? His establishment of Mozart's sufficient genius might be described as Euclidean—proof by redundancy of addition.

Stravinsky, doodling for Robert Craft, once asserted that if many composers' works might be tagged 'analytic', then his were properly 'synthetic'. Two mere words, but quite illuminating, especially if kept in mind while listening to *Pulcinella*. That perennially surprising masterpiece is not just a time-traveller's clever scoring of another man's tunes. It is a remarkable synthesis of original materials joined to the musical hares they started in the mind of an acute creative imagination. At any point in his career Stravinsky worked by a process similar to adjacency or symbiosis. This is what lies behind his 'borrowings' which Lambert and others found so pernicious. Already existing music (it could be folk melodies as well as scraps by Pergolesi and Tchaikovsky) is not dressed up by Stravinsky but suggests offspring and neighbours to him which he then layers into his own composition. This method of composing is truly synthetic in that it uses one sort of material to produce another sort. It is not collage, montage or even variation, but collateral imagination.

Such examples may be irrelevant to this argument but they can help justify employing a general terminology, the language of humane criticism, when discussing music. As the redneck puts it in Eliot's 'Sweeney Agonistes', 'I got to use words when I talk to you'. They are blunt tools but nothing else will get very far, not even an improvised workshop at the piano. Musical dissection leaves material scattered all over the dissecting-room floor.

Is there then a language of music? Deryck Cooke thought so, and wrote an eloquent book on the subject. It is indeed a good book, the product of a well-informed and sympathetic mind. It is also the issue of one man's intense love of the art he is anatomising. Cooke's musical landscape is an Elysian Fields which any music lover would be at home in. But I find it impossible to accede to his general principles, most notably because they are so general. Can musical expressiveness be categorised or pigeon-holed according to the feelings or moods which seem endemic to intervals, tonalities, harmonies, phrase shapes and instrumental timbres? Might not an interval frequently encountered in the musical depiction of one human mood be found elsewhere depicting a quite other mood? I recall hearing a young composer remonstrated with at a concert of the Society for the Promotion of New Music in these terms: 'All those minor thirds make you sound so English!' Dire warning, indeed. Only in music of the baroque and classical period (1600 to 1830) does a tendency to Sturm und Drang, a dramatically intense colouring or melancholy emphasis, seem to demand a minor tonality. Even here, Handel uses the major mode to portray sadness and the minor for stateliness.

Cooke is able to list enough significant examples of intervals reinforcing Theophrastian moods to indicate some musical tendencies, though the process of selection is necessarily biased to produce the desired result. And there are further problems in his conclusion, which might be summed up as being of the order 'the interval of the rising third often indicates sadness, or the octave is chosen to demonstrate certainty'. While agreement can sometimes be reached on mood identification in a piece of purely instrumental music with no title beyond prelude or sarabande, a more definite association requires a feeling-intense text attached. We know the feelings concerned because the words tell us what they are. Cooke's copious examples of intervals and harmonies being associated in composer's minds with particular concerns and feelings is forced to lean heavily on vocal music, where argument about musical meaning can be supported by verbal meaning. Many of his chosen quotations are drawn from the intense and even hysterical poetry of Lutheran piety and nineteenth-century Romanticism. One has to keep one's head down when discussing such matters. There is clearly an appropriateness in musical expression which is natural to our human nervous system. Exhilarating music is likely to be at a fast tempo; loud music will not usually be appropriate to meditation (though consider the F-sharp major vigil of *Don Quixote* in Strauss's tone poem); only a perverse composer would set the words of the Credo of the Mass, *'et resurrexit tertia die'*, to a descending and not an ascending scale.

There are major decorums in all arts which even the most iconoclastic spirit must take into account. Nevertheless, within such broad certainties the language of artistic expression is inexact. There is no dictionary of musical meaning equivalent to a dictionary of words. One pitch alone cannot denote a meaning. Meaning enters only when a note is sounded after another note and usually remains unclear until many other notes have joined in. I underline this truism deliberately. However you use a word, it goes on existing in the dictionary as meaning this one or some other specific thing. A note of the scale means something inside the scale but nothing outside it. The scale then relates to music in a pattern half from mathematics and half from aural experience.

This is not how meaning works in literature. Interesting literary art comes into being when the shifts and complexities of the meanings of words are exploited far in advance of their dictionary meanings. The poetry of William Empson is richer than any semantic analysis could define, but, as Empson himself demonstrates in his *Structure of Complex Words*, the ramifications of 'honest' and 'fool', short words with cataclysmic consequences, must still fall back on the ur-state of their meanings. The equivalent in music is more mathematical: the octave and the way it can be organised into greater and lesser powers, which we call keys, and the general assembly of the tones and semitones into the diatonic scale. And so on. This is certainly meaningful but it is not analogous to meaning in the literary or logical sense. Not for the last time in this article I should like to warn against overvaluing argument by analogy. 'Poetic' music is as sloppy a term as 'lyric' poetry.

There is only one way to assert meaning in music and that is through the ambiguous and loose feelings which music arouses in us. It is easier to take the mathematics of music for granted than to explain how they work. Theorists like Tartini found a moral value in music's very numeracy, and every academy and conservatorium teaches music in tried and tested ways which are rationalisations of basic mathematical predominances.

Deryck Cooke's thesis, from which I have now strayed some distance, does not take into account the shifts which have occurred in western music since it acquired its characteristic profile. The thousand years up to Guido d'Arezzo's development of a workable musical notation are really dark ages. Today we can buy a handful of discs which purport to offer music from Greek, Roman and Byzantine times. But there are few performable scores. And while poets and liturgical compilers were adapting Latin to make it sound like various vernaculars—that is, scanning it accentually and letting it rhyme—*Dies Irae, Stabat Mater* and the rest—what music was doing was confined to plainchant, Ambrosian and Gregorian. Doubtless such chants, now gathered and revised into the *Liber Usualis*, are rooted in the memory of popular forms, folk or sacred, but they are distant from our ears' present sensibility. If we take Organum and Conductus, the School of Notre Dame, as being a useful starting point of western music as it develops beyond monody, we still have four hundred years of musical production ahead of us before we get to the classical model, which is where Deryck Cooke's examples will be found.

In the twentieth century we have become used to various Promethean rebellions against the musical mainstream, and so we are tempted to assume that the orthodoxy from which post-*Tristan*

Modernism departs is nothing less than the true voice of music. Triadic, Classical, Tonal—whatever you call it—this organisation into major/minor tonalities has prevailed from the Renaissance onwards and still underpins the expectations of modern listeners. It is the ambience Cooke's language is at home in. But modal music offers different tropes. Modality's sense of a musical land-scape is as different from Beethoven as Old Norse or Anglo-Saxon are from Alexander Pope. On the horizon now many new tongues are calling. Total Serialism may have succumbed to market forces, and various repetitive, single-minded techniques restoring some of the more threadbare Triadic devices (one witty commentator speaks of them as 'the boring simplicities of Baltic Monks') may be the rage at the moment, but one can have a confident expectation that over the next four hundred years there will be further radical alteration to music's practical language. Natural sound—not just imitating Nature but recorded in and reproduced from Nature—appeals to many assemblers of new music. Pitch, harmony, the-matic structure, special instruments, orthodox notation—the minutiae of music's mathematical foundations may be dispensed with. If it gets too far from Brahms on the one hand or Ockeghem on the other, it won't be music to me, but someone writing such an essay as this in the future may find himself working along an utterly different set of coordinates. Our revolutionaries are already asserting that music is whatever they say it is.

Back in our traditional playground, we have quandaries enough to be going on with. A central concern of mine is with the relations music enjoys with words. It's a bullying relationship, but more of that later. First, how abstract is music? Surely its abstract character is one of its glories. Poets look enviously on music's not being dominated by meaning—verbal meaning that is. We got nowhere when we tried to describe a language of music, but will we do any better if we discern instead in music patterns which make sense, images and shapes which please us?

Perhaps the most viable way of dealing with such a knotty ques-tion is to abandon generalisation for a moment and consider real pieces of music heard in real time. Consider the slow movement of

Bach's Italian Concerto. It is an extraordinary piece, being a chain of notes almost like an improvisation, for the right hand over a gentle supporting bass in the left hand. Bach's weaving of this long garland of sound is intensely lyrical, but his instrument is the harpsichord, and so the lyricism is a divine cheat, being made up of individual struck notes which manage to suggest the weave of a string instrument. Other keyboard composers have excelled at this sort of writing—Chopin's cantilena also makes the piano sing. There are no special harmonic audacities in Bach's piece but the supremely beautiful line is not primarily melodic either. (The mystery of what constitutes melody is beyond the power of any textual analysis. All the interesting chiming significances—interval recurrences, implied harmonies, sequences, aroused and satisfied cadences et cetera—end up telling us nothing. Nor does the number of permutations of the notes of the octave unravel the mystery. They are innumerable, but why are some more fascinating than others? How much does any bare tune owe to a larger relationship with other tunes? The politician's greedy shout, 'There is no such thing as society!' is proved false by music. There is nothing but society in music.)

Back to Bach. Starting and cadencing, approaching and retreating from tonally important crisis points, rising and sinking—these descriptions of the upper line's movement are just about applicable to its effectiveness and beauty. You could try breaking up the line into numerical or metrical units: you could verbalise things by speaking of Bach's 'wandering' progress as though he were anticipating that walking impulse which Schubert made his own. In the end you will have only three perceptions you know to be true—the succession of notes sounded above their supporting bass delights the ear; the pattern is satisfying without its having to be perceived as a pattern; and Bach has gauged with supreme accuracy which notes to use—you could decorate his line with various further ornaments, appoggiaturas et cetera, but you would discover that he had foreseen this and propounded a processional sequence which abjures addition or deviation. What he writes lies beyond meaning in any applied sense: the music means itself.

Immediately, one must enter a caveat to such absolutism. Bach's technique in the 'Italian Concerto', and indeed in almost all his instrumental composition, is the same as he uses when setting words, where it must reflect and support specific and often contentious meanings and emotions. Dozens of passages from instrumental works, such as the 'Brandenburg Concertos', the solo violin sonatas and partitas, and the organ fantasias and toccatas, are re-employed not drastically altered in his church cantatas. How can pieces of music satisfying in their abstract musicality be recruited to reinforce the pious hallelujahs or the intractable stiffnesses of Lutheran theology? I propose to account for this by inventing a concept called 'transferable value'.

You are Bach setting the words *Unser Mund sie voll Lachens* for chorus and orchestra at the start of a cantata for Christmas Day. Then why not recognise that the text 'Our mouths are full of laughter ... at the great things God has done' requires a rollicking piece of music, and look among what you have written already to help out with just such a proposition. There it is, in the opening movement of the Fourth Orchestral Suite in D Major. It takes readily to your added vocal parts and the end-product necessarily is a different composition. It is now our turn, as Bach's inheritors, to think backwards. Does his decision to use his original orchestral music to carry his later message of Christian joy mean that the Suite possessed just such a quality all along?

The answer is yes and no. Transferable value in such cases—and there are thousands of them—is another example of music's dominance when associated with words. It is also a testament to the language of music's being so generalised that it is infinitely re-usable within a broad range of categories. What the listener who does not know Cantata No. 110 receives when he or she listens to Suite No. 4 is ebullience and excitement without a Christian message. Christianity has always baptised whatever it has recognised as a value. As Stravinsky puts it, 'One should worship God with a little talent if one has any.'

It follows that any art which is sufficient in itself, or which commands its own coordinates, when combined with another, will take on secondary colouring without losing self-possession. Either as the Suite or as the Cantata, Bach's invention delights us, though only one of the forms (the Cantata's) has a specific connotation. This pushes us back into Deryck Cooke's dilemma—how purely orchestral music can be held to use certain technical means to embody demonstrable emotions. When discussing this previously I didn't ask any of the necessary practical questions. Sticking to Bach then (who is a good case for the examination since not many of his instrumental works have been given a sobriquet or nickname from listeners' perceptions of what they are like), is the Sarabande of the Fifth Partita in G for keyboard sad, comfortable, pompous, processional, elegant, or any combination of these states? I hold it to be beautiful music, neutral in mood. It hardly suggests any clear-cut state of feeling.

However, the great Chaconne which ends the solo violin Partita in D Minor moves in and out of moods which, though not labelled as portraying anything specific, do suggest strenuous feeling. The movement's structure, being composed of variations of virtuoso violinistics on a ground bass, is what analysts choose to draw attention to, marvelling at the complexity Bach achieves with limited means. Performers are amazed by the sweat and difficulty of it, and admire those of their number who can execute the music with the least compromise. I was once in a room at a private party when the Chaconne was played, and listened afterwards to what good people felt obliged to say about it. They emphasised its nobility, its philosophical power, its undoubted profundity. Yet there are no verbal clues to latch on to and no philosophical or moral imperatives in the music beyond those its hearers can import into it. Some musicians have been very wary of the public's tendency to gush over great works. Stravinsky thought Proust's exclamations of admiration for Beethoven's Late Quartets an example of literary men's fashionable insincerity. He also characterised Pablo Casals as 'being for World Peace and for playing Bach in the style of Brahms'.

The question of music's connection with states of mind within its own value system has always troubled our understanding. It even goes back to the origins of the art. For the Ancients, as far as we know, music was almost synonymous with nature. Gurgling streams, rushing wind, bird calls—a whole armoury of natural sounds—were adjuncts to human feelings. An expertise in music was jealously guarded by the gods, as the fates of both Marsyas and Orpheus suggest. Nobody bothered to make permanent the tunes Marsyas played during his fatal competition with Apollo. It would seem that for both the Greeks and the Romans (and likely enough for everyone else in the Ancient World), music was largely a matter of that 'underlining' I noticed at the beginning for this essay. Roman *bucinas* helped put the enemy to flight in a way unimaginable for the Grenadier Guards Band. A friend once sang to me the marching-song that Caesar's army bellowed out when his legions entered Rome, the one translated by Robert Graves as 'Home we bring the bald whoremonger, / Romans, lock your wives away!'. He claimed that the tune had come down to us from the last years BC, but he didn't tell me how it had survived.

We have sheaves of lyric poetry from the classical world, much of it probably intended to be sung to the accompaniment of lyre or lute. Whatever the rules of the music it gave rise to, we now know only the forms and structures of the poems. These are often elaborate, but what scales, modes or other conventions governed the music to which such verse was set, we have little idea of. Observation of music in the classical world leads us to believe that it was always assigned a supporting role. Almost two thousand years had to pass before it became autonomous and—I have to confess as a devoted music-lover—a tyrannical art in its own right.

Music undoubtedly played an important role in the solemnities of Greek Drama. So much so, in fact, that efforts by the self-conscious archaisers of the Florentine Academy to revive music's part in dramatic poetry led, through creative misunderstanding, to the dominant late-European art of opera. Music will always be a fifth-column art: its patron saint might well be Thomas à Becket rather than Cecilia. Sent to do Drama's bidding, it goes native and takes over the whole caboodle. Let music through your defences and it will put your moral citadel to sack. As an *arriviste*, it protects itself by assuring everyone that it has an ancient lineage and is properly classical. It is, however, a savage newcomer, and, at least for those who can hear its siren call, a mistress who will brook no rivals. When the mysteries attendant on Iphigeneia's sacrifice were enacted in fourth-century BC Athens, music was on hand to empower the ritual, and, in the form of the chorus' part, to reflect on the tragedy. But by the end of the nineteenth century words were no more than a listener's right-of-way through the harmonic forest of Act Three of *Parsifal*. Wagner's art is Midas-like, it turns everything it touches into music. The most ludicrous image of artistic misapprehension known to me is that of King Ludwig of Bavaria having Wagner's libretti read to him in preference to hearing the operas performed. Not for economy's sake but because the words excited him as the music could not do. He loved the man and the words were more the man: music was the man magicked. But we later Wagnerians are in thrall to Venusberg and are likely to apologise for its creator's character. Wagner has replaced speech's best, which is eloquence, with the world-soul itself, the music that speech has conjured up.

When music and literature work together we encounter a bewitching and hard-to-analyse mélange. Let us plunge into an already well-documented world any time between the early eighteenth century and the middle of the nineteenth. By now music has wrested power from the literary arts, though that isn't always obvious to composers and poets. There are sensible and practical letters by Mozart, pointing out what was wrong when some literary consideration was spoiling a musical one. He wrote to the Abbate Varesco and Gottlieb Stephanie Jnr, librettists of *Idomeneo* and *Die Entführung aus dem Serail*, urging them to curb their own enthusiasms and find the right words to accommodate his needs. He was not, of course, dealing with first-rate and important littérateurs.

The exchange between Richard Strauss and Hugo von Hofmannsthal is a more equal encounter, or is it? Critics have found it easy to applaud the tasteful Hofmannsthal and rebuke the vulgar Strauss, but it was always the composer who was in the saddle.

It is not my purpose to argue that music is a greater art than poetry: while I covet music's freedom from direct responsibility to meaning, I also value the 'shock of recognition' which is literature's special gift. What I do suggest is that when music and literature work together music will inevitably be the dominant partner.

The history of opera proves this. Imported as a means of emphasising the eloquence of speech, music quickly took over and became the *raison d'être*. Between those classicists who set up such pioneer works as Peri's *Dafne* and collaborations of professional librettists Felice Romani and Francesco Maria Piave with Bellini and Verdi, a great gulf is fixed. Music's ability to eat 'texts' is shown as early as Monteverdi's setting of Rinuccini's *Orfeo* (1607). Verdian *brevità* is already being imposed on the text.

Music is magic. It has the full flush of original sin on it. It can collaborate only on its own terms. What it wants from words is that version of 'meaning' which verbal structures possess and music does not. When musical meaning is added to verbal or humanist meaning, we get a doubly powerful art. The cannibalism involved is not essential for musical achievement, but it is something composers have shown themselves grateful for. Bach's two books of twenty-four preludes and fugues for keyboard in all the keys would make him a great composer by themselves, but the technique which fashioned them had further work to do: to serve the world, the flesh and even the Devil in passions, cantatas and motets.

Arnold Schönberg once related how a composer goes about setting words to music. Or at least how *he* did it. Firstly he spoke of Schubert's songs. Many of them had lodged naturally in his consciousness and yet he discovered that he could not remember the lyrics of the poems Schubert set or what they were about. When he read the lyrics as poems in their own right he appreciated that they made sense quite outside his experience of them as songs. When he himself wrote songs, he was inspired by the general impression of the poet's creation and was influenced only secondarily by the words he was setting. Musicians tend to compose ideas and regard words as only the necessary assembly of syllables to carry their notes. They may be attracted initially to a phrase. In some famous arias the melodic blossoming proceeds from what seems the tritest of texts. '*O mio babbino caro*' with its dipping tune and octave leap is a teenage girl's wheedling of her Daddy to go down to the jewellery quarter of Florence, *la porta rossa*, and buy her an engagement ring.

Stravinsky always asserted the divine right of music to treat words just as syllables, being sure this would justify his iron control over both sound and sentiment. He had the Cocteau libretto of *Oedipus Rex* put into Latin for him, because, as a dead language, it was free of the tendency to over-emotionalism of a European vernacular. Perhaps also the Latin helped him serve a concept greater than local meaning or autonomous sound. The vocal line of *Oedipus Rex* disproves emotional indifference on his part. Just before the climactic Gloria which ends the first part, Oedipus sings 'Invidia fortunam odit ...': he has reached the high point of his confidence and indulges in the hubris of defying both men and gods. Stravinsky's setting of the Latin admonishment of envy is tortured, melismatic, almost unbearable, one of the most involved pieces of declamation in his œuvre. It gains by being strung along the syllables of a distancing language.

For the same reason thousands of composers have been able to make great art out of liturgy, especially the most overworked part of it, the ordinary of the mass. The words are familiar to the point of exhaustion, but the beliefs they serve are universal and inexhaustible. Most composers have the natural skill and good sense not to try to set (say) the Credo in some smart way which will call the wrong sort of attention to it. Prevailing conventions are useful without being stifling. The 'Crucifixus' is a natural crisis point and demands hushed treatment, the 'et incarnatus est' is an occasion for lyricism and the coda 'et vitam venturi sæculi' calls for triumphant setting.

The syllable-isation which music imposes on language is different from any of the localising techniques which poetry itself indulges in. Composers are attracted to poetry's distillation of effect when seeking texts, that concentration of essence which already separates verse from the more expansive patterns of prose. Despite Auden's credo that an operatic libretto must decently be in verse, I doubt that rhyme or metre have much to do with it, though the factory-produced libretti of Italian theatre hacks are always in rhymed verse. Music identifies in rhymed poetry a symmetry which is a paradigm of its own. Where effectiveness of setting is in question a composer will always be cavalier with the rhyme and metre of his text, if he has to be.

Hugo Wolf disapproved, or said he did, of over-melismatic setting of words, of excessive coloratura, embellishing of melodies, in fact the whole elaborate millinery of *bel canto*. He would not have wanted to do what Handel and so many others did in the eighteenth century—make a handful of words the hanger on which to display up to ten minutes of florid vocalising. But even Wolf didn't insist on one note to one syllable, and the reason is easy to understand. Poetry, if one sticks strictly to the metres commonly encountered in European languages, is unresourceful compared with music. Most triple metre in verse becomes tiresome or comical very quickly, and is not easily given variation by metrical change. Music has so many more rhythmic possibilities than verse. In practice, admittedly, we seldom let the official scansion of a line of poetry govern our delivery of it. Instead, we introduce humane inflections instinctively. But poetry has never developed an exact system of notation of pitch or metre. This is probably why, in English, iambic pentameter blank verse has been such a favoured form among poets, especially for dramatic purposes. In blank verse the metrical insistence is subliminal rather than profound, and the actual rhythm of each line is subject to the ebb and flow of meaning. What the speaking of poetry does so advantageously within its own metrical bonds, music can afford to do much more extravagantly.

As you consider the ways composers have managed to set poetry, the opportunities they have relished to give solo singers and ensembles such adventures among words, the more you marvel at the ingenuity of music. From plainsong melismata, such as the extensive ululation of the word 'caput' in the famous Sarum antiphon, through to the eleven-minute polyphony which is the Kyrie and Christe of Bach's B Minor Mass, music has festooned words as mistletoe covers trees or convolvulus a civic garden. Yet just as these vigorous parasites could not exist without their hosts, there remains an idea and a skeletal means of pinning it down beneath much exfoliating vocal writing—and this is embodied in words. Floridity is not the only response to texts, but it is the most interesting if we are to examine the vexed question of how words and music work together.

It is customary to write the history of music as a progressive, even a triumphant story. It is also reported as vindication, as a humanising improvement. Thus, from Schubert onwards, the nineteenth century disapproved increasingly of settings where the notes so obscure the words that audiences cannot know straightaway what is happening in a song. Centuries earlier, at the Council of Trent, the Doctors of the Church had also worried that an excess, however pious, of musical flowering was tending to bury important doctrinal concerns in the liturgy. The Fathers wished to rescue dogma, while the theorists of the Victorian age, especially Wagner and his followers, wanted to restore a paramountcy of humanism and philosophy. There are many florid moments in Schubert's songs—think of 'Des Fischers Liebesglück' and 'Am See', but the great songs at the end of his life show him matching notes to words with inspired economy—as with 'Am Meer' and 'Der Doppelgänger'.

Then came music's greatest crisis—an increasing chromaticism until all sense of key evaporates, which was flagged by Wagner's *Tristan und Isolde*. From this point radical change was speeded up. The coherent collaboration of music and humanism disintegrated into pioneering attempts to radicalise every aspect of form. Experiment concentrated on elevating technique into various local rebellions. In turn, early twentieth-century liberalisation was succeeded by a draconian puritanism where words and notes marched in mathematical uniforms. Eventually, floridity returned as composers began their long trawl back to a past which offered models more congenial to creativity than such absolutisms as Atonalism and Serialism. Stravinsky ranged across several centuries and Britten found in Purcell a way of adding brilliance to the art of Schubert and Wolf. Michael Tippett ransacked the rhythmic audacities of Renaissance madrigalists. In this century, words have been assigned an even more equivocal place in music. They are not the custom-made felicities which the eighteenth century demanded and which were literally more in theme than outline. Texts of most contemporary compositions cannot claim partnership on equal terms with scores, as was the case in nineteenth century Romanticism. Today all the arts enjoy a dubious equality: they have lost their way and a good part of their audience.

All except one, that is—and even that one owes its success to a kind of debasement. This is pop music in all its manifestations. I feel poorly equipped to discuss pop, rock, Tin Pan Alley and the like, and scarcely better acquainted with jazz, swing, modern jazz, country and western, folkloristica and ethnic music. But it seems to me that in all these forms the partnership of language and music is a more equal one. The 'book' of a show still matters on Broadway. Though many contemporary musicals are thin stuff indeed, vintage Broadway, from the turn-of-the-century through Jerome Kern, Rodgers and Hart, Cole Porter, Irving Berlin, *Guys and Dolls* and *Pal Joey* and up to Leonard Bernstein's shaky crossovers, enjoys living interaction between humanity and popular music. We tend to remember these shows for their songs and ensembles, but the best of them have not degenerated into 'highlights' in the manner of so many serious operas. Wagner would be surprised to discover that the true inheritors of his concept of *Gesamtkunstwerk* today are the best Broadway and Hollywood spectaculars.

When two artists combine, the tension set up between their contributions may wax and wane in an audience's mind. There can be no doubting primacy when one of the collaborators is a genius, so that while we are full of admiration of Lorenzo da Ponte, we would never assign him equality with Mozart. Our proper reaction is gratitude that so excellent a librettist should have served so transcendent a composer. Let us also heap praise on those less-than-original poets, professional and amateur, who provided Schubert and Brahms with their copious Biedermeier verses. These were at least well-cut and shaped for their purpose. When poetry stands eventually before the gold bar of heaven, its good deeds, in the form of the shapely verses it has bequeathed to composers, will not be the least of its mitigating circumstances as it faces accusations of vanity and triviality.

I've already emphasised the adage that no opera has been saved by its libretto. Alleged masterpieces of sophistication by Abbate Casti, Da Ponte's rival, are seldom heard, since the music they serve has been given the thumbs-down by posterity. The opposite observation, however, is spoken of less: that good musical works may be betrayed by poor books. The position here is complex, since one must distinguish between a poorly executed libretto and a decently written but outmoded kind of text. Handel's operas make an informative study in this respect. While many are mediocre examples of a questionable sort of libretto, several have books which should have guaranteed them a place in the modern repertory. *Giulio Cesare* compares quite favourably with Bernard Shaw's play *Caesar and Cleopatra*: the opera even has the same sardonic emphasis. What militates against all these Handel operas on the stage is the convention in which they are written. However good their books, modern audiences just cannot get on with *da capo* aria format. This is unfortunate, since if one forces oneself to follow the action with proper concern, then Handel's undoubted dramatic gifts begin to come to life. Mostly we look at and listen to his operas as if they were concerts. Bach's 'Passions' offer an illuminating contrast. Though they are not intended to be staged, their combination of narrative, chorus, reflective aria, dialogue in arioso and Lutheran chorale is felt as a genuine dramatic progress, almost a musical Stations of the Cross.

Here the power of the New Testament story, even though largely conducted in recitative, is the reason. This is not because the subject is sacred but because it is direct and pointful, unlike the extreme artificiality of so many operas set in classical or mythical times, with their complicated amorous intrigues. The 'Passions' illustrate music's indifference to merely literary value. Their overall theme is so profound. Bach sets the several sorts of language with an eye to their importance in the story and not to any sense of their quality as poetry. Thus the words of the Gospel, including dialogue

for Christ, Peter, Pilate et cetera, the mawkish piety of the interpo-
lated arias and choruses, written by such poetasters as his colleague
Picander, and finally the congregational hymns, are regarded as
equally demanding of eloquence. The whole pattern is a simu-
lacrum of the divine order: the theme is 'Divine Grace is dancing'.

The same sense that the whole created world is animated by
God's spirit informs Bach's Church Cantatas. Here there is a place,
as there is in Milton, for the malign parts of Creation, especially
the Tempter Himself. In No. 130, 'Herr Gott, dich loben alle wir',
he introduces the dragon of the Apocalypse in a hair-raising bass
aria accompanied by three obbligato trumpets and tympani, which
goes further towards giving the Devil the best tunes than almost
anything I know in music: 'Der alte Drache brennt vor Neid'.
Music, more than words, does not comment on the universe; it
invents it. Its unmatched palette for lamentation, pastoral, ferocity,
exhilaration, even equanimity is not commentary but the transformation of secondary states of mind, familiar from verbal annota-
tion, back into primary assertion. We are born knowing music's
language and need no special Pentecost to comprehend what it is
saying.

The sad liaison of good music and bad or undramatic verse continued through the nineteenth century. Perhaps there has been no
one musico/dramatic form as doomed as the classical opera of the
entrance-and-exit-aria kind, but poorly constructed major operas
and oratorios have carried generations of inventive composers into
limbo. Just to name *Alfonso und Estrella*, *Euryanthe*, *Genoveva*,
Rusalka, *Der Corregidor*, *Palestrina* and *Moses und Aron* is enough to
show the waste of good music on bad texts. It was left to the often
lowbrow or vulgar geniuses with an instinct for drama to propel
opera into the modern theatre and make it a popular art. Hats off
to Rossini, Bellini, Donizetti, Verdi, Bizet, Massenet, Puccini,
Richard Strauss and Britten—all men who exploited language in
the interest of musical effectiveness. And, of course, the presiding
Spirit of Overreaching, the Great Beast himself, Wagner.

We should consider an even older habit of mankind—the
tendency of our invention, music, to imitate nature. This is not

Emily

949-7868

surprising since such imitation may be the origin of the art. But in its more sophisticated garb it shows a process of considerable complication working for a fairly simple-minded end. Or is it a case of the end only seeming simple, and being, in fact, a gestalt, a symbolism with widespread significance. The myths which suggest music's origins in the imitation of natural sounds are anecdotal metaphors. The shepherd cuts a reed, makes holes in it at calibrated distances, and is able to imitate the songs of the birds which surround him.

Poetry is born, again according to myth, through shepherds discovering the potential of 'numbers' which imitate nature's own 'divisions' of sound. These notions, however, are likely to be back-derived, explanations of important données made after the event. Music's and poetry's creation are lost in time, and happened presumably through complex inspirations. What is still audible, after many years of a highly developed art, is music's imitative faculty. This is more than just a question of 'onomatopœia', one of the most overworked and overvalued of concepts. Again, specific examples will help more than abstract commentary.

The quaver murmurings in the piano accompaniment to Schubert's song 'Gretchen am Spinnrade', suggestive of her spinning wheel (and the same figure transferred to the violin and viola parts of the opening movement of his A Minor Quartet Op. 29, where it is the mood of the song rather than its spinning-wheel echo which is evoked)—this would be Exhibit A in any catalogue of musical empathy with Nature. Further examples abound—the strings creating the movement of river water in the opening chorus of Bach's Cantata No. 7, 'Christ unser Herr, am Jordan kam'; the E-flat pedal sounding from the depths of the orchestra and continuing throughout the first part of *Das Rheingold*, representing the *ur-laut* of the Rhine itself; the instances are too numerous to go on with. In Schubert's songs alone there is a plethora of imitation of brooks, mill-wheels, storms and hunts in full cry. Perhaps these examples are too crudely imitative. But music is also able to extend its lyre-bird passion to metaphorical landscapes through a generous and audacious aural sympathy. Debussy's *La Mer* evokes sounds of the sea, the play of winds and waves in recognisable patterns, but over and above this, it constitutes a great sound-map of the sea, a veritable campaign of philosophical identification. Mozart is especially wise in such things. The string figures in the trio of Act One of *Così Fan Tutte*, 'Soave sei il vento' are reflective less of the actual sounds of gentle zephyrs than of the languishing feelings of Fiordiligi and Dorabella as they watch their lovers wafted out of sight and touch, and away into the sentimental keeping of memory, where they will remain untarnished by reality.

Music's imitative faculty is its equivalent of literature's 'on-the-spot' recourse to simile. They are aural hieroglyphs, or at best cuneiform or semaphore. Music never abandons its artificiality. It has no need to because its language is a system of sounds-as-signs appealing to a pre-ordained knowledge. We discover the meaning of music by experiencing it. What remains unexplained could never be explained.

Having declared that you cannot describe music by using music and having been forced to depend on words about it, I am left with one special department to look into. This is music's own comprehension of music. Is there any way of accounting for musical shapes and how they satisfy the requirements of adepts? Are the patterns of music encoded by the types of instruments employed or is the truth the opposite of that, vice versa? Certainly music's rules are taught and analysed technically. Indeed, analyses of compositions are all too familiar, with their armoury of technical terms, tonic, dominant, subdominant, inversion, exposition, development, recapitulation, and so on. They make sense of what happens in a musical work but only because they are self-referential. They were made for a pre-existent reality rather than their being in at its making. They are the *Gray's Anatomy* of music.

Bernard Shaw parodied academic musical analysis by applying its rules in a mocking way to one of Hamlet's soliloquies. Grammar is not mathematical in the way music is and so such analysis of a passage of poetry is bound to sound ludicrous. Many people who have studied harmony and composition might be surprised to learn that academic analysis is not analysis at all. It is a post-hoc attempt to present what went on in the composer's mind while he was choosing the sounds he needed for his inspiration. Sound first, rule book afterwards.

Once you have become familiar with classical music you find no difficulty in moving among its shapes and structures. To the tone-deaf these are meaningless. On the face of it, there is no reason why the materials which make up a movement of a Haydn string quartet should ravish our souls, but indisputably they do. One reason why commentators prefer the social language of academic analysis is the illusion of precision. In all the arts there is a nervous tic brought about by envy of scientific objectivity. We have learned to be suspicious of romantic and personal interpretations. Literary people have written comical things about music—for instance, E. M. Forster's embarrassing reaction to Beethoven's Fifth Symphony. And popular legends and radio and record commentaries are usually pretty irrelevant. However, none of this is as annoying as the smart jargon of modern reductive theory. Before the present age, when so many composers are earning their living not by their works but by teaching, the masters rarely referred to the grammar of music at all. Wagner complained to his devoted Cosima, herself a musician's daughter, 'these wretched key signatures, but one must be neat'.

Music is not difficult to appreciate. People may learn a language by living among those who speak it. When W. H. Auden and Chester Kallman shared a house on Ischia, Kallman became fluent in Italian by mixing with sailors on the quay, while Auden kept stumbling on the vernacular after taking formal lessons. A good test of how well someone knows music is to question his or her powers of identification. Not just recognition of a specific composition but wider familiarity with epoch and style. Most of us, hearing a piece on the radio which we cannot put a name to, will be able to categorise it in some way—for example, to state that it seems to be from the second half of the nineteenth century, and to sound Czech in style—possibly something previously unknown by Smetana or Dvořák. The work may turn out to be by Foerster, Fibich or Novak, and our guess will have been pretty close.

However and whenever a work was composed, once it is performed it is living in the present. A mass by Josquin or Dufay is instantly labelable stylistically but in our ears it enjoys full contemporaneity. The mind makes instantaneous conversion of its expectations the moment the music begins. Our chief musical event, the public concert, would be impossible if experience were not rooted in the present. The distillation of pleasure is not affected by time-travelling. We may prefer the music of some ages to that of others, but we are all ransackers of the past and we enjoy our looting wherever we find it.

Because there is so much music in existence, and because it is not tied to historical events as other arts are, the history of music should be less controversial. Unfortunately, it is not. Composers' competitive urges are hermetically sealed and often savage. Music's very Protean quality, its Tarnhelm-like capacity to turn itself into any shape it desires, leads to a form of 'killing the Father' more extreme than in literature or painting. It is also given to legend-making, to a dangerous propensity for vindication which fills whole books of exegetical biography. The titanic hero struggling to make himself heard among the conventional certainties of his time is the archetypal composer of public fancy. Peter Ustinov recalls being reprimanded at school for answering the question, 'Who was the greatest composer who ever lived?' with one word, 'Bach'. The right answer, according to the schoolmaster, was Beethoven.

On the brink of the new millennium, music lovers may be swayed by arcane worlds which wait beyond the folds of time. But it is more likely that they will see themselves as custodians of a rich inheritance, responding, for instance, to the genius and fecundity of Schubert, whose anniversary is upon us. Contemporary composers will stay in their ghettoes, the experimental workshops and the university music departments. Something may be on the point of being born, though whether it will be a Golden Age or 'the rough beast' feared by W. B. Yeats we shall have to wait to find out. Certainly, if music ever had a universal language, it does not have one now. Instead, we pick and mix across a wide range. The twentieth century has taught us, as W. H. Auden wrote, 'Man' ... (has) ...

no more nature in his loving smile / Than in his theories of a natural style'. We may weep that at one time our most glorious synthetic construction, music, sounded so human and moved us so readily, but we cannot assume that we know the reason. Nor what we should do now to recover such potency. Those who call on history for help will get only siren answers and new rocks to founder on. Seeking rules from our oracles, we may be told there are no rules.

Much of what any avant-garde attempts is by definition that which cannot be done. Accordingly we should remember that music, as with any art, prospered by pursuing the possible. Ears and wrists have been the real virtuosi. For centuries improvisation was an important technique nurturing composition. Bach may have happened upon some of his finest ideas at the keyboard, and some musicologists believe that Domenico Scarlatti's sonatas were writings-down of his explorations at the harpsichord. Put the instruments in place, including the human voice, and mind and fingers will seek the music waiting platonically for them. As with poetry, a creative artist hardly knows what he wants to say until he has begun to say it. Our ears are highly experienced at responding to what our improvisation can uncover.

To end this peculiar chronicle I have run up a few assertions which are more bits of talking to myself than wise instances or noble maxims.

—We should depend on axioms, not analysis.

—Extreme complexity may be a smokescreen for a new sort of simple-mindedness (hear the works of György Ligeti, *passim*).

—'More a matter of feeling than a question of painting'—yes, but the foreground is painted in in considerable detail.

—*Prima la musica e poi le parole* is still true.

—Subtraction is usually more deleterious than addition.

—No one has ever believed in *Gebrauchsmusik*: music will suffer no rival near the throne.

—You cannot tell a composer's moral character from his or her compositions. Nevertheless, Wagner may not have been as vile a man as his biographers make him.

—Literary men must be expected to misvalue music. Their greatest vulgarity is to swoon over opera and ignore instrumental music.

—The composer composes the world, not the text.

—'I looked in meaning for whatever wasn't meant'. So with Wittgenstein, so with Beethoven.

—There are no parallels in the arts and few analogies, just a handful of metaphors. As with poetry, the doing cleanses the obscurity without destroying the mystery.

—Keys have affinities (F major, 'pastoral'; E major, 'richness' and so on.). But you will encounter 'pastoral' in D and 'richness' in C.

Those who would thrust sublimity on music will only cheapen it.

—'Intervals, tonality, inversion, chord of the diminished seventh, stretto, pedal point'—now wash your mouth out!

—The meaning of music is music.

There are many ways of paying tribute to this beautiful and generous art. The best is to use it—to play, to listen and to be grateful for such a pleasure. If the skilled doctors upbraid us for our lack of academic understanding, we should just turn the volume up and ignore them. At music's apotheosis, words will be invited, but only as observers. Perhaps occasionally, they will be permitted to help as paid bards praising their betters. Here is how one poet, who loved music, sang his praises of it—the second section of W. H. Auden's 'Hymn to St Cecilia', written by Benjamin Britten:

> I cannot grow;
> I have no shadow
> to run away from,
> I only play.
> I cannot err:
> There is no creature
> Whom I belong to,
> Whom I could wrong.
>
> I am defeat
> When it knows it

Can now do nothing
By suffering.

All you lived through,
Dancing because you
No longer need it
For any deed.

I shall never be
Different. Love me.

If we love music enough, we will always know what it means.

1997

HELEN GARNER

Mr Tiarapu

ONE SUMMER I WENT TO SYDNEY to visit my friend in hospital. He had just had a brain tumour removed and was lying, on a very blustery day, in a ward with flapping blinds and no air-conditioning. My friend was recovering well, considering. He was quite shaven, and half his head was bandaged.

When I arrived he was propped against his pillows, eating oysters out of a flat grey cardboard box. He offered me one and said, 'Pity you didn't arrive ten minutes earlier. Because do you know who gave me these oysters? Patrick White. I was hoping you'd arrive before he left; but another friend of mine came instead, and when I introduced them she looked terribly excited and said, "Not *the* Patrick White?" and he said, "No. *A* Patrick White".'

We ate the oysters. When we had finished them, my friend said, 'But I would like to introduce you to the bloke in the next bed. Because he's from Tahiti, and lives in Noumea, and he can't speak English—perhaps you could talk French with him.' He sat up with his bandaged head and called to the man, who appeared to be asleep. 'Eh, M'sieu.'

The man turned his body slowly towards us. He was a very tall man with a big head, perhaps forty-five years old, and evidently in pain: his brown islander skin was greyish and his cheeks were hollow.

My friend, in his carefully enunciated fourth-form French, explained that I was someone who spoke French better than he did. The Tahitian put out his hand and took hold of mine.

'*Enchanté, madame,*' he said.

We exchanged courtesies and platitudes about our experience among the French.

'*Les Français sont des racistes, des hypocrites,*' he said. 'They speak to you politely, then they massacre you behind your back.'

He told me that he lived in Noumea, and that he had a wife and six children at home. He did not know what the matter was with him, except that he was unable to walk, and had not been able to for some months. He said that he had been taken to hospital in Noumea for this unexplained weakness of the legs, and that suddenly hospital officials had told him he was to be sent to Sydney 'to have some tests done'. Since his arrival at the Royal Prince Alfred Hospital, he had not understood anything that had happened to him, nor anything that had been said to him, until he had been moved into the bed beside my friend with the opened head. 'Your friend,' he said, looking earnestly at me, 'is a very very nice person.'

I asked him if he would like me to stay till the doctors came, and try to interpret for him. He said he would like this very much, but that I was not to put myself out if I had something else to do. He said that he had not been given time, in Noumea, to see his wife and children before they had bundled him on to the plane. He said that he would like to write to his wife to tell her that he was all right and where he was and that he was waiting for tests to be done. He said he had not been able to write before, because he had not been able to ask for paper.

I asked a nurse for paper and a pad was procured, also an envelope and a biro. He sat up as far as he could and leaned on a magazine and wrote, in a large formal hand, a long letter. While he wrote, I talked with my friend. It was very hot indeed and, because there was a nurses' strike on, the nurses who wanted to strike but who did not wish to leave their seriously ill patients unattended were working dressed in ordinary street clothes instead of uniforms. This gave them a less brisk, less intimidating appearance, but it did not help the Tahitian man with his language problem. One of the nurses said to me, 'They arrive at the hospital from Noumea in plane loads.'

I asked when the doctors would be coming round, and the nurse said they would be there any minute. The man, whose name was Mr Tiarapu, finished his letter and addressed the envelope and stuck it down and then lay there with it against his chest, as if not sure what to do next. He looked from side to side.

I said, 'Would you like me to take it downstairs and post it for you?'

He said he would like that, if it were not too much trouble.

Two doctors entered the ward. They were very young men, younger than I was, and one of them was Australian and the other was Thai. They came to the end of Mr Tiarapu's bed shyly, as if they and not I were visiting. They looked at the chart attached to the foot of the bed.

I said, 'I can speak French, and wondered if I could explain to Mr Tiarapu what is the matter with him, because he doesn't know.'

The doctors looked at each other like two schoolboys, each waiting for the other to speak. The Thai said, 'Well, we are going to do some more tests.'

I said, 'Can you perhaps tell him more than that, because he must be very anxious, not knowing what is the matter with him.'

The Australian said, 'Does he want to ask us any questions in particular that you could translate?'

I translated this for Mr Tiarapu who was lying with his big head held up in a strained position, as if trying to understand by sheer effort of will.

He said, 'I would like to know if I will be able to walk again. It is my legs, it is awful, not to be able to walk. Will you ask the doctors why I can't walk, and whether they can do anything about it?'

The doctors, speaking in duo, said that there was a blockage in the spine somewhere, and that the tests they would do were to determine the possibilities of a cure. 'If it is only a blockage,' said one of them, looking slightly helpless, 'tell him he will be able to walk again if he does the exercises we will give him. If he does the exercises, he can only improve, if all he has is a blockage.'

I translated this. Mr Tiarapu looked much less anxious. He did not seem to want to make further inquiries, and the doctors said they would come back at a certain time the next day and that they would appreciate it if I could be there to interpret again. I said I would be there.

Mr Tiarapu took my hand and thanked me. He looked at me in a way that made me feel very bad, and sad, as if I were a kind of lifeline. I would have liked to kiss his cheek, but I was afraid of overstepping some line of protocol that might exist between white and black, or well and ill.

I said goodbye to my friend, and to Mr Tiarapu, and picked up the cardboard box with the oyster shells in it and dropped it in the rubbish bin on my way out of the ward. I took Mr Tiarapu's letter across the road in the gritty wind and into the post office, and got them to put the right stamps on it, and posted it.

Next morning, I returned to the hospital. The weather had not broken. When I walked into the ward I saw that Mr Tiarapu's appearance had undergone a shocking change. His face was no longer brown at all; the colour had left it, his cheeks had sunk right in, and he seemed to find it difficult to open his eyes. But he saw me and took my hand and held it.

I said, 'You look tired. Didn't you sleep well?' I did not know whether to call him *vous* or *tu* so I said *vous*.

'Not very,' he said. 'I was thinking of my wife, and I was worried.'

Before the doctors came on their round, the door at the end of the ward burst open and two cheerful nurses entered. They approached Mr Tiarapu's bed and seized his chart. 'Yes, this is the one,' said one of the nurses. She directed a powerful, jolly smile right into Mr Tiarapu's face. 'We're moving you today!' she announced. 'Different ward!' She grabbed a corner of Mr Tiarapu's blue cotton blanket.

Mr Tiarapu's face was grey now with fear.

I said, 'He doesn't understand what you are saying. He doesn't understand any English at all.'

'Oh,' said the nurse, stepping back.

At this moment the two doctors came into the ward. They said good morning to all concerned. Mr Tiarapu gazed from my face to theirs, waiting.

'Can you explain to him why he is being moved?' I said. 'Because he has only just got used to being here and talking to the bloke in the next bed.'

The doctors looked at each other. One of them said, after a short pause, 'We have to move him to another ward to do tests.'

I translated to Mr Tiarapu that he was going to another ward in order to have more tests. This information did not cause the look on his face to alter.

'Which ward?' I asked the doctors.

'Oncology,' said one of them, and he looked me right in the eyes with an expression at once blank and challenging. He said oncology. He did not say cancer. And I was not absolutely certain, not one hundred per cent certain, that oncology did mean cancer. And I couldn't ask because Mr Tiarapu was holding my hand and staring at me and the doctors with his grey face, and the French word for cancer is so similar to the English that it would have been impossible to disguise it.

'Do you want me to explain what you mean?' I said to the doctors.

They looked embarrassed, moved their feet on the spongy lino, and glanced at each other. 'If you like,' said one of them.

'But do you think I *should*?' I said.

They both shrugged, not because they didn't care but because they were very young, and because they probably didn't know any more than I did whether he was going to live or die. The longer we talked and gestured like this, without my translating anything, the clearer it became to Mr Tiarapu that there was something someone didn't want him to know. The responsibility for the transmission of information had been shifted squarely on to me, and I was not adequate.

I said to Mr Tiarapu, 'They are moving you to a different ward because they have to do the tests, and they're still not sure what is wrong with you, and they can't do the tests here.'

Mr Tiarapu nodded, and lay back down.

I said to the doctors, 'Don't you have interpreters here? Because I have to go back to Melbourne tonight. I can't stay any longer.'

'Oh, yes, I think so,' said one of the doctors. 'There's supposed to be a woman somewhere round, but she's renowned for her lack of tact.'

The nurses got Mr Tiarapu ready for the move. I stood between his bed and that of my friend, who had been watching this without speaking. When Mr Tiarapu was on the trolley and it was time to go, he took my hand again and said, 'You have been very, very kind to me. I will always remember your kindness.'

My friend also said goodbye, and Mr Tiarapu was wheeled away.

1980

PETER GOLDSWORTHY

The Biology of Literature

THE FIRST LITERATURE CREATED BY another species was a short poem by the chimpanzee Washoe, most advanced of the apes who were taught to communicate some decades ago using a rudimentary form of American Sign Language.

Annoyed with her teacher, Washoe signed the insult 'shit' at him, using the word, or handshape, in a way which was—at least for chimpanzees—completely new.

Washoe and her friends had previously adapted known Sign words in new, composite ways—labelling a radish a 'cry-hurt-food', citrus fruits 'smell-fruit', a duck a 'water-bird'. Such imaginative naming is extraordinary, but to call something that is not a shit a shit is something else again: a knight's move creation, a jump from one frame into another.

A poem.

Washoe's shit-metaphor came to her during a moment of high emotion, suggesting what is perhaps obvious: that metaphor carries a special emotional charge, whether in the form of crude insults—'prick' 'cunt' 'piss off'—or in the most powerful and resonant poetry.

Debate continues over the depth of language ability of the signing apes. A concise criticism, from a Chomskyan perspective, is contained in Steven Pinker's excellent book, *The Language Instinct*

(Penguin, 1994). But many native Signers who have watched the apes are convinced that *something* is being said, even if it lacks grammar.

Koko the gorilla seemed to take the metaphoric capacity a step further. The usual poetic juxtapositions of Signs were shaped by Koko—'white tiger' for zebra, 'bottle match' for cigarette lighter, and 'bottle necklace' for a six-pack of beer-cans. I'm not sure if this last counts as metaphor in gorilla-think, or as a confused description, but when she was forced to drink water through a straw, after being denied fruit juice, and described herself as 'a sad elephant', another primate poem had surely been created.

This metaphoric ability also suggests something less obvious: that certain kinds of thinking might come naturally to us, that certain patterns of thinking have been forced on us (and apparently on related species) by the imperatives of evolution.

The sign-speech of Washoe and her friends has been used to cast doubt on Chomsky's notion of a deeper structure for language, hardwired into the human brain, part of the actual brain anatomy. One of the signing chimps was even christened, memorably, Nim Chimsky. But Washoe's shit-sign points more surely in the opposite direction, suggesting that modes of thinking (at least in the common mammal-brain, which forms a large part of our own) are to some extent in-built, or instinctive, and one of these is comparison: matching like with like.

This goes with that.

Rather than discrediting nature in the Nature-versus-Nurture Hundred Years War, the signing chimps, and their shit-metaphors, surely strengthen its hand.

❃

What other of the standard ingredients of literature might be, at least to some extent, hardwired into the nervous system?

One test of this might be our physiological responses to what we read or hear. The threshold response of laughing (or not) at a joke is the most obvious, and immediate. Jokes are binary—either/or; yes/no. They either work or they don't. Likewise the Robert Graves

Test of Poetry: whether the hairs stand up on the nape of the reader's neck. What I'm talking about is what might be called natural literature, in the sense that stories, jokes, myths seem natural: they have a transcultural universality that goes far beyond the taught or received or culturally determined.

Particular jokes might well be culture-specific at a surface level. Hunter-gatherers are apparently unamused by fart-jokes, presumably because farting is not taboo in those societies. But the deeper structure of a farting-joke—the breaking of a taboo—is universal, and our responses to the structure seem at some level instinctive.

If metaphors and jokes are engraved in our brains at some deeper structural level, so surely are other transcultural practices which find their way into accepted literary forms: the reverie, the speech, the description.

Enactment also? The acting out of dramas is common to all cultures, mimicry appears to arise spontaneously in all children—and in chimps.

Even the so-called 'conventions' of 'realist' narration ('There was'; 'he said'; 'then she said') on deeper examination, especially an examination of ancient texts such as the Old Testament, or Gilgamesh, or the Mahabharata, or the Aboriginal Dreamings, are anything but conventions. Their grammar might well be as intrinsic to us as Chomsky's deeper structures of language.

Rhythm and rhyme certainly seem natural to the human brain. There are good reasons for this, explored by the philosopher Daniel Dennett (*Consciousness Explained*, 1991), among others. According to Dennett, evolution has saddled our brains with a memory that is not as reliable, or as quick, or as 'random access' as the 'dry' memories we can now build with silicon. That is, memorising in the human wet-brain is fallible, and often requires intense rehearsal and repetition for memories to stick. Our brains have therefore developed various tricks to help—rhyme and rhythm among them.

Rhyme and rhythm are cultural universals. The usefulness of rhyme as a mnemonic is obvious, and clearcut—but the music of a rhythmic or alliterative maxim or epigram or proverb or slogan would also seem to ease memorising. All cultures store knowledge in the form of proverbs, or sayings, or slogans or epigrams. Much human wisdom is formatted in this way in our wet-brains.

There is a worrying implication in this: not only do we tend to remember the substance of a sentence because of its style, we are also more likely to *believe* it, irrationally. An ugly, awkwardly spoken complex truth may in fact be more useful or correct than a beautiful lie, or simple line of poetry—but that's not the way our brains prefer to store information. We find slogans memorable *and* convincing.

'Rhymes and rhythms exploit the vast power of the pre-existing auditory-analysis system to recognise patterns in sounds,' as Dennett put it in *Consciousness Explained*.

This analysis system preceded the acquisition of language by the human brain. Grammatical language was a latecomer, arriving well after the big growth spurt in the brains of early hominids. Therefore—Dennett claims—language had to be jury-rigged by evolution (and culture) onto this huge plastic organ, which was constructed more for tasks such as 'food-seeking, face-recognition, and the ballistics of throwing and catching', than for speaking. Evolution often makes do with what is at hand, with what might even be second—or third-best—rather than mutating an entirely new apparatus. One example might be the small bones in the mammalian ear which transmit sound from the ear-drum to the inner-ear—developed from the jawbones of reptiles. The QWERTY keyboard is a nice metaphor, used by Dawkins and others, for these evolutionary processes—and their legacies that remain with us, and which we can never quite escape. QWERTY keyboards evolved in the early mechanical clunky typewriters as a method of keeping the most commonly-used keys separate, thus preventing their frequent jamming. As the mechanics of typewriters improved, this quickly became superfluous—even more so now, with electronic keyboards—but the cost of changing to more rational keyboard system is prohibitive. QWERTY is with us at least until voice-activation. Evolution often leaves us with such legacies, allowing a temporary gain in fitness perhaps, but in the long run not the best fork to choose in the choice-tree of development options.

Our powers of memory seem to be jury-rigged in this fashion, especially our power to remember sequences of words which make use of the various mnemonic tricks such as repetition, poetry and music which I have been talking about.

❂

If such *aide-memoire* are hard-wired into us, genetically and biologically, then so too is the telling of story. Stories might be seen as possessing the mnemonic power of rhythms, in a longer version—although the rhythms of story are not musical rhythms or the rhythmic cadences of language, but the rhythms of sense. Semantic rhythms.

How deeply is story inscribed into our nature? Is there some deep structure, hotwired into us in the way a sense of rhythm or rhyme or assonance would appear to be?

Many of the elements of story recur in completely unrelated cultures. From Frazer's *The Golden Bough* on, anthropologists have noted the astonishing congruencies between stories, myths and folk-tales. In *Morphology of the Folktale*, the Russian anthropologist Vladimir Propp has attempted to find a common essence in these stories. According to Propp, the archetypal male stories, 'Quest' stories, can be seen as a pattern of key, recurring elements. A Quest story always begins with some injury, or need. The hero is told to go somewhere. He has adventures which usually involve meeting a man, or creature, who sets him various tasks or tests; these often involve combat.

In the end, after various adventures, following a standard pattern, the hero is always rewarded, or married, or becomes king.

If we look at the dominant myths of our secular time—provided by the movies, and to a growing extent, computer games—the Quest is still the central male story-telling form, at least among adolescents.

In his recent book, *Creation of the Sacred*, the Swiss anthropologist

Walter Burkert has suggested that the Quest story maps, on a biological level, the basic daily need of early Man: the quest for food.

Another recurring form is the female quest, or female fairy-tale, 'The Maiden's Tragedy'. These elements are again common, and transcultural: a virgin leaves home; there is a period of seclusion or wandering. A catastrophe interrupts, usually the introduction of a male. Various tribulations, trials or imprisonments follow. Finally, there is rescue, by another male, and the story finishes in marriage, and childbirth.

Burkert believes that this tale follows the biological changes and tribulations of menarche, intercourse, pregnancy. Its tracks can be followed through much of Mills & Boon, and even into *Gone with the Wind*, the theme of which seems to be that No-Means-Yes if the male pursuer is a hunk/rich/wild lover.

Initiation stories in both sexes also seem to follow, or map, the biology of pubescence.

In pre-literate societies, such stories are a matter of life and death. Quest stories, or songs, in the Aboriginal Dreaming also provide maps of the clan or tribe's territory; they act as mnemonics or reminders of where essentials such as food or water or ceremonial materials can be found; they are exactly and precisely rooted in place. For this reason they form the prime evidence for a skin-group's claim to native land title. An enormous amount of vague, pseudo-spiritual hippification and 'Californication' of Aboriginal beliefs has taken place in recent years—which can be seen as another form of whitefella exploitation. Such New Age ectoplasm usually loses sight of something simple: the Dreaming stories had sacred elements, but they were also a plain fact of life—and their knowledge was above all immensely practical, and in a harsh environment crucial to survival.

Whatever other purposes they serve, they are an encyclopædia.

Necessary information about life takes the form of tales, including sung tales, in all pre-literate societies. Information is stored and communicated through tales. Because many tales are similar to each other, they are also easily remembered.

We remember a story even better if we can sing it as well.

Melody, and the repetitive rhythms of music or poetry, are also superb *aide-memoire*. But even without music, we don't remember strings of facts, or numbers, with anything like the ease with which we remember stories of equivalent length. We hear a good story once; we can instantly repeat it.

The invention of writing put paid to the necessity for the vast feats of memory of pre-literate societies, whether these were the Odyssey, Gilgamesh or the Aboriginal Dreamings. But the neurological templates are still there. The reason stories still fit our brains, hand in glove, is, to quote Walter Burkert, because 'the organising principle of the tale, the soul of the plot, is found to operate at the level of biology'.

Chomsky's ideas on language—that the mind is not Locke's 'blank slate,' but is to some extent pre-programmed—resonate here. Children perform certain grammatical transformations without ever having been taught them. Children from a very young age also pick the crucial elements from stories, and refuse to allow alternative readings that miss, or change, the sequence of these elements. This applies even to stories they have not heard before.

Chomsky is necessarily more interested in syntax than semantics—in form than meaning. His method is structural, language is seen as a system of formal relations—it does not explore the function or evolutionary necessity of speech. Likewise the various structuralist approaches to story seem to ignore this side of story—that it is an emotional, often cathartic experience; that it has evolved to act on a human mind and is primarily a process of transport, and rapture. Its grammar is a grammar of the emotions, its unit elements as much those of suspense, laughter, horror, satisfaction, as stasis, closure, kernels, process.

We see a sad movie twice—and still weep the second time, knowing not only the outcome, but also—of course! how tiresome to have to repeat it—that it is entirely a fiction. The emotional mammal-brain is only partly hinged to the rational human forebrain—something that appeals to the forebrain alone might be marvellous—but it is not, finally, story. Structuralist approaches, by definition, are more interested in structure than content. But it's precisely the *mixture* of structure, metaphor and specific content that provides the power of myths, and the mythic power of the best stories.

Its story structure may help us to remember, say, the Rain Dreaming in the Tanami Desert—the story fits the brain like hand in glove—but the structure alone won't help us find a cache of white ochre unless we also hear the elements specific to the clans of the Walpiri tribe who are the local guardians of that huge Dreaming.

Our instinct for metaphor seems especially obvious in the workings of the unconscious. Every writer experiences the way the unconscious mind makes connections and finds patterns—patterns which are often powerfully metaphoric. Dreams also have this power, and often work in the realm of symbol, or metaphor. Examples of dream creativity abound. Kekulé von Stradonitz's discovery of the benzene ring is perhaps the most famous. The problem of how to join six carbon and six hydrogen atoms together in a way consistent with their valency had perplexed chemists for many years until Kekulé dreamt of a snake swallowing its tail. His solution seems obvious, almost facile, in retrospect— arrange the carbon atoms in a circle—but it required a knight's move jump: from linear thinking to circular.

We also often understand stories at this unconscious level before, or parallel, to any conscious appreciation. The unconscious seems to be the level that myth primarily works at. Good stories are usually very simple—so simple that we often don't understand them. Their truths are hidden in full view, if sometimes in symbolic form, as with the benzene ring.

I can best argue this point by telling a story—a story within a story. I remember reading as a child the Arabian Nights story of the genie corked inside a bottle at the bottom of the sea. At the end of the first year of imprisonment the genie vowed to shower rubies and emeralds on anyone who would set him free. At the end of the second ... gold and silver. By the end of the seventh year he vowed to kill whomever set him free. (I think it was the seventh; if it wasn't the seventh it was probably the third: threes and sevens are for some reason recurring numbers in stories.)

I read the story as a child, and thought it ridiculous. Who on earth would kill someone who set him free? But the story stuck in my mind, and stayed there, itching. Its sheer absurdity fascinated me—surely because it had a metaphoric power that spoke to deeper parts of me.

Years later, a novel of mine was shortlisted for the Miles Franklin Award. My then publisher rang me a few days before the announcement of the winner, and said he had good intelligence that I'd won, and was sending me an air-ticket to Sydney. Write a speech, he suggested.

I didn't write a speech, but I was ultra-pleased.

The next day he rang back with an apology: Oops, wrong intelligence.

Then I wrote the speech. It went something like: 'I know my novel has faults, but I didn't think it was quite bad enough to win the Miles Franklin Award ...'

At that moment, under the emotional pressure of a wounded narcissism, the Arabian Nights story came back to me. For the first time I began to consciously understand its bitter kernel, although I suspect that even as a child some deeper, darker part of me had always understood, even as I puzzled. It's the story of human bitterness, a long, sad Dreaming whose song-lines can be tracked through other stories, from Aesop's fox and his bitter grapes to the folk-wisdom of phrases such as cutting off your nose to spite your face.

If we don't always understand the stories that we read at first sight, we also don't always understand what we write. One of the great pleasures of writing is similar to a great pleasure of reading: setting out on a journey with an unknown destination. Each time we pick up pen or page we are boarding a Mystery Flight. In the process of writing we discover how much we know, we discover what we know. Sometimes we discover that we know more than we thought we knew, and if we are very lucky, we might even write something more intelligent, or sensitive, than ourselves. Here, again, we are in the domain of the unconscious, and its pattern-seekings and obsessions.

Another story. Some years ago I was assisting a plastic surgeon remove a tattoo from a young woman's body: her ex-boyfriend's name, engraved on an intimate part of her anatomy. All morning the surgeon had been removing such tattoos: unwanted names and redback spiders and cobras and rattlesnakes and even, amid the predators, the odd cute butterfly. I found myself wondering what happens to the tattoos after their removal. What is the actual fate of each miniature work of art on its canvas of skin? In fact, the material ends up in the hospital incinerator—but I wondered if something more interesting might happen. I didn't know *what* at the time, but I felt the stirrings of a story, and jotted the idea in my notebook.

I didn't give it another conscious thought. A year or so later I was reading again the famous story about Vincent van Gogh severing his ear and mailing it to the woman who had rejected him. My tattoo story popped into my head complete; I knew how it ended. Imagine a woman whose ex-lover won't accept that the relation-ship is over. What better way of getting the message across than to return his name to him, to actually hand it back, ritually?

A vulgar notion? Perhaps, but the story also had a deeper, metaphoric resonance which I liked. On another level it's a story of growth, of a girl turning into a woman, of someone who doesn't wear labels, who isn't property. Propp might even claim it as an element in a female quest, or initiation, story.

Whether it is or isn't, and whether it's a good or bad story, is beside the main point I want to make: no conscious connection was made.

The crucial story-structure came together at a deeper level.

The deep structure of our story-seeking might be glimpsed in the 'confabulations' or fictions which patients suffering from the severe short-term memory deficit of Korsakov's Syndrome continuously invent to paper over the gaps in their memories.

For some years I worked with victims of Korsakov's Syndrome in an Alcohol Dependence Unit, and was always struck by the power and absurdity of their inventions. Korsakov's Syndrome is an end-stage disease in alcoholics caused mostly by vitamin B deficiency, which damages the mamillary bodies in the brain. It was also common in malnourished Australian prisoners of the Japanese in the Second World War, a part of the clinical spectrum of dry beri-beri. The chief manifestation is a severe short-term memory deficit, although long-term memories—of childhood, say—often remain intact. In severe cases, victims can remember no further than a few seconds into the immediate past. Other brain functions are often untouched—mental arithmetic, say, or logical thinking. In the acute, early stages, amnesia seems to bring a tremendous imaginative power to the fore, constructing fictional bridges across the gaps in the record. Passing faces, places and events are pulled into a continuously improvised web of story which is, above all, a system of explanation. I was often a shifting character in these stories—a nephew or son, a former mate, even an Army mate, although our ages might vary by forty years. The hospital itself might be conscripted into a barracks, a hotel, a pub—the stories themselves, remembered for only a few sceonds, would shift and change depending on the current input.

Oliver Sacks has written powerfully of such patients in his essay, 'A Matter of Identity.' A victim of Korsakov's Syndrome, he writes, 'must literally make himself (and his world) up every moment. We have, each of us, a life-story, an inner narrative—whose continuity, whose sense, *is* our lives.'

The Korsakov's sufferers are veritable Scheherazades, improvising thousands of stories to cover whatever anomaly or unremembered face impinges briefly and confusingly on their consciousness. These 'confabulations' are patently lies to any outside observer—full of absurd contradictions, and easily disproved—but they are utterly, if transiently, believed by the patient.

Can they be regarded as a kind of 'default' narrative in the brain when reality fails it—a default programme whose principal imperative is 'only connect'? The brain must still come up with some connecting thread of story, even if the story has the same wild and surreal feel as the stories that are improvised by comedians on *Good News Week* to connect the various mismatched objects they are offered.

In another essay, 'The Lost Mariner', Sacks introduces us to a patient with retrograde amnesia to the forties. Still stuck back in 1943, the patient can remember nothing after his navy discharge. Each morning he wakes and it is the same morning, he is still seventeen, Truman is President, as if in some real-life Ground Hog Day. Past the acute phase of his Korsakov's Syndrome, he no longer confabulates but has settled into what Sacks calls a 'permanent lostness'. Now middle-aged, he is offered a mirror by Sacks. In a profoundly memorable passage, Sacks describes how his face drains of colour, and a look of panic crosses his face as he stares bewildered into his much older face.

Fortunately he forgets this anomaly a few seconds later; but the power of confabulation may have been a blessing at that moment if he could have improvised some self-deluding story to explain why his seventeen-year-old face looked like an old man's.

The inner story-telling drive might also show its hand in dreams. Dreaming is a form of programme clearance according to current theory—an erasing of unwanted data. But at the point of waking, as the data screens past a waking consciousness, the narrative instinct attempts to link the stuff together into Story, and shape something plausible out of it.

This seems the essence of the art of fiction-making.

✪

To precisely what extent are our responses to literature part of our in-built 'nature'? How much is learnt, or received, nurture? Of course the only sensible answer is a mix of culture and biology— as with the rest of our behaviour. Perhaps the exact proportions don't finally matter. But to ignore, or patronise, one side at the expense of the other is necessarily limiting, and debilitating. It seems to me that this century—the century of the elevation of nurture over nature—many of the natural elements in writing have have also been pushed to one side.

In the world of pop literature—of the airport novel, say—it is easiest to see what is missing. Popular writers such as Michael Crichton tell wonderful stories. Their books are gripping, and often unputdownable—like movies, they keep bums stuck to seats. Yet Crichton, say, couldn't write a memorable sentence to save his life. Story is present in pop fiction, but the musical elements of language at full stretch—cadence, epigram, assonance—are mostly absent.

In the world of high literature—the world, say, of the 'serious' or 'art' novel—it is more difficult to see what has gone missing, at least for those of us who grew up with the received—i.e. university-approved—version of High Church Modernism. It can also be difficult to see through the mountain of reviews and glosses and commentaries. There often seems a comic dimension to this world of high book-chat: we know more than we need to, and our discussions often sound more pompous and important than the things they concern. But surely there has been a dislocation, or alienation, from our story-telling nature in this world. The art forms central to our time have little to do with the contemporary Serious Literature that is taught, say, in universities. (Serious Literature is such a resonant term—it always reminds me of Serious Drinking.) If Homeric or Mesopotamian epic poems were the forms of earliest antiquity, Athenian drama of fifth century BC, blank-verse drama of the Elizabethans, and the novel essential to the eighteenth and nineteenth centuries—in this lineage (to cite the Western story-telling tradition only) ours is, above all, the movie script.

I'm not talking about the study of poetry or essays—just about Made-up Stories. This is something new in history; the stories of the past that we now regard as classics never had to be taught at the time they were first written or sung or spoken. For one thing, they were mass entertainments—from the Epic of Gilgamesh to Dickens. They were the popular cultures of their time. They were also profoundly memorable.

Memorability is a key key, if not *the* key.

Only the texts of our century—the texts of Modernism—have ever been unpopular, and unmemorable, enough to require teaching. (What are they? It's an elastic-sided list, but always includes Kafka, Beckett, Joyce, Woolf in the world of fiction.) Yes, there are lines from all these writers that I know by heart— all are capable of writing beautiful lines, or stanzas. These writers are poets, in a sense; their novels can be seen as over-long poems. At the level of the sentence, the poetic unit, we still find memorability—unlike a pop writer such as Crichton. We also find many other things that are memorable, but this is not the place to explore those relative merits and limitations, or my limitations in reading them. I merely want to make a point about a disproportion: whatever else these writers can do, most can't tell a story. Surely the unpopularity of their books is due—in part—to the fact that story was something that Modernism lost sight of very early: the fact that any pub or dinner-party raconteur can tell a better story than, say, Virgina Woolf chooses to do. Not write a more subtle essay, or a more elegant and memorable sentence (think of some of the languorous sentences in *Mrs Dalloway*, for instance)— but tell a better story. Granted, there are other ways of structuring a 'fiction' than with story, but the writing of such 'fictions' (a pretentious, precious term that I detest) has become an essentially decorative art; its beautiful sentences an end unto themselves. Its satisfactions seem transient, and lacking nourishment.

As with the repression of the sexual drive (with food-seeking, the most ancient of instincts) the repression of other aspects of our nature cannot be complete. We can, and often must, divert those instincts, or channel them, or sublimate them—but we cannot ignore them. I am using a deliberately overblown metaphor— comparing story-telling with sex—but I am suggesting that, like sex, story will out. Whether in film, in computer games, in biography or history, or in the novels we read on planes, narrative will always find willing eyes and ears that seek its deeper satisfactions when novels fail it.

Was the search for such satisfactions a force in the work of Jorge Luis Borges towards the end of his life? Claimed as an archetypal modernist, Borges never strayed far from story. The great early stories—'Funes the Memorious', 'Pierre Menard, Author of the Quixote', 'Tlon, Uqbar, Orbus Tertius' et cetera—at first glance seem to be a literature of essay and irony only, a literature of the head, lacking human dimension. Borges himself grew tired of this early work, and spent the last years of his life writing gaucho 'cowboy' stories about characters who were less expressions of an idea than human beings, but the story-telling lessons he learnt from his favourite writers—Stevenson, Chesterton, H. G. Wells—underpin the narrative trajectories of even the most literary of those early stories.

With Borges, we always want to know what happens next.

He also teaches another crucial lesson: unlike many of those he influenced, Borges understood that it was necessary to keep the cleverness short and sweet.

The best thing about the wave of deconstruction that swept Australian universities in the eighties was its irreverence. It served in this sense as an excellent antidote to High Church Modernism and its fetishistic book-worship. The central problem of Deconstruction—which is, after all, a further step in the European tradition of scepticism—is that it has taken scepticism perhaps as far as it can go, and risked everything, including itself.

In evolutionary biology we might find an antidote to these nihilistic end-games; biology might offer us a hand up out of the current mud of sticky subjectivities, and provide measures by which we can understand better our responses to literature, and why they arose in us. It might also provide some useful bedrock on which to stand and make judgements, independent of individual or cultural taste—or at least parallel to taste.

I have only lightly sketched some of the possible intersections of biology and literature. More will probably emerge over the next decades, because cognitive scientists and neurobiologists seem to be offering a final deconstruction of human thinking processes which is far more profound than the fun and games of Derrida and company. The full reach of this new scientific triumphalism remains to be determined, but there seems little doubt that at least *some* of the central questions of epistemology, say, will undergo rigorous experimental scrutiny.

For now, we can at least reclaim that part of literature which belongs to us, biologically. Pop culture has continued to understand this—in its tear-jerker and feel-good movies, its romance novels and thrillers. The world of pop culture has always understood the human heart (read instincts) far better than the world of high culture. High culture—so-called 'serious' culture—understands the complexities of the head in far subtler ways. Of course we need both—the complexities of the head, and the simplicities of the heart. We also need mind *and* brain—to map, roughly, the terms of the Cartesian duality onto my argument. We need both nature and nurture.

I would like to see a more perfect fusion of the two: of story and essay, heart and mind, content and form. I want Crichton to lie down with Woolf, beneath one cover.

The intellectual fashions of our century, as still taught in the leading fashion houses, and promulgated in the leading fashion magazines, have tipped too far in the direction of obsessive formalism at the expense of content.

A high culture which values essay over story, taste over energy, mind over body, is a lifeless museum culture. Its literature will be ruled too much from the forebrain, without the nourishment of the heart—a literature which the simple, over-emotional poetry of Washoe the chimp might tell us was not worth shit.

1997

———————————— ❖ ————————————

BILL COPE

 The Language of Forgetting

A Short History of the Word

NOW, ANSETT FLIES TO GROOTE EYLANDT three times a week. When my uncle, an Anglican minister, first visited Groote thirty years ago, he had to stay two weeks. That's how long it used to be until the next flight out.

'Observe the fasten seat belts sign ... tray tables. Flight attendants ... ready for landing ... Welcome to Groote Eylandt ... We hope you ... Thank you for flying Ansett ... again next time.'

The words are predictable and forgettable. English words which are repeated in exactly the same way from one stop to the next, learnt and replicated from the Ansett book of customer-friendly yet insistently practical corporate words. The words are forgettable because they are so predictable. They are written down anticipating forgetfulness. They are repeated for people who are not really listening.

The missionaries are now all but gone from Groote. The Anglican minister is an Aboriginal man, and, except when there are funerals, only a handful of people go to church. A linguist is still translating the Bible into Anindilyakwa and a couple of other whites are working with the Church Missionary Society on things like substance abuse ...

✸

Whites have been fiddling around with words here for decades. First it was the word of God.

Arnhem Land was made an Aboriginal Reserve in 1931, a place where missionaries were the only whites allowed. A. P. Elkin, anthropologist and inventor of the idea of assimilation, was instrumental in getting the government to create the Arnhem Land reserve. The missionaries were there to help the natives assimilate.

Even before this time, the moral mission to minister to the Aborigines had been on the fringe of the Church of England's institutional conscience. First it was a matter of smoothing the pillow of a dying race, of showing compassion for the vanquished, of bringing the word of the Lord Jesus to ease the souls of a people dispossessed.

> *We have developed the country, but we have certainly done very little to preach the Gospel to the people we have dispossessed. In the course of a generation or two, at the most, the last blackfellow will have turned his face to warm mother earth ... Missionary work then may be only smoothing the pillow of a dying race, but I think if the Lord Jesus came to Australia he would be moved with great compassion for these poor outcasts, lying by the wayside, robbed of their land, wounded by the lust and passion of a stronger race and dying—yes, dying like rotten sheep—with no man to care for their bodies or souls.*

These were the words the Bishop of North Queensland, used to put his plea to the Church of England Congress of 1906.[1]

The Roper River Mission began its work of spreading the word in 1908, followed by missions on Groote Eylandt in 1921 and at Oenpelli in 1925. These were just the Anglican missions in Arnhem Land. There were others too, across Arnhem Land and beyond— Presbyterian, Lutheran, Catholic, Methodist, Baptist, each with its own ethnic variation on the missionary theme. Between about the 1880s and the 1930s, most of the Australian continent, the parts where Aboriginal people had still been living relatively undisturbed lives until the missionaries came along, came to be carved up into a series of ethno-moral fiefdoms. This wasn't a very different business from the colonial carve-up of the world in the nineteenth century, at the end of which a place like Africa resembled only an imperialist patchwork, each putative country representing quirkily different ethnic variations on the same story, with a single historical moral: civilisation through progress and development. In Australia, Aboriginal countries were replaced by missionary countries and the imperialist moral was the same.

Dick Harris came to Groote in 1943 to set up a new mission at Angurugu. Over the years, in the spirit of many a white pioneer, he led the building of a mission settlement with a church, a school and a dormitory for the girls. The girls were locked up each night to protect them from moral danger and consequences of promised marriages and polygamy. For at least fifty years, the dormitory system had been a frequent feature of Aboriginal missions.

> *And to godliness, brotherly kindness; and to brotherly kindness, charity.* (II Peter 1.7)

But it turned out that the word alone was not enough. It needed to be enforced by lock and key. The lock and key were a consequence of the word. Lock and key was the way through which people were helped to forget the culture of the past. By 1943, the dormitory system was controversial and needed to be defended. This was when Dick Harris wrote to Sydney, to the Reverend W. J. Ferrier, Secretary of the Aborigines Committee of the Church of England.

> *May I also say that I believe the most important element in dealing with the native is the character and perhaps the experience of the missionary. I think, if II Peter 1.7 is made part of one's life, the native can hardly think of the dormitory system or any other effort made for his best good as an 'open declaration of mistrust of the native'.*

Open declaration of mistrust. These words of accusation, levelled at his approach to the bringing of the word, must have made Dick

Harris feel uneasy, and this unease called him to invoke the words of his God.

> *I personally am quite happy that he should think of it as a declaration of distrust in his present mode of life. I would emphasise the word 'brotherly' in the text quoted and I think of charity as 'the love that God has toward us'. I may not understand the subject anthropologically but if I understand my calling aright, one phase of it is 'to keep men from sin'.*

There was inherent virtue, it seems, to monogamy and modernity. Harris made no bones about what he was offering the natives who were the object of his brotherly love. He told the word straight.

> *Wherever the Gospel has been preached throughout the world, women have gained their freedom, and if we are allowed to continue here, your women will gain their freedom too. If you do not like that, you had better tell us to go away.[2]*

This was the theme of one of his sermons.

Anthropological understanding aside, this was the point at which the word of God, according to Dick Harris, met the secular word of assimilation. Assimilation was a word coined by anthropologist A. P. Elkin in the 1930s. By the 1950s, assimilation had become official government policy. Assimilation was the secular coming of the word of modernity.

> *The Australian Native has, through the centuries, developed as a nomad, producing nothing, storing nothing, and relying for his survival upon Nature completely unchanged. At every point, therefore, his evolution has been under influences, the direct antithesis of those which have evolved the civilization into which it is now hoped to admit him ... If assimilation is to be successful,*

> *it will be necessary first to remould his character in harmony with*
> *the new social structure. To this end, he must be subjected to*
> *influences and stimuli which have evolved our own race.*[3]

This is the word of Dr C. E. A. Cook, from the Commonwealth Department of Health, told to an Australian Institute of Political Science Conference in 1954. Racial survival was dependent on the Australian natives forgetting the past, on the working of 'new influences and stimuli'.

Disturbances at Angurugu turned into violence in 1957–58. The Chief Welfare Officer of the Northern Territory, E. C. Evans, and Patrol Officer, E. J. Egan, were called in to investigate the causes of the trouble. 'The main reason ... is that the people are not convinced Christians ... I consider that a serious mistake was made in not educating the people to the stage where they are ready for monogamy before actually insisting on its implementation,' said Egan in his report.

The point of contention was not the principle of forgetting but the technology of forgetting. How could people best be made to forget? Was it not better to educate them to forget? These were subtle points in the whites' conversation about assimilation and the future of the Aborigines.

Yet there did seem to be a degree of acceptance of Christian principles among the people at Angurugu. Egan reported that all the women were adamant that they wanted monogamy. All the single men were equally adamant. From what the whites thought they were seeing and hearing, it looked as if some of the natives wanted to forget. The old men, however, were hard to find. These must not have been things they felt they needed to talk to white people about.

Egan did also note 'the antagonistic attitude of the Natives towards the missionaries, the equal of which I have not seen on the few missions that I have visited ... The "forbidden fruit" atmosphere of the girls living in the dormitory may be the cause for a feeling of hostility on the part of the men on the Mission, but none of the men want the dormitories abolished.'[4]

What was required in Angurugu, Egan said,

> *was a more concentrated effort to Christianise the people. They*
> *must be educated in Christian doctrines before they are*
> *required to be subject to those doctrines. I firmly believe that,*
> *provided there is sensible co-operation between the missionaries*
> *and the natives, together with a concentration on the Christian*
> *teachings regarding marriage, there will be no great difficulty*
> *in gaining the complete acceptance of monogamy by the native*
> *people.*[5]

❂

As the Ansett plane comes in to land at Groote, you can see the community of Angurugu right beside the airport. Angurugu is squeezed between the long straight scar in the bushland that is the airport and the moonscape of an open-cut mine. This is the manganese mine of the Groote Eylandt Mining Company Limited—GEMCO, which is a part of BHP.

Trucks the size of small apartment blocks take 150 tons of ore at a time to the concentrator plant. Angurugu is called an Aboriginal community. The mine can be heard rumbling at night; everything is covered in charcoal grey manganese dust. It's not dangerous to humans, they say.

These sorts of places are called communities right across the continent of Aboriginal Australia. Mostly they are ugly, architecturally disjointed places, generating a sense of discomfort that is peculiar to the built spaces of modernity. But here the unease is even more acute. Community is a euphemism for a place that can no longer be called a mission.

From the plane, you can tell that Groote, the island itself, is a paradise on earth, a place of beaches and bays and rocky headlands. It is the sort of destination that would-be tourists shut up in airconditioned offices in some metropolis or other might dream about, if only there were a colour photo in some tourist brochure to prompt such dreaming. But there isn't one. You can't visit this place, unless you have something to do with the mine, or if you are on community business.

Community is the whites' word, a word which gives the impression that the place is at least the sum of its people and maybe more, that there is some sort of local and spontaneous relationship between the people and the settlement: the houses, the school, the medical centre, the council. The description 'mission' is actually still closer to the truth because the people are only living together at this particular spot by reason of the missionary history.

The missionaries chose this place, Angurugu, because it was away from the beach and the sea and the places where the people had liked to live and considered significant. This was a place away from distractions, away from reminders of the past, and forgetting was a necessity if they were to become focused on God and work.

The institutions represented by today's buildings are sovereign white institutions, not mission buildings, different ones. Though the new technology of the word won't allow for such a simple admission.

❂

The Ansett plane lets off the miners, who all live by the sea at Alyangula, about ten or fifteen kilometres away from Angurugu. The mine's remoteness belies its moral position at the heart of white modernity, producing one quarter of the world's manganese. It's been two hours by jet from Darwin, and it's more than that if you're flying on to Cairns. The others getting off must be people with permits, doing Aboriginal community business. Like I am.

One quarter of the world's manganese is mined on Groote Eylandt. By my calculations—and the modernity of us whites is one in which numbers are the measure of most things—this adds up to one quarter of the Volvos and one quarter of the Toyotas, one quarter of the New York skyscrapers and one quarter of the Sydney skyscrapers, one quarter of the fridges in Buenos Aires and one quarter of the fridges in Johannesburg.

One of the strange things about modernity is that you never

know whose land it is that has been dug up to make these things, to know whose land it is you are touching or to know the identity of the tangible object other than its surface visibility, to know which quarters end up in which cars, which skyscrapers or which fridges. The numbers seem to matter, but they are meaningless. But as you stand and hear the rumble of the mine, the numbers do warn you that Groote is the heart of industrial modernity.

A GEMCO publicity brochure explains that 'the ore was deposited over a gently sloping basement in shallow sea water during a period of rising and falling sea levels. This deposition occurred during the "Cretaceous" period some 95 million years ago.'[6] These are things we believe as unknowingly, with as little tangible experience to back them up, as the quarters in the world's steel.

The missionaries, to their credit, pulled out with some degree of secular grace as well as the grace of their God. In 1955, BHP geologists found manganese samples on Groote. In 1960, Mr Peter Dunn of the Commonwealth Bureau of Mineral Research saw manganese outcrops on Groote and mentioned them to the Church Missionary Society workers at Angurugu. This prompted the CMS, in the name of its mission superintendent, to take out a mining lease on 530 square kilometres, or about a fifth of the island. When BHP decided to mine, CMS struck a 1.25 per cent royalty deal on behalf of the local community, and the people of Groote Eylandt become the first Australian indigenous people to receive mining royalties.

When the mine began, the community was asked how it wanted the land rehabilitated: market gardens, fields for cattle, forests that could be harvested for timber? After all, it seemed there that there might be some residual advantage in having had the land cleared. White people have made a virtue of cleared land for centuries.

No, the people said. They said that none of this was any use to them, they wanted the land put back the way it had been.

'The mission having held the original rights, we were able, after some hard bargaining, to ensure that considerable compensation will come to the island people once mining actually starts.'[7] This is what was written in the official CMS records. Mining started in 1966.

✲

I'm here on a project examining the English language and literacy in the development of workplace and training competencies.[8] 'Competency' is one of those terrible neologisms that come and go as white bureaucratic systems slide from one set of euphemisms to another.

Simply, each skill needs to be learnt or sufficiently well learnt. How well it has been learnt needs to be observed and assessed. Competencies, the training involved and the assessment of competency, are created by training modules—bounded, clear, definable pieces in a skills construction that can be assembled neat little piece by neat little piece. Each module, each skill, is made up of units and elements whose scope is clearly delineated, no less and no more for each skill. And in competency systems there are clear prerequisites, stating what you need to have done first, clear lines of articulation indicating how training modules interrelate, a whole lot of words of structure and utility, an engineered edifice of individual development, whose purpose, whose end, is the whole worker, the multiskilled worker. So the skills framework builds up.

The engineers of competency systems imagine them to be emancipatory; they make explicit what is required in a job, and this is important for all people who come from outside the mainstream culture of work: migrants, women, Aboriginal and Torres Strait Islander people.

'Things are turning around now because there is new management at the mine. There's Mabo and they want to extend the mining lease, so the directive has come down from Melbourne: hire some blackfellas,' says a white trainer in the community.

So here am I doing community business, competency business, where a previous generation of whites, my people, had done missionary business.

The easiest place to get started is in rehabilitation—in planting trees after the manganese has been removed and the overburden replaced. If 'they' like that work and are found to have built up the requisite competencies, they can then move on to work in the mine itself. These are a few small steps on the path to employment and, ultimately, community self-determination. Self-determination. This is, of course, a different modernity from the one Dick Harris brought. His modernity was one where all the skills were for the purpose of assimilation, and not for self-determination, as it's described now.

For the rehab team, it's Nursery Skills, end of module, then irrigation and tractor implements, end of module, and, and, and.

❂

The flying boats of Qantas Empire Airways used to stop at Umbakumba Bay during the late 1930s and early 1940s. Umbakumba is on the opposite side of Groote from Angurugu. Fred Gray, a trepanger who had set up house there, used to supply the flying boats with produce from a vegetable garden in which he used Aboriginal labour.

The Director of Groote Eylandt SkillShare was previously employed as a specialist in cross-cultural psychology. SkillShare is a federally funded community training and employment pro- gramme. One of the outcomes of SkillShare on Groote is the devel- opment of literacy and work skills relevant to employment in the GEMCO mine. SkillShare has an office in the restored 'Bark Hut' at Angurugu, one of the mission's first buildings.

'I was employed by the community. They are the sponsoring body, the Aboriginal elders of the communities. At the interview for the job I asked what work they wanted to do, what enterprises they wanted to have. They said they wanted to get the old ways going again. They remembered Fred Gray's gardens. They told me to go away and look into what they could grow. I chose heliconias for their cultural compatibility.'

Heliconias are large waxy flowers that originally came from

Hawaii. SkillShare is a national programme of community-inspired and community-managed employment and training activities. Self-determination has replaced assimilation and the mission buildings have been registered by the National Trust as representative of a time that has now passed.

'They are not attractive to the community. This is why I chose them. You couldn't grow watermelons because they would all be taken. Heliconias have a long vase life, so you can get them out on the Ansett flights. They sell for thirty dollars a stem down south. Also, the plants will last, so if everybody goes off to a ceremony it won't matter. With pumpkins or mangoes, you'd be fighting the culture.'

The Umbakumba people in the Heliconia project—some days nobody turns up and some days a few people—are all doing a Certificate in Horticultural Skills (Aboriginal Communities) at Northern Territory University. In the words of one trainer, this course uses a tick-and-flick approach. 'Can describe the shape and arrangement of leaves', the competency module form reads. Describing the shape and arrangement of leaves is an observable competency, and once observed, the trainer ticks and flicks.

The trainer's manual for the Certificate in Horticultural Skills (Aboriginal Communities) puts the cultural differences in general terms. It uses five cells to describe a history of two centuries' worth of differing.

> As a trainer in an Aboriginal community, the following
> diagram which summarises some aspects of European and
> Aboriginal styles of learning may be helpful to you:

EUROPEAN SOCIETY	ABORIGINAL SOCIETY
Expected to learn by themselves	*Learn from older wiser people*
Learn by being told	*Learn by doing*
Learn in made-up situation	*Learn in real life activities*
Learn for future	*Learn for today's activities*
Society in constant change	*Traditionally stable society*[9]

❁

A decade or two ago, there were perhaps sixty Aboriginal workers in GEMCO, not just in rehab but in real jobs driving trucks and working in the concentrator. By last year, the number had gone down to seven. The problem at least in part is the language demands of competency. People might be able to do the job, but the culture of the written word in the competency-based training and the competency-based assessment keeps them out.

This is why we are there, to work out paths to access and thus to self-determination, to work out how people might get the literacy skills they need to get jobs. Where the workforce is not English speaking or reading or writing, or insufficiently so, language and literacy skills development is an important feature of competency training. They need white written words for self-determination.

In the Bark Hut, the SkillShare team has installed a bank of computers as part of the adult literacy programme, a programme to develop work-related competencies. They are mostly used for playing games, and the SkillShare people consider this to be a good start. It is a first step towards competency and self-determination. The most popular and useful game of all is one called 'Lemmings'.

'Aboriginal people are present-oriented and unable to plan. They are people of the concrete here and now; they do not think abstractly or about the future. The main thing you need to look at is not literacy, but what work means. Leanne comes in and says she is interested in a job. So I say, well if you want this job, come in and talk to me about it tomorrow morning at 9.00 a.m.—just to see if she has any idea about time and white man's work. The "Lemmings" game on the computer is ideal in beginning literacy. It teaches people to think forward. "If you do this ... then that." "What if you did this instead, then what ... ?"'

When I was a child my mother got me to include the black children in my prayers—a broad group. The children of the Arnhem Land missions merged into a longer list which included missionary outposts in Tanganyika and Kenya. My prayers traced the ethnic English lines of brotherly love that overlaid imperial self-interest. The African missionaries of my mother's generation, the ones she used to get me to pray for, have all come back to Australia now and retired. She still prays for Julie Waddy who's been on at Groote, at Angurugu, for eighteen years now. The mission no longer enforces the word of God with lock and key.

'People have demanded that the Bible be produced bilingually. There are enough people who can see the point of reading in their own language now. They want to keep the culture strong; it's a statement of identity when the culture is under threat.' This seems to be a substantial change of heart since the time when Dick Harris was at Angurugu. The minister is now an Aboriginal Person. The community is self-governing. Julie Waddy's role is an ancillary one, as a linguist and a Bible translator.

'Anindilyakwa is the world's hardest language.' That's what Julie's white offsider, another CMS worker, says about the grammar, and the authority for that is an American linguist by the name of Heath, who documented Nunggubuyu, a language on the mainland opposite Groote which is supposed to be just about as hard. No other language has the number of pronouns, the number of cases, the number of tenses, the amount of inflection.

'There are five noun classes for non-human things, eighteen personal pronoun prefixes, including distinctions such as between first-person inclusive and first-person exclusive.' The CMS representatives have to know all this now because the word has to be brought now in a very different way, a new technology of the word, in a new culture of remembering.

'They want to keep the culture strong; it's a statement of identity when the culture is under threat.' Things seem to have changed. Dick Harris could never have said that, yet his was the same God as Julie Waddy's, and the same word. Just what does it mean to 'keep the culture strong'?

In the schools at Angurugu and Umbakumba, there's culturally sensitive education, two-way education, both-ways education. The old Dick and Jane readers have been thrown away, and now it's all 'empowering' writing, 'relevant' reading and writing.

'The Aboriginal Schools Curriculum Materials Project ... is a Commonwealth-funded project to improve Aboriginal access to, participation in and outcomes from education ... Language, subject matter and methodology used in the materials are relevant and appropriate to the needs of teachers and students.'

Access is a thing created by 'empowerment'. Relevance is achieved by granting the need for 'culture'. Skill in reading and writing—literacy—is relevant to access.

Black children are being empowered through culturally sensitive education which is delivered to them through the 'genre' approach to the teaching of reading and writing. All writing, all types of writing, this approach explains, are either one or another type of 'genre'. Genre is a 'staged, goal-oriented social process', the teachers' notes tell us.

Narrative genre is one very important genre, and it is, like other genres, 'staged'. That is, it needs a number of parts, a structure, to achieve its purpose; the fact that, like all genres, it has a purpose, is what makes it goal-oriented. Its purpose is 'to entertain' and 'to help people think about the meaning of life and experiences in life'. Narrative, the literature says, opens the door to the world of literature. Its structure, its generic stages are: 'orientation; complication; crisis; resolution'.

These are authoritative words from the white science of language. Cultural sensitivity is delivered by employing local stories—'relevant' narrative. But first, for the teacher/trainer's sake, the stories have to be structured into their generic stages, so that they can be taught usefully.

An East Arnhem story—one used in culturally sensitive education—is 'staged' thus:

Orientation: 'Long, long ago, a giant serpent called Inganarr lived in Arnhem Land. He ate people wherever he went. He moved from west to east, eating people as he went.'[10]
Complication: 'Inganarr went to North Goulburn Island and ate all

the people there. He returned to the mainland and rested. Two boys, out hunting, were surprised when their spears came back to them when they threw them in a certain direction. When they moved closer to the area they saw Inganarr. They raced back to tell their father. All the tribe took their hunting weapons and ran to kill Inganarr. They couldn't. Instead, the people were swallowed by Inganarr.'

Crisis: 'Inganarr slowly made his way to eastern Arnhem Land. He had eaten too many people. He felt sick. Suddenly, he opened his mouth and threw up.'

Resolution: 'Out came all the people, still holding their hunting weapons. They settled down in eastern Arnhem Land and never returned to the west. And that is why, to this day, there are no people living on North Goulburn Island, and there are more people in eastern Arnhem Land than in the west.'

'Myths,' say the same materials, 'tell of relationships between gods, spirits or supernatural powers and humans and nature, for example, creation stories.'

Would Dick Harris have called the creation stories he told a myth? Is the creation story about the depositing of the ore some 95 million years ago in the GEMCO publicity material a myth? Was the purpose entertainment, or mere edification, or was it an entrée into the world of literature?

Doing myths seems to be a matter of remembering culture, a matter of recognition. Doing local Aboriginal myths at school seems to be a matter of making the school a genuinely community thing. So, the school—because it is all about cultural sensitivity—teaches the stuff of 95 million years ago as fact. The indigenous is turned into stories.

This is how culture is being brought into schooling. The purpose of story—all textual purpose—is simplified entirely within the terms of a society where social processes are staged in simple and linear ways, and goal-oriented with a relatively limited focus. Rather than bringing culture into schools, it is forced through the cultural filter of school literature. This is a way of reinventing culture, of transforming it fundamentally.

The 95 million years referred to in GEMCO's literature end with a large hole in the ground and BHP making a lot of money. This is fact. It is also staged and goal-oriented social process. Anything else is ancillary to this fact, this goal, including self-determination and the pragmatics of the new Aboriginal employment objectives.

It looks like Aboriginal culture is now being done in the school and self-determination is being done in the mine. In reality, new technologies of forgetting are in place, more effective ones than before. And whites are again firmly—more firmly—in control of the culture of the word, the written word.

The Inganarr myth is narrative genre. The narrative, *Little Red Riding Hood*, the materials tell us, works the same way—orientation, complication, crisis, resolution—entertaining, helping people think about the meaning of life, opening the door to the world of literature. This is the cultural orientation of the English written word, and things Aboriginal are being reconstructed as a variation on *Little Red Riding Hood*.

The Bible translation continues. This is after the vowel wars—ten years during which two white linguists fought over whether there were just two vowels or six vowels in Anindilyakwa. Until that conflict was resolved, bilingual teaching was very near impossible. Culture through language in school had to wait. One of the linguists has now retreated and the six vowel version has prevailed.

'People have demanded that the Bible be produced bilingually. This is why the Bible is in both languages, translated back into English at about third grade level. The translation back into English avoids passives, the clause order is different from the regular English Bibles, implicit information is made explicit, the negative is posited before the positive and the use of abstract nouns is avoided—these are the principles of all Aboriginal languages.'

This is the business of being culturally appropriate, of making the Bible simpler.

'Aboriginal languages break things down into their component parts. This means that translation takes much more space than the original. There is lots of redundancy. For example, both pronouns and verbs indicate person. In writing the Bible down, a lot of the redundancy is removed, edited out.'

This is the business of completely transforming Anindilyakwa by writing it down, of making it simple after the style of the culture of writing.

Now that the vowel stuff has been resolved, the old Dick and Jane readers have been replaced by Anindilyakwa readers. The kids sit up straight, doing genre-narrative: staged, goal-oriented social process—doing school.

'The language is strong here because there is only one language, and it is an island.'

This is a nonsense, just a linguist's convenience, convenient for translators and the writers of dictionaries who fix words and meanings into straight lines in fixed order. The truth is that there are nineteen clans on Groote. Nineteen clans means nineteen languages. One clan means multiple languages of age, of gender, of moiety.

Doing culture and language appear to be ways of meeting Paul Keating's injunction when he was Prime Minister, to recognise the 'oldest culture in the world', after the shame of genocide and protection and assimilation. Culture and language, however, turn out to be white man's inventions, another way of forgetting, although this time it's a smarter, more surreptitious, more effective, more devastating technology of forgetting. It is forgetting by reframing the remembering.

Once the epistemological scaffolds have been set in place—the reconstruction of Anindilyakwa as a written language, the forcing of texts from another life into the genre of myth-narrative; the charade of competency as self-determination—once this cultural frame has been internalised, then the scaffolds can be allowed to fall away and it appears that the culture has been preserved and that the people are determining the course of their own lives. Keeping up the appearances of remembering, a new culture of forgetting is set in place.

Liberal sensitivity to difference is a white lie.

Now, whites officially regret the genocide which happened right across the continent. And they officially regret the policy of protection that at least replaced genocidal fervour and isolated Aboriginal peoples in reserves as a mark of regret about the genocide. And whites now officially regret the policy of assimilation that at least replaced the policy of protection, and that attempted to give Aboriginal peoples a 'fair go' as a mark of regret about the protection. At least self-determination includes regret about assimilation, for wanting to wipe out their culture and replace it with ours. Respect for other people's cultures, cultural sensitivity, is now the name of the game.

> *From their music and art and dance we are beginning to recognise how much richer our national life and identity will be for the participation of Aboriginals and Torres Strait Islanders ... ATSIC emerges from the vision of indigenous self-determination and self-management ... Imagine if our spiritual life was ridiculed and denied ... All over Australia, Aboriginal and Torres Strait Islanders are taking control over their lives ... Imagine if ours was the oldest culture in the world and we were told it was worthless ... The Mabo judgment constituted recognition of an historic truth ... The cultural shift is occurring.* [11]

These are Prime Minister Paul Keating's historic words, and a sign of a new politics of remembering, a politics of culture and self-determination.

Groote Eylandt is now a place of historic truth, a place of self-determination and a place where the past can be freely remembered. There are no longer restrictions on 'their music and art and dance', the representatives of the 'oldest culture' can hold their heads high.

But the 'historic truth' of Mabo is old hat here, old hat because the land is already all Aboriginal owned and the Church Missionary Society did their job of making sure that the indigenous people would receive mining royalties. The future's already here at Groote.

✪

'DEET [the former Department of Employment, Education and Training] demanded a white person as the chairperson of SkillShare, a "person with extensive financial and administrative experience",' says the Director of SkillShare.

'I am here, on Groote, as a consultant employed by SkillShare. SkillShare is run by the elders. They tell me what to do. But a lot of the time, I tell them what to do. They just trust me, and I do the work. If they didn't trust me, they'd let me do it anyway.'

Every July, at 'clan time', the 'clan money'—the mining royalties—is distributed among the nineteen clans. Depending on whether GEMCO has had a good year, it might be $3 million, it might be $5 million.

'We trainers shut down for two weeks at clan time,' says one of the trainers. 'The miners call it Black Christmas. We all go off to Bali for a couple of weeks. There are gunshots in the streets. Boys race round on the back two wheels of new motor bikes until the petrol and the money runs out. There are big card games. The white miners who live in Alyangula put junk furniture out in the street and ask exorbitant prices for it. The car dealers come out from Darwin with photo albums of second-hand cars. These people have $80 000 to $90 000 family incomes and it's all spent in a week. For the rest of the year they're on the dole. The dole money is called sit-down money. There's still a hunting and gathering attitude here. They gather the money on dole day as if it was mangoes or yams. These people are very traditional. These guys are still hunters and gatherers and the dole money and the clan money is a part of the gathering. The money holds back their moving towards western culture. It keeps them living in the here and now, it keeps the hunting and gathering going.'

Here is a new mission for whites, a mission that needs this sort of cross-cultural understanding.

'We're stoked, we love it here. We love mucking around in other people's cultures.'

✺

The white principal at Angurugu school is taking early retirement. This has been the worst year of her career. A fourteen-year-old boy had been sniffing petrol in the school grounds for weeks on end, sleeping there by night. She took the petrol can and rang the police. The cops took him away and returned him to his mother. There was not much else they could do. Next day, the mother came back to the school and demanded the can of petrol back. He died in the school grounds a couple of days later.

When in Groote, even community visitors like us usually stay in miners' accommodation at Alyangula, about ten kilometres from the airport and Angurugu. Each day we drive to Angurugu to do our community business, crossing the boundary between the world of the whites and the world of the blacks.

By tonnage, this is Australia's busiest road, an almost straight stretch of bitumen from a hole in the ground beside an Aboriginal community to a white community by a beach and a shipping wharf from which the manganese is dispatched to the world of industrial modernity. The distance is measured out by exactly one hundred high-tension power poles, each with a number painted near the base. It's hard not to count out the distance each day, from one to one hundred, in a world of numbered rationality.

Groote has the highest rate of crime per capita in the world, another fact in the universe of numbers. The police won't even go to Umbakumba, nor will the ambulance, it's too dangerous. Random gunshots ring through the night. The ambulance people say that if you can't get yourself in to Alyangula, the white miners' town sixty kilometres away, you're not going to survive anyway.

✺

Christian revivalism sweeps Arnhem Land in waves. One of these waves had recently been through Maningrida, just as Groote is swept along from time to time.

The day after a big revival meeting, a large white cross still stands in the open field in the middle of the Maningrida. The field is empty now, but yesterday it was filled with expectation of the last days and the coming of the Lord and the fruits of repentance.

Everyone seems to be on edge. A meeting under a large raintree follows through on some of the arguments of the previous day. Questions of meaning and purpose cannot be raised and just left to another Sunday; and they cannot be said without there being reverberations in the whole renegotiation of history going on right now.

A woman speaks into a loudspeaker, weaving in and out of English and Kriol and language:

> *Dreaming not culture.*
> *Drinking not culture.*
> *Fighting not culture.*
> *It's not God's way.*

Culture, this woman seems to be saying, is an antidote to the life of Dreaming, Drinking and Fighting.

'Cross-hatching', she says, 'is the work of Satan!' This is a deliberate pitch for a certain sort of modernity, the ideal culture of a promised and imminent future without drinking and fighting. The irony is that our contemporary definition of Aboriginal culture insists on 'cross-hatching'. And the irony is also that the 'cross-hatching is the work of Satan' argument—the white missionary definition as it once was—is now a wholly indigenous one.

'The Dreaming is evil.' Again, this is what white missionaries used to say. The things she is saying are things that whites cannot say any more. A new white framing of culture means that even the missionaries who are left at least have to keep up the appearance of respecting the difference that 'culture' seems to make visible. The woman is not using 'culture' here the way whites now do.

'Culture is the work of the devil!' The woman's next sentence reverses the semantics of 'culture', as she has been using the word. Culture is now tradition, including Dreaming and cross-hatching, but in this meaning it is something to be left behind just as it is hoped drinking and fighting can be left behind. But who invented this idea of culture? Culture slips into this part of her argument as an English word, a word that the whites have brought of late and which an Aboriginal woman is now directly repudiating. The semantic shift works perfectly.

We meet with Milak Winunguj, Council President at Maningrida. An older man is already in the room talking with him. The discussion about culture over the loudspeaker is still going on in the distance. The older man is accusing people of selling out, including the Aboriginal members of the council, including Milak. It seems that the preacher has been sentenced to death, and Milak and the old man are talking about that.

'Balanda not true. Culture is true. You're half way between culture and Balanda,' the old man accuses Milak.

Balanda is the Yolngu (Northeast Arnhem) word for whites, from the word 'Hollander'. The Yolngu knew the Dutch had found their way to Batavia long before any whites knew the Yolngu existed. They had been told by the Macassans and some Yolngu travelling to Macassar may have even seen whites. Yolngu discovered the whites long before the whites discovered the Yolgnu. They had a word for the whites before the whites had a word for any of the indigenous inhabitants of Australia. This is significant for white history in which there is truth in 'discovery'.

Milak rages and threatens to throw us out of his office when we ask the old man what he means. We are questioning community. This stuff is community business, not white business.

'Traditional culture is a key to education. Balanda education is very, very hard, but our education is just as hard, just as good. Our kind of thinking is in two worlds. We need to use Yolngu tactics in introducing things in the curriculum, learning about the core of the place that you belong to, the territorial boundaries, where you come from. I know that very, very well, that's where my education comes from. The species, the contours, short or long beaches, type of trees that we recognise very well, that's where our education comes from. Seasonal changes that fit in with our song cycle, that's where our education comes from. Learning at campfires, sitting around, that's a key to education. Observing each other's conversation, learning from it, footprints on the beach, recognising whose they are, this is part of communication. Yolngu tactics are important, a key to education. We want to use Balanda tactics, too, but white teachers are just coming here for the money. We're coming home, but they could go anywhere.'

The argument about cultures and tactics is one that whites can never carry on as cogently as this because the world of the whites has reached ends—work competencies, schooled learning, the authority of the written word—that are far less negotiable, far less open to possibility. Milak's rage at us is proper. Whites have no right to intervene in the argument, no right even to have a view on arguments so fundamentally outside their experience.

'European society: Expected to learn by themselves. Aboriginal society: Learn from older wiser people.' Learning by ourselves, personal responsibility for personal development—these are classical white myths.

'Myths tell of relationships between gods, spirits or supernatural powers and humans and nature, e.g. creation stories.' Our personal selves figure heroically in educational stories of self-creation. This is self-delusion. The truth of the culture of writing is otherwise.

I won't believe until I have read it. (Martial, 103 AD)

Human beings around the world hold true to a wide variety of beliefs, some mainstream, some unusual and some bizarre. Whether you want to know about the world's great religions, the thoughts of famous philosophers, or what makes politicians tick, there are books and journals that will tell you all that you need to know.

(National Book Council. Reading Rewards. Sponsored by Australian Paper Manufacturers and the International Literacy Year.)

These are the words of a poster on the wall of a classroom, a call to self-creation through literacy.

'There are books and journals that will tell you what you need to know.'

Our revealed truths are fixed in print. This is our style of learning—we learn from the older, wiser people of white written words—and this style of learning removes far more negotiating power from the learner than the oral tellings of Aboriginal elders ever did.

'European society: Learn by being told. Aboriginal society: Learn by doing.' The abstract word stands opposed to the culture of the concrete here and now. Where does this leave the staged, goal-oriented doings of competency frameworks? Where does it leave the tellings of Aboriginal elders? These little cross-cultural keys seem handy ways of sorting the world out, but they never work.

'European society: Learn in made-up situations. Aboriginal society: Learn in real-life activities.' This must mean that Inganarr is real-life activity and competency training is all made up.

'European society: Learn for future. Aboriginal society: Learn for today's activity.' It seems from the activities of white educators that this is a crucial difference. The future is abstract, the present concrete, so the European is future oriented, the Aborigine oriented to experience in the present.

'European society: Society in constant change. Aboriginal society: Traditionally stable society.' The sung words of Anindilyakwa and other Australian indigenous languages told of almost everything except a concrete present. They told of the immanence of distant pasts and of imminent futures, in people, in objects, in symbols. These were languages of abstraction, of metaphor, of overlaid references so complex that their meaning required dedicated lifetimes. A word was a person, a place, a god in a cosmological narrative, an object in the natural world, a clan.

Songs were sung, and resung, but never twice the same way. Songs were points of negotiation, of living with constant change by constantly making change, of renaming the world, of always throwing sovereignty into question by reopening the discussion about words and people and places.

The white schemas of cultural difference could be as wrong as this, or more. Difference and sensitivity are nicer than the way things used to be done—a kinder, gentler, white liberal racism.

❁

The white principal had drawn up a timetable on the whiteboard in the school staffroom. 'Constant change is here to stay,' was written across the top of the board, yet all the cells in the grid were still white blanks—alike in their dimensions and still empty even though it was several weeks into term.

The world referred to in Anindilyakwa was not a fixed world. As a person died and his or her name could no longer be mentioned, the whole world had to be renamed. As a person progressed through life, the world was renamed in progressively more complex languages of age. Women named their world in ways different from men's. Clans named their lands and other people's lands in dialects of affected differentiation.

Everything was always up for renegotiation, for reappropriation through renaming, for singing again, for telling again, for creating the world anew by remembering and refashioning its sung and spoken words. This was not a stable, unchanging society; it was one of continual recreation, of people remaking their history all the time.

'Constant change is here to stay.' But the words of English, the language of ostensible change, are fixed in dictionaries, signifier representing signified, in a probably more static and non-negotiable relationship than any other language, ever. English has been standardised, which means that there is a right and wrong spelling and grammar, tick and flick. The logic of Anindilyakwa was one of differentiation instead, of marking land ownership and clan identity and gender and moiety and age by the different ways in which you could name the world. Depending on who you are and how you experience it differently.

This was the way the language worked, before dictionaries and language revival, that is. When Anindilyakwa is put into lists of straight lines in a dictionary, all meaning and reference is frozen in the same way that writing English is based on frozen meaning, frozen referents. It can be taught in schools. It can be read in Bibles.

The world of white words is a world of replicated time and space, a world where creation can be reduced to numbers— 95 million units of homogeneity. It is an additive world where we can claim as a virtue that English has 150 000 words, more than any other language, even though most of them are practically useless to us almost all the time.

But the grammar, the pronouns, the relating of ourselves in the world—you can count English pronouns on a little more than one hand, versus the hundreds in Anindilyakwa. There are just a few English tenses compared to the manifold complexity of Anindilyakwa pasts in relation to presents in relation to futures.

We whites live in the world of the concrete, the predictable and the repetitive. This is the culture of the written word.

As you spend time on the vast continent of Aboriginal Australia, you realise that an anthropology of the whites is the thing that is needed. Whites bring the words of culture and language, they use them as a way of seeing what they understand to be differences, but what do these words mean? When might we have an Aboriginal linguistics of white naming instead of a white linguistics of Aboriginal naming?

So we can understand ourselves and what we are doing.

✺

'We want to learn the roots of the Balanda way,' says a teacher-education student, 'the way they teach, the secret lessons.'

The problem is that the whites themselves don't know what they are doing and won't until there are Aboriginal anthropologies of the whites. They simply don't know what English really is, what dictionaries really do, what kinds of faith underpin competencies and what kinds of secular modernity underpin Bible translations. Whites don't know what they are. Whites use their secrets but they do not know what they themselves are, so they can't say what their secrets are.

'We should do assignments on western knowledge. We want real life. We want to know about both ways. Now the content is Yolngu, method is Balanda; we want to swap this around. Now we are like the children of Israel, slaves, whites making us do things about our own communities, forcing us to do this and that.'

I am writing all this down as field notes, so we can piece together an ethnography of literacy and so we can consider the questions of cultural relevance (sensitivity) and competence (self-determination). I am writing it down because if I don't, I'll forget.

I am a slave to the culture of writing, a culture in which we have lost the ability to remember even a few sentences, let alone the hundreds of hours of songs fading through perhaps six or ten languages as they travel across the land and its history.

❈

Stephen Brown is the Aboriginal Employment Officer with GEMCO. In the last year he has managed to get the number of Aboriginal employees up to twenty-three.

'We don't want to be on the dole. Every time I drive up into Angurugu, I can't drive through that town without someone asking me for a job. We don't need more training either, we need jobs. Blackfellas are the most trained people I have ever seen. Forty thousand years of dreams and 200 years of fucking nightmares, that's what I say. I wanted pre-employment programmes run through SkillShare. I say, this is what we need you to run. They say, no, this is what you need. They run it their way and think that blackfellas don't know what is good for them. The heliconias, noxious fucking weeds, they don't belong to here. We're planting natives in the rehab programme. The computer games—they must think we're fucking stupid.'

Out at Noonkanbah in the Kimberley, Dickie Cox tells us what he doesn't like about the Mabo legislation. He had been one of the leaders of the land rights struggle of the seventies and eighties.

'What we're saying now, we're one people in the community, we run this as a cattle station, more than one million acres. But some people are saying, this bit's my land, I'm going my own way. Mabo says you have to prove links to the land. A lot of people are getting confused. They're making money out of Aboriginal people with all this.'

Mabo expunges liberal consciences by reinventing tradition and by forcing the communities that were created in white missions and white cattle stations, to reinvent themselves in terms of liberal notions of culture, within a white framework of supposed remembering. This is creating fabulously well-paid jobs for anthropologists and linguists, not a few of whom are former missionaries, to provide expert assistance in the remembering.

On Groote, it may mean that only two of the nineteen clans, the ones on whose lands the mine was built, will get all of the royalty money, and people fear the terrible consequences this would produce.

'*Orait, longtaim bifo enijing bin jidan, det Wed bin jidan, en det Wed bin jidan garram God, en det Wed na im God.*' This is the first verse of the Gospel According to John in the Kriol Bible. 'In the beginning was the Word, and the word was with God, and the word was God.'

Kriol is a completely new Australian language. Lance and Gwen Tremblett are Anglican Bible literacy teachers. Now they live at Ngukurr, the old Roper River Mission, and help in the ongoing task of translating the Bible into Kriol. In the last days of the mission Lance had been town clerk at Angurugu.

'You might hear people say that language is alive but you try and ask any child to speak one of them and they can't. There's a handful of speakers of each of the eight languages represented here at Ngukurr. They're trying to write the languages down but they only come up with word lists: animals, birds and the like. They haven't got a lot of the words that they need, they have already disappeared. Kriol is becoming a language of Aboriginal identity. That's what our Aboriginal Preacher, Michael Gumbuli says. He's from Groote and speaks five languages. He says that all the old languages will be gone in a decade or so. He's a realist.'

Soon we may have lost the resources we would need to be able to do an anthropology of the whites and a linguistics of their written words.

There's been a funeral at Ngukurr, and ceremony has been going on for several days now, moving uneasily between Christian hymns, a sermon from Michael Gumbuli on the evil of grog, and the clapsticks and didgeridoos of a culture the Trembletts believe is disappearing.

❂

Kevin Rogers was the first Aboriginal principal at Ngukurr. He used to work operating heavy equipment for GEMCO on Groote when the mine first opened. Now he's doing an MA in linguistics.

'There's been a revival of ceremony; it's a way of linking up with your people, of establishing traditional tracks. I wouldn't call it real estate. This language revival thing is really a big task. The increase in ceremonies has been triggered by the schoolhouse. People are starting to talk to the children in language. Things used to be done for you, now you've got to look after yourself, do things for yourself, putting things back on Aboriginal shoulders, looking further down the track. Without the language, you have no land, you're not what you are, you're just a coconut, black on the outside and white on the inside.'

A new world is being remembered, a world that in the remembering is like no past worlds except when it revives their capacity to recreate, to reinvent, to rename. There is more radical recreation, reconstitution, reconstruction happening here than is ever possible in the words and spaces of metropolitan modernity, in the white world of the written word.

Nancy Lalara is married to Grant Burgoyne, a white man, and they both work for the council at Angurugu. 'Self-determination was handled appallingly. It's just words. You see so many white people come and go, people don't give a shit. Corrupt principals, teachers, bludge in the bush. The white people here are basically dead wood. They're conservative and interested in themselves. They want to earn money, get a good mortgage for a house somewhere else. Things couldn't be worse if all the white people left. Nothing's happening because it's bludge city here.'

I wonder what I am doing here now. Things would be no different if I weren't working on competency. Obviously, consciously, deliberately, I'm not doing what the missionaries were doing in the days of my prayers. But competency is just as much a matter of expecting Aboriginal people to obey white words, only now we try to ease our consciences by calling this 'skills for self-determination'. As subtle as this conceit may be, it doesn't seem to be working.

It really wouldn't matter if all the white people left, left to allow indigenous peoples to engage with the world of modernity in the ways that they want to, when they want to, on their own terms. When there is recreation and reinvention now, it is despite the white presence.

On a whiteboard in the Anglican church at Angurugu the Aboriginal minister had written:

> *What happened to our ancestors? Was there a signpost for them?*
> *What is the meaning of the story about the fresh turtle meat*
> *and the three-day-old turtle meat?*
> *When I die, will I know everything, or maybe nothing till*
> *judgment day?*
> *Sinners from a long time ago, where are they now? Maybe*
> *somewhere around here?*

A long time ago ... somewhere around here ... judgment day.

These are all questions whites have given up taking seriously. At Angurugu the answers to these questions cannot possibly come in the terms of what whites now call 'culture' and 'language', yet they are questions that insist on answers.

✳

So this is the history of the white culture of forgetting. In the beginning there were the white people who came to Groote with a word, telling the inhabitants that they had to forget, and the word was assimilation.

Then the white people changed their minds, they said, 'Remember your past and determine your own future.' But it was still the same word, a word now so much more subtly imposed, imposed with all the sensitivity of a people which claims to know and like difference. This was a word by which, through remembering, you forgot.

In the last days, the white people just have to get out, to allow the renegotiation of words and space, to allow remembering that can recreate and reinvent a new future. Then, whites should only come back on the terms of indigenous invitation.

✳

On my last day, I am yet again counting the one hundred poles from Alyangula to the airport beside Angurugu, identical and evenly spaced. The research I have been doing here seems at best pointless, at worst it seems like I'm applying the latest technology of colonialism, a technology of the word called 'sensitivity to difference' and 'self-determination'.

I know that it is the world of the whites in which I live that desperately needs the orientation to nature and sociality that is in the grammar of a language like Anindilyakwa. It's a grammar all but lost to the culture of the written word, and one that remains largely unnoticed by the white linguists who only really listen to the language of difference so they can write it down on their own terms.

I can't believe any more in the brotherly love of the missionaries and a modernity made of quarters of manganese. The existence of the whites is a miserable wreck with a fearfully limited 'future orientation'.

To know there could be an alternative to this particular world of written words, this the reason I am here. This is my self-interest.

The Ansett lady issues us all boarding passes, imposing a numbered order on the straggle of people waiting for the plane. The whites end up at the front of the plane and the blacks at the back.

The plane takes off and below lie the bays and headlands of Groote. A white person near the front of the plane is reading a book with a sunset red cover. I'm thinking what I'm thinking. The title of the book is almost unbearable. *Aboriginal Fables and Legendary Tales*, it's called.

1995

[1] Quoted in Keith Cole and Dick Harris, *Missionary to the Aborigines* (Bendigo: Keith Cole Publications, 1980), p. 6.

[2] *Ibid.*, pp. 45, 61–2.

[3] Australian Institute of Political Science, *Northern Australia: Task for a Nation* (Sydney: Angus & Robertson, 1954), p. 201.

[4] Cole, *op. cit.*, p. 64.

[5] Cole, *op. cit.*, p. 64–5.

[6] BHP Manganese GEMCO, *Groote Eylandt Manganese*, publicity booklet, 1993, p. 6.

[7] Keith Cole, *Groote Eylandt Aborigines and Mining: A Study in Cross-Cultural Relationships* (Bendigo: Keith Cole Publications, 1988), p. 21.

[8] This writing is based on several different projects, several periods of time and several trips to Groote Eylandt and other communities in the Northern Territory and Western Australia, in 1993 and 1994. Texts are quoted verbatim. However, to protect the identities of some of the persons and activities discussed, in some places, projects and sites have been elided and transposed, and characters disguised.

[9] Institute of TAFE, Northern Territory University, *Certificate in Horticultural Skills, Trainer Manual*, p. 1.

[10] A short version of [an] Arnhem Land myth, as told by Esther Djayhgurrnga, 1992, *Getting Going with Genres: Narrative Genre* (Darwin: Northern Territory Department of Education, 1993), p. 19. Interpretive gloss, pp. 1, 15, 27–34.

[11] Speeches by Prime Minister Paul Keating, Redfern, 10 December 1992; Sydney, 28 April 1993.

BARRY OAKLEY

At the Third Stroke

POOL: THE SOFT KISS OF THE P, the swooning vowels, the lulling closure. The perfect summer word, carrying, between its first and final consonant, the suggestion of smooth water ... The old Olympic Pool in Batman Avenue in Melbourne. The sign in the dressing room: Do Not Pollute the Water. Not one pool but three—Paddlers, Diving and Olympic. Its chlorine tinged, blue lucidity, its jellied depths, dazzling in the December sun.

When you swam, time stopped. You left it behind with your clothes in the locker. Slip into the mirror-water and you entered a realm where everything moved in slow motion. The world of clocks and friction fell away, you inclined from the vertical to the horizontal—it was like flying or dreaming. You moved whichever way you wanted, gracefully and without effort. You had spent the first nine months of your life floating and your body sank back into the medium with relish, as if it were its true home.

If the Olympic Pool was paradise, the Richmond Baths was the river of hell. It was where the school swimming sports were held. Like the Styx its waters were cold and uninviting. Like Hades it was cavernous and sunless, and the noise, booming up to the tin roof and back again, sounded like monstrous lamentations. I was never a very good swimmer, so the sports were a time of dread. I used to represent St Francis House in F-Division, the lowest grade possible, and had trouble completing the 33^1/$_3$ yards, earning my house no points at all. At the Richmond Baths you were made to see that the Olympic Pool was a fantasy, that there was no escape from the realities of life. Competition ruled, in as well as out of the water.

❋

The third pool to lap at the sides of memory was at Maryborough, Victoria, where I once taught at the Technical College. In winter it was a long scoop of concrete, lying dormant behind the pines of the park. In September it was watered and came to life, and by November the whole town seemed to gather round it, like Hindus by the Ganges celebrating rebirth.

The first summer I just watched and listened to the pagan joy of it from the landing of my first-floor flat. During the second, when I'd met my future wife, we joined in the celebrations. We had a courtship in and out of the water, submarine and ultramarine. Which led, ineluctably, to pool number four, a small rectangular one of military green canvas, with room for just one adult and two little kids, lying not swimming, in about a foot of water. It cooled us through the first family summers in outer-suburban Carnegie. Then came the move into Richmond and pool number five—an above-ground model with uncertain aluminium walls, a sensation in a neighbourhood that had neither the space nor the money for such a luxury. That summer the Richmond Baths were closed for repairs, so the Oakley pool became a local attraction. Our children's friends jumped into it from the flowering gum tree near the front gate, while others peeped longingly through the tea-tree fence. It needed frequent emptying and replenishing. The first time I tried to do it by simply pulling out one of the aluminium panels, and sent a small tidal wave tumbling into the street, frightening an old lady on the opposite footpath. It roared through the fence, crossed the road and was only just held by the gutter near where she had broken into an elderly half-canter with her stick.

❋

In our eighteen months in London we lived across the common from the Peckham Rye pool—one of only about a dozen public ones in the entire city. We were there for the famous heatwave of 1976, when hundreds of thousands of pale English bodies turned pink, footpaths melted, and buses stopped running because their drivers said it was too hot to go on. Peckham Public Swimming Bath (it was singular, so small and dingy it didn't deserve the 's') couldn't cope with the numbers and queues formed outside, and the green water turned brown, like soup. When we came back to Australia and took a flat in Manly over the road from the beach, our kids ran across the sand, even though it was only August, the delirious way dogs do when they're let off their leashes in parks, and hurled themselves into the water—because that was what they'd missed most.

The final pool is in the backyard of our daughter's house in Hornsby Heights. The scene is Boxing Day. The shade tent is up, the champagne is uncorked, a family lunch is about to begin. Emilia, our granddaughter, is learning to dog-paddle, but hasn't quite mastered it, and makes small splashing lunges from the steps and back again. She sees her grandmother in the middle of the pool but her grandmother doesn't see her. Unnoticed, she paddles off in her direction and then disappears. My wife turns at that moment, sees the bubbles and just gets to her in time ... Every pool is really two pools. Below the clear blue Olympic there's the sunless underworld Richmond one, green and cold and waiting to drag you down.

1995

Atavism

THERE WAS A GOOD DEAL OF THE SCOTS in Kenneth Slessor, but not as much as the *Sydney Morning Herald* had in mind when, in November 1995, it paraded the poet as a famous Australian with a Scottish name. 'Kenneth' maybe, in deference to his mother's family, who had emigrated from the Hebrides: but the poet got 'Slessor' from his father, who got it from his father before him. In those days it was pronounced 'Schloesser', and it remained 'Schloesser' until Slessor was thirteen, when, after the outbreak of war in 1914, his father changed the name to conceal its German origins.

But there was another, much older process of effacement at work, which had begun generations before. Few would recognise Kenneth Adolphe Schloesser as one of Australia's great poets: but until Geoffrey Dutton's 1991 biography, only a handful of people could have known that Slessor on his father's side was as Jewish as he was German. Slessor's great grandfather Louis was a distinguished musician, a valued acquaintance of Beethoven and a friend of Berlioz—his position as Kapellmeister at the Court of the Hesses in Darmstadt presumably required some down-playing of his Jewish origins. Slessor's father noted that his own family was 'entirely free of any religious observances or creeds'. Yet his mother was a Salomon, and the family tree boasts distinguished Jewish names on both sides, Schloesser and Salomon, Emmanuel, Cohen, Nathan, Baruch.[1]

Slessor evidently cherished this inheritance, since papers relating to his family history, and a copy of the family tree dating back to the eighteenth century, are to be found in his papers in the National Library of Australia. But it seems to have been largely a secret possession, a hidden aspect of what was, by all accounts, a personality marked by repression and inhibition. In the Sydney of the twenties and thirties, which is when Slessor made his mark as a poet, and in the artistic and journalistic circles he moved in, Jewish forebears were probably best left in the closet.

The anti-semitism of Lionel and Norman Lindsay is well-known: the one presented modern art as a pernicious conspiracy foisted on an innocent public by international Jewish financiers, the other saw the Jew as a threat to all that was noble and joyous in human creativity. Slessor was close to the Lindsays, and to Norman in particular. Yet as late as 1959, as editor of *Southerly*, Slessor could publish an essay in which Lindsay railed against 'the monstrous amalgam of sadism, masochism and nihilism' which Christianity had got from the East, by which he meant Judaism. 'Is there any need to question a mystery in the hatred of the Jew,' Lindsay asked, 'the only Eastern race which has penetrated Western civilisation and imposed on it its own religious cultisms and its racial cunning?'[2] Lindsay had developed this line of argument at length in *Creative Effort*, almost forty years before. One wonders what Slessor did with his Jewish part when Lindsay spoke of these matters in private conversation, as he surely must have done during their long period of friendship. The one reference to Jews in Slessor's poetry is a slighting one, when the poet imagines himself as a retired sailor or sea captain walking down William Street, 'With a tin trunk and a five-pound note, looking for a place to eat,/And a peajacket the colour of a shark's behind/That a Jew might buy in the morning ...'. Ironically, Slessor's sea captains often exhibit Jewish characteristics. But in this poem, called 'Metempsychosis', the Jew is definitely other, and inferior—one of Lindsay's Jews.[3]

How completely can one efface the past from which one has come? 'Five Visions of Captain Cook' is one of Slessor's most famous poems. In its short compass it does more to establish Cook as a heroic figure in the Australian pantheon than many larger works of scholarly or hagiographic intent. Faced with the task of imparting a mythical resonance to the figure of the great explorer, Slessor's imagination drew on atavistic sources. Slessor presents Cook as a Jew. Not as the Jew that Lindsay, or the cartoonists of Slessor's own *Smith's Weekly* enjoyed caricaturing, a swarthy, lecherous, cunning, usurous, rather slimy figure—but as a Magus, a wizard or alchemist, one of a fellowship of Kabbalist sea captains, 'daemons in periwigs, doling magic out':

> *Who read fair alphabets in stars*
> *Where humbler men found but a mess of sparks,*
> *Who steered their crews by mysteries*
> *And strange, half-dreadful sortilege with books,*
> *Used medicines that only gods could know*
> *The sense of, but sailors drank*
> *In simple faith. That was the captain*
> *Cook was when he came to the Coral Sea*
> *And chose a passage into the dark.*

Indeed Slessor goes so far as to dress Cook in phylacteries, the small boxes containing holy script which orthodox Jews bind to head and arm while at prayer, 'It was the spell/of Cook did this, the phylacteries of Cook'. The poet Heinrich Heine defined the phylactery as the means by which 'faith is fastened on to the arm'. In Slessor's use religious faith has been replaced by the power of magic, in line with his general sublimation of the Jewish element—that element characterises Cook, but only because it has been washed clean of the taint of deceit or malice or cunning, and refined to the highest degree of heroism. At this level of refinement, even Lindsay would have been able to claim the Jew for his own cause, and in fact did so. Slessor's Rabbi Cook is like no-one so much as the magus in Lindsay's 1927 etching, 'Enter the

Magicians': the same glittering stare as Cook, the trappings of the astrologer-alchemist, and with a Star of David emblazoned on his sorcerer's cap. 'The magicians, of course, are the artists, the creators', Lindsay noted in a gloss on the etching, though he had elsewhere seen the Jew as the death of creativity.[4]

Slessor would not have needed to look deep into his unconscious in order to find an expression of Jewishness so acceptable, and even attractive, to his contemporaries, that it might not have seemed Jewish to them at all. The association between alchemy, astrology, divination, and the figure of the Jewish magus is a persistent one.[5] It gained renewed currency in the use made of the Kabbalah by the various occult movements of the late nineteenth and early twentieth centuries. It is possible that Slessor and Lindsay read the same books—Blavatsky, Eliphas Levi, A. E. Waite, or the fugitive writings of Aleister Crowley. But Slessor clearly has more invested in the figure of the Kabbalistic magician or alchemist than Lindsay, for whom it is just one in an eclectic cavalcade of exotic figures, most of whom are young, nubile, and in a state of undress.

In the poem which stood first in his first volume of poetry, and which was aptly titled 'Incongruity', Slessor pictured himself 'robed in the stoles of alchemy' in the midst of the Australian bush, in a scene charged with apocalyptic promise, waiting for night to fall so that he might exercise a magical power that would stop the planets in their tracks. Towards the end of his poetic career, in 'Five Bells', his elegy to his friend Joe Lynch, and to his own powers as a poet, Slessor's stance is still essentially that of the Kabbalist or the magician, seeking in vain to attach meaning to the name, and to conjure the past back into existence, through a divination unsuccessfully practised on the fragments furnished by memory. Slessor defined poetry as 'music and magic', and the notion of the poet as a magician, always carrying a sense of incongruity or diminished power, in recognition of his circumstances, in Australia, in the twentieth century, is apparent both in the perspectives of his poetry, and through displacement and projection, in the gallery of heroic and mock-heroic figures that appear there.

Some of these figures may seem far removed from the strict representation of the Kabbalist, with the Jewish element leached out, but with the oriental quality, and the sense of homage to the patriarchal ancestor intensified, as in the mandarins and mages portrayed in poems like 'Marco Polo' and 'Taoist', 'those wise old men/Dozing all day in lemon silken robes,/With tomes of beaten jade spread knee to knee'.

At other times, Slessor's orientalism is given a European twist, which allows Jewish attributes to enter in a disguised form. In 'Earth-Visitors', the heroic figures from the East who appear without explanation at a wayside inn, fascinating the onlookers and tumbling the girls, display all the features—the beards, the dark furs, the gypsy eyes, the foreign garments, the strange words upon their tongues—commonly associated with the *hasidim*, the Kabbalistic sect with German roots with which Slessor might be expected to have the closest affinity. Of this branch of Kabbalism Gershom Scholem noted, 'nowhere else in Judaism has man the magical creator been surrounded with such an halo'.[6]

Slessor presents his 'strange riders' as figures of desire, haloed in light and casting a 'wild radiance' in their wake—and he goes out of his way to dignify them, calling them princes, barons, kings, before deciding they must be 'Archdukes'. The 'archdukes' is a measure of how far the 'riders' might have had to travel from their otherwise lowly origins, how deeply Slessor felt the need to give them exalted credentials. The epithet 'sweet as pineapple' applied to their 'strange tongue' shows a similar urge to exaltation—overdetermined, even in this ornate context, the detail is worth setting against the caricature of the Jew current in Slessor's time, which has him spitting and lisping his way in an insinuating fashion through the English language.

This suppressed negative underside to Slessor's exoticism is clearer in his use of dark or black fur as a poetic detail. In the poem 'Two Nocturnes', where the detail is applied to the portrayal of night, it is first a sign of grandeur ('cloaked in black furs, like some magnifico/come mourning to the catafalque of day/night swaggers down the sky to Arakoon') and then a sign of intrusion, as 'the swarthy wash of night' comes like a Jewish peddler into the middle-class comfort of a Sydney suburb. There is the 'fur of the night', which chokes the lips of the dying poet in 'Heine in Paris', and the grapes, 'half-savage with black fur' in 'Wild Grapes', 'out-laws of a strange bough' that carry in their exotic sweetness the taint of murder. In these negative connotations one senses as well a certain horror in the very reach backwards, as if the conjuring with the past were also a form of necromancy, and atavism a trade with the devil.

In some cases, Slessor's fascination with powerful ancestral father-figures and precursors, like Dürer in 'Nuremberg' and Heine in 'Heine in Paris', takes him back, quite explicitly to Germany. Here the reference points marked out by Slessor's atavism can be quite precise, though still veiled from the common gaze. Heinrich Heine was of particular interest to Slessor as a poetic precursor, not only because he was German, but because, like Slessor's own paternal forebears, he had had to submerge his Jewish origins, and profess himself a Protestant. Heine's satirical and scornful poetic stance is not unlike Slessor's own—Heine was an exile in Paris, Slessor in his poetry clearly conveys the sense of a poet exiled from his sources of inspiration.

There are certain family resemblances: between Heine's Uncle Salomon, the Hamburg merchant, and Slessor's own ancestors, Falk Schloesser, listed in the Slessor family tree as Court Provider of Foods to the Darmstadt Brigade, and Jakob Baruch, listed grandly as 'banker', of Frankfurt-am-Main. Jakob Baruch's son Löb Baruch was an essayist and journalist who had changed his name to Ludwig Börne in order to relieve the stigma of being born a Jew. Subsequently, like Heine, who was his friend and fellow-exile in Paris, he changed his religion too. Börne was Slessor's great-great-grandfather's brother, according to the family tree—a famous writer, and one of the leaders, with Heine, of the 'Young Germans' literary movement, he was an ancestor well worth claiming. Slessor claims him in 'Heine in Paris', but so subtly, and so ambiguously, that their affiliation must have remained unknown to all but the poet himself:

Men crumbled, man lived on. In that animal's face,
'Twas but a squirt aimed at the moon, to fling contempt.
Meyerbeer, Börne, and Klopstock vanished, but in their place
New Klopstocks, Meyerbeers blown again, and Börnes
undreamt,
Sprang up like fungi, and there remained no trace
Of lashings past ...

Slessor would have been, according to this line of descent, one of those undreamt Börnes, springing up like fungus, in a foreign land.

Atavism is, by its very nature, a complicated and mysterious transmission. In Slessor's case the transmission is further complicated by a sense that the past is both a source of riches, and a blight upon the present. Slessor's ancestral figures are not all cut from heroic stone. In his poetry there is a line of descent from the Kabbalist through the Jewish merchant and wanderer—magicians of another sort, transforming matter through exchange, bearing strange talismans from other worlds, avid readers of the stars—to the retired sea captains who capture his imagination in the later poetry, anchored in the calm waters of old age, conjuring tropical visions of paradise from old maps and ledgers, mementoes and memories. These captains are somewhat foolish figures, benign but impotent, marooned in a past that holds them in its spell—yet they bring the poet an important gift. Because they have been travellers in tropical waters, through their eyes Slessor's imagination enacts another eastern displacement, east and south this time, to the enchanted beaches of the Pacific, and to the east coast of Australia. Slessor's Captain Home, whose body moves in Scotland amidst 'the vague ancestral darknesses of home', but whose eyes are 'dazzle-full of skies and water farther round the world', embodies this paradoxical trajectory of atavism, which by coming from home, finds itself at home, in a place very different from that it had started from. One of Slessor's great achievements as a poet is to have seen his own place, Sydney, with an ancient gaze attuned to the possibilities of magic, and to have seen it truly.

But if time has given Slessor's sea captains this visionary power, it has also rendered them impotent. Behind these figures there is a deeper fear, of time falling backwards into the past, since it is from the past that the present draws so much of its significance. Joe Lynch, the friend whose drowning in Sydney Harbour Slessor mourns in 'Five Bells', may have had an oppressive father: but nothing quite prepares one for his appearance in the poem, the type of the ancestral father whose very influence, exercised in all innocence, is a burden that weighs heavily on the present:

> *In Sydney, by the spent aquarium-flare*
> *Of penny gaslight on pink wallpaper,*
> *We argued about blowing up the world,*
> *But you were living backward, so each night*
> *You crept a moment closer to the breast,*
> *And they were living, all of them, those frames*
> *And shapes of flesh that had perplexed your youth,*
> *And most your father, the old man gone blind,*
> *With fingers always round a fiddle's neck,*
> *That graveyard mason whose fair monuments*
> *And tablets cut with dreams of piety*
> *Rest on the bosoms of a thousand men*
> *Staked bone by bone, in quiet astonishment*
> *At cargoes they had never thought to bear,*
> *These funeral-cakes of sweet and sculptured stone.*

Slessor was descended from a line of distinguished musicians, and Lynch's fiddler-father is reminiscent of his own ancestor, Falk Schloesser, Court Provider and violinist. The past seems to carry for him too, this double aspect: as sweet nourishment, as terrible cargo.

There is a distinctively Jewish attitude to history which sees it as a terrible cargo, a burden of sorrow born of exile and persecution, from which one can never fully escape. Ludwig Börne referred to this melancholy outlook as 'the immense *Judenschmerz*, a rich dark treasure handed down from generation to generation'. Heine offers a vignette in his 1840 memoir of Börne which begins 'He who does not know exile will not understand how luridly it colours our sorrows, how it pours the darkness of night and poison into all our thoughts.' At least, he went on, the German writer exiled to France still finds himself in a familiar kind of landscape, and an almost identical climate. ' "How terrible exile must be, where this likeness does not exist," Börne once remarked, as we were strolling in the *Jardin des Plantes*. "How terrible if one were to see only palms and tropical vegetation, and strange wild life, like kangaroos and zebras." '7

That is precisely the kind of world in which Börne's undreamt-of Australian relative found himself. Much has been made of Slessor's supposed pessimism, the determined cynicism with which he confronts, not only his surroundings, but his own pretensions as a poet. This power of mockery and scorn is an important feature of the work of Heine and Börne, where it is often attributed to the oppositional stance forced upon them by the fact of being Jews, and underwritten by a literary tradition running back to the Hebrew prophets. The same kind of affiliation might be claimed for Slessor, who is usually seen as an *angst*-ridden modernist, were it more widely recognised that his gestures of negation are usually performed with a self-conscious deliberation, and with a theatrical aplomb often bordering on self-parody.

In some cases the gesture has gone completely unnoticed, as in the first of the 'Five Visions of Captain Cook', when Slessor observes how, faced with the choice of sailing north towards the safety of home, or westwards into the unknown, Cook had proved more courageous than his predecessors, and sailed into the west. 'So Cook made choice, so Cook sailed westabout,' Slessor wrote, 'So men write poems in Australia.' Slessor is usually seen as pressing a claim here for the Australian poet, on the grounds that Cook's heroic choice made it possible for other heroic acts, like writing poetry in Australia, to take place in turn. But if you read the lines with a resigned emphasis on the repeated 'so', and a disillusioned shrug of the shoulders, Slessor's ironic inflection becomes obvious. 'So Cook sailed westabout, / So men write poems in Australia': so if only Cook had sailed north, he—Slessor—would be writing poetry in Paris or New York.

Elsewhere, Slessor's negative stance is so flamboyant, and so melodramatic, that it really invites one to see it as drawing on an established repertoire of gestures, a rhetoric of indignation and moral outrage. Slessor's adoption of the prophetic role in 'Winter Dawn', looking across the rooftops of Sydney, is perhaps the most obviously traditional of these gestures:

> *O buried dolls, O men sleeping invisible there,*
> *I stare above your mounds of stone, lean down,*
> *Marooned and lonely in this bitter air,*
> *And in one moment deny your frozen town,*
> *Renounce your bodies ...*

But his habitual conjuring of the bush as blighted wasteland or lurid stage-set, furnished with monsters, or ruins, or poisonous exhalations, and his celebrations of the city as a place which the ghostly and the damned, the criminal and the outcast, may justly feel at home in, also belong to the same basic drama of exile and alienation.

The editor and critic A. G. Stephens was right in one way when he noted in his diary, 'Slessor looks like a Jew; an undercurrent of disapproving Jeremiah in his work'. There *is* something characteristically Jewish in Slessor's determination to look on the dark side of things, insistently, with dedication, gaining from his gloomy ecstasy an ironic purchase on the vicissitudes of existence. Others have seen something else—'a grim Calvinist stressing our doom of predestined mortality'—thus pointing to the fact that Slessor's dark side may owe as much to the Scottish Presbyterian in him as it does to the Jew.[8] In view of its history of immigration and displacement, Australia is fertile ground for *schmerz* of many kinds, from many different sources: Slessor is by no means the only Australian writer, in outward appearance at home in his surroundings, to have drawn in his writing on the legacy of exile. You don't have to struggle to hear this dark atavistic note, as if it came, with a weakened intensity, from far away, and a long time ago—it resounds through Australian literature.

And on the other hand, what of the legacy of hope? This note is easy to miss in Slessor, because it leads a bright, but fugitive, existence in his poetry. At the end of 'Five Bells', as the nightmarish encounter with death fades, the poet's attention is captured by the light glittering on the waters of Sydney Harbour:

> I looked out of my window in the dark
> At waves with diamond quills and combs of light
> That arched their mackerel-backs and smacked the sand
> In the moon's drench, that straight enormous glaze ...

This outbreak of radiance lasts only for an instant, before it is swallowed up by the pitiless drench of the moon's dead light. This happens often in Slessor's poetry, a sudden effulgence of light, which is just as suddenly frozen, congealed, or turned into shiny coating or crust. There is a good deal of the alchemist in Slessor's poetic method as well as in his stance as a poet, in the way his imagery is constantly subject to transmutation, fire into water, water into air, air into stone. There is a similar trade in metals, as natural details are transformed, upwards to copper and silver and gold, but more often downwards, to iron, pewter and lead. It is poetry as a kind of negative alchemy, with darkness and deadness as the common end, but with light as the vital spirit, breaking out of and returning to entrapment in the material world as it flees before the process of transmutation. Indeed so active is Slessor's light, so dazzling in its effects, though it may turn to paste or to scale, that the force of darkness in his poetry really seems to be owing to the withholding of light, as if in its retreat, light sucked darkness into the world in its wake.

There is a Kabbalist concept called the *Shekhina*, which has its roots, again, in German hasidism, whereby the glory of God is visible to man as a divine radiance, scattered by the Fall and held captive as sparks and particles of light in the matter of this world. From this dispersion it will be recovered by the acts of the righteous, and restored to its original splendour. Gershom Scholem saw in this image of a scattered and fractured radiance, a particularly compelling retelling of the great myth of exile—but with this consolation, that it offered the reassurance of an ultimate homecoming. Norman Lindsay has a rather twee, secularised version of the *Shekhina* in the foreground of 'Enter the Magicians', where in the midst of an extraordinary burst of radiance you can just make out a naked young girl. As for how this magical light reached Slessor, by what refractions and displacements, we are left only with conjectures. Atavism, like the radiance of the *Shekhina* itself, is unpredictable and intermittent in its operation: it does not submit readily to the rigour of proof.

But there is this interesting line of descent, through the medium of a third party, from the Kabbalah through Madame Blavatsky to Kenneth's father, Robert Schloesser-Slessor. Robert Slessor was a mining engineer, an expert on the extraction of metals, an alchemist of sorts. He was also an amateur philosopher, and filled notebook after notebook with his thoughts on important topics, and his dreams. In the first of these notebooks, titled 'Night Thoughts/ Daylight Discounts', in an entry dated 5 May 1916, he noted:

> *The only acceptable conclusion (concerning the evolution of the soul) to my mind is the Theosophical doctrine that God gave forth 'divine sparks' which descended into gross matter and gradually evolved up and up, till the divine spark is reabsorbed in the Deity—that seems to me today the satisfying and reasonable conclusion for the conviction that 'God is immanent everywhere'.[9]*

Whether it travelled by this path, or by some other, the light in Slessor's poetry sparks with a radiance which belies the distance it has come. Nowhere is it more dazzling than when it blazes out of the Pacific visions of Slessor's retired sea captains, and nowhere more at home than when it shines in the glittering waters of Sydney Harbour.

> *Darkness comes down. The Harbour shakes its mane,*
> *Glazed with a leaf of amber; lights appear*

Like thieves too early, dropping their swag by night,
Red, gold and green, down trap-doors glassy-clear,
And lanterns over Pinchgut float with light
Where they so long have lain.
All this will last, but I who gaze must go
On water stranger and less clear, and melt
With flesh away; and stars that I have felt,
And loved, shall shine for eyes I do not know.

1996

1   Geoffrey Dutton, *Kenneth Slessor: A Biography* (Ringwood: Viking, 1991), ch. l; Slessor Papers, National Library of Australia, MS 3020/9/481.

2   *Southerly 1*, 1959, quoted in *Norman Lindsay on Art, Life and Literature*, Keith Wingrove (ed.) (St Lucia: UQP, 1990), p. 194.

3   All references to Slessor's poetry are to *Kenneth Slessor: Collected Poems*, Dennis Haskell and Geoffrey Dutton (eds) (Sydney: Angus & Robertson, 1994).

4   Heine, *It Will Be a Lovely Day: Prose Selections*, trans. Frederic Ewen (Seven Seas, 1965), p. 252; Lindsay, letter to Charles Shepherd, quoted in Ursula Prunster, *The Legendary Lindsays* (Sydney: Art Gallery of NSW, 1995). Permission to use a detail from 'Enter the Magicians', for the purpose of illustrating this essay, was refused by the copyright holders.

5   See, for example, Raphael Patai, *The Jewish Alchemists* (Princeton University Press, 1994).

6   *Major Trends in Jewish Mysticism* (Schocken, 1961), p. 99.

7   Börne cited in Solomon Liptzin, *Germany's Stepchildren* (Jewish Publication Society, 1944), p. 33; Heine, from *Ludwig Börne: A Memorial* (1840), in *It Will Be a Lovely Day*, p. 280.

8   'A. G. Stephens's *Bulletin* Diary', ed. Leon Cantrell, in Bruce Bennett, *Cross-Currents* (Longman, 1981), p. 83; T. Inglis Moore, 'Kenneth Slessor', in *Critical Essays on Kenneth Slessor*, ed. A. K. Thomson (Jacaranda, 1968), p. 114.

9   Slessor Papers, NLA MS 3020/2/11, pp. 63–4.

The Holocaust on Fast-forward

WE WERE STANDING AT THE COUNTER in the Elite Cafeteria trying to decide on popsicles when the Richters came up through the soles of my feet and started shaking the salad display. There weren't many of them—a puny 3.7, according to the television news later—and at first I didn't recognise them as an earthquake. The floor just sort of rumbled quietly and the columns supporting the ceiling swayed a little. My first thought was that somewhere below, on one of the lower floors of the Museum of Tolerance, a particularly interactive exhibit had swung into action. What could it be, I wondered? A cattle car, perhaps?

Then a woman jumped up from her coffee and rushed to the nearest door frame. 'You do this, don't you?' she asked the room in general. 'In an earthquake, I mean ...' Her words trailed off in embarrassment. The trembler had already come and gone, leaving her lack of cool hanging in mid-air. Her companions chuckled indulgently and stirred their cappuccinos in an understanding sort of way. 'This is Los Angeles,' one of them said. 'What did you expect?'

We had arrived the day before from Las Vegas—man, woman and eleven-year-old boy—on a plane alongside bone-weary Korean businessmen and off-duty discipline mistresses in rhinestone-studded leather. We had three days in LA and we knew just how to fill them. Tomorrow, Universal Studios. Tuesday,

Disneyland. Today, Dad's choice, the Simon Wiesenthal Centre Museum of Tolerance. Not the big $US168 million Holocaust Museum in Washington, mind you. But a smaller, more modest attempt at the same objective—the application of American imagination and technology to the representation of genocide. Imagineering the unimaginable. Schindler's theme park.

So far, my companions were sceptical, but appropriately tolerant. We bought our popsicles, went downstairs and handed over our tickets to a pretty girl in a floral dress. 'Hi,' she said. 'I'm Mitzi, your guide for today.' She skipped ahead of us down a spiral ramp. 'Welcome to the Tolerancenter™, a unique workshop featuring hands-on exhibits spotlighting the major issues of intolerance that are part of our daily life.' This will be our orientation area. Here we will be provided with the framework with which to understand what follows, the Holocaust Section.

Interactive devices are scattered through a large display area. 'The current theme of the Tolerancenter™ is "Understanding the Los Angeles Riots"', explains Mitzi. 'Although you may prefer the word "Uprising".' I touch the screen of a video monitor and a timeline scrolls by—Watts 1965 becomes South Central 1992, National Guard troops with M16s become Korean appliance store proprietors with automatic pistols. Touch me, the screen invites, for suburb-by-suburb demographics, response polls, media reaction, police views, eyewitness reports. Break the statistics down by race, income, profession. What percentage of Latinos considered the looting justified? Touch screen to select.

There is a tug at my sleeve. My son leads me into a darkened tunnel. 'Greasy spic,' someone whispers in my ear. 'Dirty kike, asshole.' The walls are talking, their voices triggered by our passing. 'Bull dyke bitch,' they hiss. 'Fatso.' 'Fatso?' says the kid. Piss weak. We emerge beside a large map of the US covered with flashing lights—a push-button, state-by-state breakdown of current neo-Nazi activity. The boy sidles back into the tunnel, charmed.

Our tour group is bustled onward, twenty-five whites, two blacks, past a wall of screens. 'I have a dream,' proclaim a dozen simultaneous Martin Luther Kings. On we move, our guides polite but firm. We must maintain the schedule. We are sat before a flickering silent movie. Watch this. Model-T Fords. Daredevil biplane antics. Neck-to-knee bathing beauties. The Roaring Twenties. Above us a digital clock counts down the minutes we must wait. Charlie Chaplin. Clemenceau. The Charleston. Five minutes to go. The Thirties approach in flickering monochrome.

Doors swing wide and we are ushered forward to be issued with an ID card. Mary Steinhauser, mine says. A blurred picture shows a button-nosed little girl of about three staring out from under a pixie hat. No other information. For the remainder of the tour, this will be my identity.

Before we can proceed, however, there is one more essential step. Lest we have come this far without realising it, we are to be reminded of what it is we will see today. In a diorama of a modern design studio, three animated mechanical mannequins discuss the problems inherent, from a museum point of view, in constructing an accessible Holocaust. Sources are discussed, the difficulties of authentic simulation, curatorial and technical issues, the nature of representation. Politics are not mentioned.

We are led down the reproduction of a Berlin streetscape, circa 1933. Posters proclaim Hitler's imminent victory. At an outdoor cafe complete with Kurt Weill muzak, spot-lit dummies in period costume discuss the future. 'Ve vill haff to liff viz zees Nazis' is the consensus. Some see career prospects. Ze vord 'fascism' iss nicht gesprochen.

Further up the street, we are fast-forwarded through a roomful of Nuremberg rallies and invited to insert our ID cards into video machines. I, Mary Steinhauser, daughter of Jakob and Jenny, was born in Vienna two months after the *Anschluss*. Aged one, I embarked for Shanghai. No further information is provided. At the machine beside me, my real-life son's card shows that in 1939 his alter ego had just begun high school in Romania. My wife is a teenage Berliner called Ulrich Arnheim.

Through a plate-glass window we see a reconstruction of the Wannsee conference. A boardroom table with agenda papers and carafes of water, a soundtrack heavy with more terrible accents.

Onwards, past air-conditioned, back-lit rubble, the Warsaw Ghetto told in slides.

Suddenly the floor changes, carpet becomes rough-rendered concrete and we are standing in a bricked-in yard lined with barbed wire, observing a map of the Greater Reich, an ominous black blob veined with railway routes and sprinkled with death camp sites picked out in lights. Above arched portals signs read 'Able Bodied' and 'Children and Others'. I am not sure which to take. My ID card persona is safe in Shanghai by now, isn't she? My son is surer: he moves towards the 'Able Bodied' door. My wife takes his arm and leads him under the Other sign. The *Sophie's Choice* scenario.

In any case, both pathways converge. We have entered a vaulted concrete chamber and the door has closed behind us. I look up and examine the ceiling, half-expecting the clunk of a dropping canister. Is such a thought unfair to the good intentions of the people who have made this place, I wonder? We sit on hard benches and listen to a tape. In this setting, however contrived and grotesque, my pen and notebook seem out of place, a profanity. I put them away.

We sit in wincing, self-conscious silence and listen. The story we hear is poignant and horrible and concerns the means of selection for murder of a group of young boys. The detail that sticks in my mind is Josef Mengele's mode of transport. The Angel of Death rode around Auschwitz on a black two-wheeler. The tape ends, but the silence does not. Then the door swings out onto a well-lit, beige-toned dénouement. We file out and read the names of the righteous (not many) and what became of the guilty (not much).

A machine consumes our ID cards and replaces them with full-page biographies. At the end of the war, I read, unlike a million and a half other Jewish children, I was still alive. For all I know I still am. Perhaps I live here in Los Angeles. Maybe that was me I passed coming out of that Chinese restaurant outside of Pico Boulevard. My son's surrogate had fared less well. His high school student survived deportation and forced labour only to die five days after liberation. Ulrich Arnheim was murdered before his fifteenth birthday. But their identities live on, endlessly recycled by the interactive processes of modern museology.

Standing in line to sign the visitors' book, I feel it is again OK to take out my notebook. I copy these remarks from the comments column beside the day's signatures: 'Should be similar displays for other ethnic groups'; 'I wish there was more on the repression of women'. Even in victimisation there is competition. In several places words have failed entirely, or may have never been there in the first place. Three separate visitors had simply made their marks—a circle, two dots and a curve.

As we spill, subdued, into the street, my son hands me his biography to look after. 'What did you learn from that?' I ask. He shrugs. 'Well, it wasn't Disneyland, that's for sure.' Realising I expect more, he gathers his thoughts. 'The tunnel was good, but,' he offers. 'Fatso.'

1994

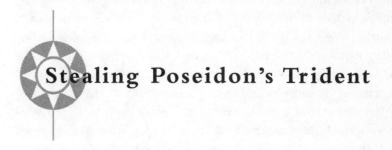

PETER STEELE

Stealing Poseidon's Trident

'NOW HE SUBMERGES ONCE AGAIN into the sea of the unread and then surfaces puffing and rejuvenated, as proud as if he had stolen Poseidon's trident.' Elias Canetti writes this in a journal entry, perhaps of himself. Whoever he had in mind, I take it as a sketch of many readers in action, at many stages of life. That sea, that surfacing, that rejuvenation—they all sound familiar. And now for a few strokes of my own in the oceanic territory, where even puffing can be revealing.

✪

At the southern tip of Attica, on the bluff of Sounion, there stands a temple of Poseidon. Ruined over its twenty-four centuries but much restored today, there it is, in a locale as dramatic as it is beautiful. Many visitors have cut their names into its stones, including that romantic ruffian George Gordon Lord Byron. The sun blazes over a theatrically blue Aegean, the columns rise at once austerely and elegantly. If the whole thing were more striking it would be intolerable. And if Poseidon existed, he would have to be pleased.

✪

To the ancient Greek mind, pleasing him could take some doing. God of the sea and of water generally, brother of Zeus the sky-god and Hades the keeper of the underworld, he had his home in a golden palace in the depths of the ocean, from which he would emerge, using his trident to lash the sea into fury, and causing either earthquakes or the welling up of new springs. He was the originator of horses, the builder of Troy's walls, and a copious begetter of various gigantic or ferocious offspring. He was the god of navigation and a god of vegetation. Black bulls were sacrificed to him, and bullfights were held in his honour. He was worshipped as a physician. Restless to the last, he was rarely shown as seated. Not a figure to take lightly, whether you went by sea or by land.

Canetti, who knew so much and so many kinds of things, would have known this and more about Poseidon. A splendidly original reader himself, he could think of the moody god as having an interest in the oceanic realms of the written. For that is what they are, not only in the sense that the words stream out, day after day, by the billion, but in the sense that meanings interleave and overlap and sleek their currents through one another, making climates of their own. Going with some zest into reading is like going down to the sea in ships.

For even the most enthusiastic and tenacious of readers, an incalculably large proportion of the readable is unread. While you read that sentence, millions of words were printed. Unless we are one of the obsessives of whom Canetti wrote so well elsewhere, we don't want to keep up with it all—wanting that would be like seeking the King Canute Prize for Verbal Greed. But even if what drives us is some narrower interest—in the political economy of Patagonia, in the durability of textiles, in the shifting nomenclature of rock bands—we haven't much of a chance. There are such things as experts, of course, and they know (as we say) what's what; but reading in hopes of keeping up with the entire archive is under the disadvantage mentioned of a certain academic conference—not only did everything have to be said, but everybody had to say it. Being conscientious in such a world is a good way of getting what used to be called a 'broken head'. Not to mention the heart.

Still, it keeps coming, and so do we. After all, we do like abundance for its own sake—not always and everywhere, but often and in many places. I have no wish to traverse the Sahara Desert, but am obscurely gratified by the fact that it is big enough to accommodate something the size of Australia. It is very pleasing to know that during an Ice Age, the present site of Chicago was under a mile of ice. And what could be better than to read, of our battered planet's early fortunes, that it once rained for millions of years? Perhaps such information takes us back, beguiled, to the days when we were Lilliputians in an upscaled world, which was, as Milton says of Adam and Eve's world at the end of *Paradise Lost*, 'all before them, where to choose'. Since then, the knowledge of exile has set in pretty convincingly for most of us, but we can still get a whiff of pomegranate from time to time.

I tell my students that if they can't read slowly they can't read, and they look at me either as if I am telling them that sodium chloride is a salt or as if I am heterodox to my fingertips: but it is still true. More of this later. Let us now, instead, praise scurrying, voracious, intemperate readers. When we began to walk, it was with little elegance, but in runty, lurching fashion: catwalks might, for all we knew of it, exist only on the moon. But it caught on, as we did, and here we are, doing it every day as if we had done it all our lives. It isn't that we want it to happen all the time, otherwise there would be no palanquins, sedan chairs, or Festiva Hatches: but sometimes nothing will do but Going For a Walk, the appetite its own justifi-cation. At such moments, the blundering zest of our early days is vindicated anew, and we course our own little worlds like so many lords of creation.

And so it goes with reading. Perhaps our elders—sometimes, but not always, our betters—thought that no good would come of us if we did not proceed with a proper decorum, going dutifully from one small, well-made sentence in which the cat sat on the mat and kept its mouth shut, to larger quarters in which one clause let guardedly into another before the patient gaze, and so on until we hit the varied show in which Cicero ate fire in one patch, Montaigne did swallow-dives from one trapeze to another, and Shakespeare clowned it perilously among the big cats. And per-haps the elders were right, most of the time. But the mind, like its sibling the heart, is a larrikin some of the time, and needs to live riotously. Larrikins and prodigals remember what their more proper relations are inclined to forget: that every major human resource is veined through with magic, and as such is only partly biddable. We do not learn to love reading simply by being courtly: we have to do some courting as well, and that is usually all the better for some impulsiveness.

Memory is a rummage-sale much of the time, and no surprise, either, given the way it has been fed items even by so apparently orderly a source as the inscribed or the printed page, let alone our eerily-flickering friend the computer screen. When the mediæval scribe fills a blank patch on his vellum page with ape and curlicue and a terse complaint about the chill in the scriptorium, this is all flourish: but then so is much of the sacred tale-telling to which he is devoting his energies. It is not the mockers of the Bible but its most assiduous exegetes who bring into luminousness its variety, its contrapuntal gambits, its sprawling ménage of types, incidents, behaviours, contrivances, destinies, upheavals, solacings. Split it into chapters and verses, web it over with echoes and foreshadowings, orchestrate it from Genesis to Revelations, and it still comes up with a fiesta of astonishments.

I wonder whether, in the many studies of the Bible's impinging on human imaginations and its stimulating book upon book upon book like its own deprecated Babel, enough account has been taken of its role as exemplar or provocateur along these lines? Without some predictability we can't live, and without some novelty we don't want to; and until pretty recently the biblical ensemble catered in a degree to both needs, just as they had no doubt played upon its complex origins. But even for those who are comparatively untouched by the Bible's reverberations, writing which is not exclusively technical is laced through with rhetorical energies, all bidding for attention and allegiance. However we may be when we read it, the written word is having a fine old time.

❂

I was young—'pre' most things—when I went with my parents and brother to Bunbury, for a holiday. We were not much for travel in those days: unless somebody sent you to a war, you stayed home, and were glad of it. But Bunbury was near enough to count as one of the purlieus of Perth, and had a beachy languor about it. My father and I sauntered along its wide main street, and came across a sale of second-hand books. With a common joy, we bought and began to read S. J. Perelman's *Acres and Pains,* pure quirk dashed through with irony. Nowadays, when my own behaviour or someone else's seems the stuff of which hemlock is made, I occasionally think, 'But there's still Perelman.' My Perelman is the one of 'Kitchen Bouquet', or of 'Short Easterly Squall, with Low Visibility and Rising Gorge'. Respectively, they begin like this:

> *Yesterday morning I awoke from a deep dream of peace compounded of equal parts of allonal and Vat 69 to find that autumn was indeed here. The last leaf had fluttered off the sycamore and the last domestic of the summer solstice had packed her bindle and caught the milk train out of Trenton.*

Peace to her ashes, which I shall carry up henceforward from the cellar. Stay as sweet as you are, honey, and don't drive through any open drawbridges is my Christmas wish for Leona Claflin. And lest the National Labor Relations Board (just plain 'Nat' to its friends, of whom I am one of the staunchest) summon me to the hustings for unfair employer tactics, I rise to offer in evidence as pretty a nosegay of houseworkers as ever fried a tenderloin steak. Needless to say, the characters and events depicted herein are purely imaginary, and I am a man who looks like Ronald Colman and dances like Fred Astaire ...

What elfin charm, what pawky and mettlesome humor, tessellate the pages of Oliver Cudlipp's new garland of whimsical papers, From a Misanthrope's Inkwell! *The title, so gruff that the unwary may not descry the impudent grin lurking beneath the domino, is a wickedly disingenuous one, for if ever author were untainted by the cheap cynicism that characterizes your modernist, 'avant-garde' scribbler, it is Cudlipp. Mellow, fantastical, un feuilletoniste bien spirituel, he wends his roguish way, gently puncturing our foibles with his unerring quill but never overstepping the bounds of good taste. If, occasionally, it is impossible to tell what he is driving at, do not be fooled into thinking him insipid. Pompous, attitudinizing, unreadable, yes, but never insipid ...*

This is torrential behaviour, possible at all only because that is one of the mind's ways. We are alarmed and despondent when, against our will, mind and mouth are given their head, and the issue is manic, or outright mania; it is the mental equivalent of avalanche, and we recoil from the spectacle, let alone the experience. But like it or not, the mind is a fast breeder, intelligence is torrential after all, the natural history of the senses is of sumptuousness as well as of discriminations, and we swim with the skill of a porpoise through the krill of consciousness, the incessant storm of event. And every so often we can be glad to yield, expressly, to the tumult—can be elated by the outrageous. Wit is all very fine, rapier flicking off rapier, but the sweep and plop and splash of comedy is also something for which we have a healthy appetite. A Perelman on the loose is our crumpled sibling, and something important dies in us if we deny him room.

James Joyce, reporting that he had spent a morning on a sentence, and asked whether he was looking for the *mot juste,* said that, no, he had all the words—he was looking for the order. Perelman was out of that stable. An unbroken stallion, he was still bridled by distant, formidable intuitions of the way things must go. Having written for Marx Brothers films, he remembered this with hatred, perhaps because, for all the precision that could be seen in those performances, it is hard to isolate finesse: and what Perelman was always after was ebullience crossed with finesse.

Jonathan Swift wrote a whole book in which he deployed cliché as though it were a gift from heaven, electric with the divine intervention: Perelman, in both of the passages quoted, takes to cliché as the dark ground across which the bright mind can play— buoyant, fleering, exuberant, a maker of splashes. 'A deep dream of peace compounded of equal parts of allonal and Vat 69' conflates one of Leigh Hunt's more lustrous poems with one of life's direr and more self-indulgent blends. 'Peace to her ashes, which I shall carry up henceforward from the cellar' plays (as he might have said) fast and loose with Victorian mock-classical lingo while taking the beset householder not only down to earth but into it. 'Stay as sweet as you are, honey, and don't drive through any open drawbridges' is an incantation that I used to recite to myself for years, as a mantra, in the face of the inevitable, the unintelligible, and the gratuitous. It has none of the spiritual warrant of (say) a phrase from the Psalmist, but it has pretty well the same claim on memory.

Talking, after all, is often a way of trying to find out what the devil is going on: and even the most suavely suited and grandly capped individuals are bushed about that for much of the time.

Solemnity is commonly about three-quarters bluff, and the existence of countless institutions which might be called Solemnity Clubs dotted over our fragile ball of dirt and water does not change that fact. Auden, near the end of his poem 'In Praise of Limestone,' says, 'The blessed will not care what angle they are regarded from,/ Having nothing to hide.' Not being the blessed, and having much to hide—above all, our not being the blessed—we care greatly. Perelman does not care, and storms upon us accordingly.

Unlike various would-be-grandees of cultural life, Perelman knows that there is no way out of the ignominies of the verbal circus. St John's Gospel, in the tender and momentous formulation, says that 'the Word was made flesh'—the best words in the world, so far as I am concerned. But human flesh, and its language, is also 'flash', as in that great Australian expression, 'as flash as a rat with a gold tooth.' All of our flair is the flair of approximaters, compromisers: as, first, an American Mr Big, and then an Australian one, said in response to the question, 'what do you do?'—'I do the best I can.' Language does the best it can—is gesticulant, often unshaven, not always well coordinated. Language both makes a gift of us to one another, and gives us away. It is what we all are, for better and for worse. And when, in the second of Perelman's beginnings, the speaker goes on locking one small shield into another—'unwary ... not descry ... disingenuous ... untainted ... unerring ...'—this, while ludicrous, also makes overt a permanent anxiety. Language is often padding, but padding as buffering. We keep saying things lest silence should say its terrible word to us. All of those wielded negatives carry the flash of fear.

To have that, too, come home, along with more precious things, it is necessary to take time, at least occasionally; slow is beautiful. The curious convention of poetry whereby, usually, it is out there on the page's white arena, space around it made obvious, can also suggest to us an advantage in time's being made 'spacious', time's being given its time. For some reason, it is not our practice to attach to poems the regulatory signals we take for granted with music—no 'allegro', no 'prestissimo'—but psychic pacing is of an importance which can hardly be exaggerated, in poetry. Getting that wrong is like getting wrong the timing of a space-capsule's docking. Still, poems offer such cues as they may, and a poet like Emily Dickinson is keen to celebrate precisions which we cannot easily calibrate except in poems' own terms. She writes, for example,

> The Spider holds a Silver Ball
> In unperceived Hands—
> And dancing softly to Himself
> His Yarn of Pearl—unwinds—
>
> He plies from Nought to Nought—
> In insubstantial Trade—
> Supplants our Tapestries with His—
> In half the period—
>
> An Hour to rear supreme
> His Continents of Light—
> Then dangle from the Housewife's Broom—
> His Boundaries—forgot—

Dickinson wrote a bracket of spider poems, and no surprise perhaps. She was herself a secret worker, a maker of small, tensile poems, a framer of light, an entrapper of vagrant consciousness. Thickness for thickness, spider silk is stronger than steel: 'the spider taketh hold with her hands', says the Book of Proverbs, 'and is in kings' palaces'. Love it or hate it, your spider is anything but commonplace.

Thinking about what makes this poem, too, anything but commonplace, I notice such things as these. That 'Silver Ball' is prized as well as coloured, is magical almost after the fashion of W. B.

Yeats' 'silver apples of the moon': perhaps it is related to silver orbs held, often, in the all-too-well-perceived hands of rulers, but it is at least more than an item, is a striking entity. Those 'unperceived Hands' are stranger than the tiny claws disclosed to microscopic examination, are a juggler's, a weaver's, a magician's. That he is 'dancing softly to Himself' has an eerie promixity to, and deviation from, a singing to oneself: dance has a silent eloquence and is at the same time body-rapt, self-referring, to a degree impossible in singing. The 'Yarn of Pearl' is the kind of conception for which Dickinson is famous, combining as it does extension and concentration, one element and another, an instrument and a treasure.

'He plies from Nought to Nought—/In insubstantial Trade'—he may, but she doesn't, even if the whole poem is a kind of shadowing of Dickinson's activity as a poet. All of us, so far as we can see, come from zero and exit into nullity, clinging the while to that great O, the world. And we 'ply' in several fashions, adapting, negotiating, travelling, arguing: every applying of ourselves is a species of plying. All this is part of the human 'trade', a mixture of exertion and concession, of things brought off and things left off. Between gulf and gulf, the hardest thing for us to be doing is nothing. To Dickinson's gaze, the spider enacts all this, 'insubstantially,' which might be read as 'on a tiny scale', as 'in vacuity', or as 'fleetingly', any or all of which could be a pointer to the vanity of human wishes.

'No gin without bitters' could be this poet's slogan, though she might think that vulgar. But, in that short-hand for life's passage, 'an Hour', what go up are 'Continents of Light'. Part of Dickinson's attention was always on the expansive possibilities of common enough words, and in 'Continents' she has things both ways— giving us continental span and also a containing agent or space: she may also have in mind the more abstract sense of a summary or concentration. Plainly, in any case, the vulnerable silk is to her eye a kind of grid for consciousness, a pause-giver. As happens in dozens and dozens of her poems, part of the implied or the explicit theme is mortal transition, but nobody better justified than she did the claim of a later American poet that 'death is the mother of beauty'.

❂

In the Poseidon story, the god is not only earth-shaker and ocean-perturber, but palace-dweller and wall-builder. Somewhere between these conditions is the origination of horses, those creatures which can stand either for untrammelled vitality or for disciplines and harmonies. Most if not all of what we read has a stake in both sides of this relationship. Rhetoric, whether seen or heard, is like music at least in this that it is completely unintelligible unless it takes place between the poles of formulation and investigation. The purposes in question may be very various—instruction, edification, entertainment, surprise, description and so on—but there is a basic dynamic that can never be eluded, however eager the writer may be to do that. Much of the time there is no such eagerness, and the words become a kind of festival of accepted contrast. A favourite of mine in this regard has always been G. K. Chesterton, an essayist to the last—which is to say, a maker, savourer, and releaser of tensions. Here he is, on 'The Advantages of Having One Leg':

> To appreciate anything we must always isolate it, even if the thing itself symbolize something other than isolation. If we wish to see what a house is it must be a house in some uninhabited landscape. If we wish to depict what a man really is we must depict a man alone in a desert or on a dark sea sand. So long as he is a single figure he means all that humanity means; so long as he is solitary he means human society; so long as he is solitary he means sociability and comradeship. Add another figure and the picture is less human—not more so. One is company, two is none. If you wish to symbolize human building draw one dark tower on the horizon; if you wish to symbolize light let there be no star in the sky. Indeed, all through that strangely lit season which we call our day there is but one star in the sky—a large, fierce star which we call the sun. One sun is splendid; six suns would be only vulgar. One Tower of Giotto is sublime; a row of Towers of

*Giotto would be only like a row of white posts. The poetry of
art is in beholding the single tower; the poetry of nature in
seeing the single tree; the poetry of love in following the single
woman; the poetry of religion in worshipping the single star.
And so, in the same pensive lucidity, I find the poetry of all
human anatomy in standing on a single leg. To express
complete and perfect leggishness the leg must stand in sublime
isolation, like the tower in the wilderness. As Ibsen so finely
says, the strongest leg is that which stands most alone ...*

People will, and should, write about anything—Montaigne on
'thumbs' is a case in point—because people will do anything.
(Many decades after Chesterton wrote his essay, the London *Times*
reported, on the 18th of July 1957 that a Sydney orthopædic specialist was leading a research party into Arnhem Land to investigate
the Aboriginal phenomenon of standing on one leg.) Chesterton's
assumption was that, since everything is ultimately connected with
everything else, all may shed light on one another. This is not to
say that there is no such thing as implausibility, and those who dislike either his opinions or his demeanour are quick to point this
out. In the course of his long and immensely copious life as a
writer, Chesterton would sometimes jib at being called a paradox-
monger, but that is what he became on off-days or when one King
Charles' Head or another bobbed up over his horizon. Still, the
sloshing around of paradox when nothing else came to mind was
a carelessness about something for which he usually cared deeply
and passionately, namely his conviction that for us to be at all is at
once gratuitous, essentially benign, and relational. In that sense, he
did know where he was going to come out, whatever he was
writing about: but it is a pretty expansive 'where'.

He wrote, as many do, partly for the drama of the thing, and one
avenue to drama is the subjunctive. His 'If we wish' and 'If you
wish' are signals to the reader to be on the *qui vive*, challenged and
challenging. Chesterton seems to have assumed that the human
mind is usually on the verge of wandering off—an assumption
which I believe to be perfectly true—and that it had constantly to

be twitched back into concentration. No doubt his view was in part a consequence of his being a journalist, but many a writer who has had little to do with that trade writes as though we need all the psychic exercise we can get if we are to go the writer's way. More significantly, the drama of writing and of reading can be an implicit ritualising of everything that is large and pervasive in the conduct of our lives, which, from their most to their least material conditions, are a tissue of firmness and fluidity, of stopping and going.

At its simplest, verse celebrates this; its rhythms, crude or subtle, answer to rhythms in our seated or lying bodies as well as in our bodies on the move. Verse's 'measures', however described, have a constant traffic with our minds' 'measures' in the face of the blizzard of events through whose thousands or millions we make our way daily. And prose is another device whereby we do more than itemise, more than denominate: it exercises us in continuing insight, and helps us, as we say, to realise things. Chesterton was, often, a better-than-average versifier, though rarely a good poet; the prose, by contrast, was a milieu in which he could, time after time, be reborn as a knowing being.

One thing he knew, and continued to report upon, was that, if we need to move through oceans of significance, we also need, frequently, to fling through the air of play; Chesterton was a kind of dolphin of the mind, moving fast through complementary elements. His love of play was partly a love of art, partly a love of life. All those subjunctives—his, but also the millions of them that thread their way through writings remembered and forgotten—are in part play, are esprit, just as every artistic innovation, not only from one performer to another but from one performance to another, is gambitry, in liberty. And what Yeats calls 'life's own self-delight', whether in urchin can-kicking or in Olympic virtuosity or in the invention of the telescope or the gene-shear, all this is spirit on the wing, whatever its great or little palpable yield. Writing cannot and should not be saying this expressly all the time; sometimes we need the tranquil, and sometimes we need the dire. But play will out wherever life shows its hand in a big way, and Chesterton found it his business and his pleasure to be there and say so as often as possible. He could also, as with Ibsen, mock without hating—a rarer gift than it sounds.

✪

Inventiveness and conjecture, however vibrant, share a cosmos with all the matters of fact, and sooner or later have to cut deals with them. In the seventeenth century, Andrew Marvell, like many of his intellectual comrades, could go on entertaining possibilities with an almost unending fluency—'Meanwhile the mind/from pleasure less,/Withdraws into its happiness:/The mind, that ocean where each kind/Does straight its own resemblance find;/Yet it creates, transcending these,/Far other worlds, and other seas ...' But Marvell also had the business of being a Member of Parliament for Hull, not the most oceanic of milieux, and other poems of his have the reek of the pragmatic and the politic. The rest of us, however enchantable, wake to worlds in which we too have to manœuvre, sometimes flummoxed, sometimes cynical, frequently provisional, and always, whether or not we like it, exposed. Here is Diane Ackerman, in her *A Natural History of the Senses*, doing the daily thing in a more-than-ephemeral way:

> *Look at your feet. You are standing in the sky. When we think of the sky, we tend to look up, but the sky actually begins at the earth. We walk through it, yell into it, rake leaves, wash the dog, and drive cars in it. We breathe it deep within us. With every breath, we inhale millions of molecules of sky, heat them briefly, and then exhale them back into the world. At this moment, you are breathing some of the same molecules once*

*breathed by Leonardo da Vinci, William Shakespeare, Anne
Bradstreet, or Colette. Inhale deeply. Think of The Tempest.
Air works the bellows of our lungs, and it powers our cells.
We say 'light as air,' but there is nothing light-weight about our
atmosphere, which weighs 5,000 trillion tons. Only a clench
as stubborn as gravity's could hold it to the earth; otherwise it
would simply float away and seep into the cornerless expanse
of space.*

*Without thinking, we often speak of 'an empty sky.' But the
sky is never empty. In a mere ounce of air, there are 1,000
billion trillion gyrating atoms made up of oxygen, nitrogen,
and hydrogen, each a menagerie of electrons, quarks, and
ghostly neutrinos. Sometimes we marvel at how 'calm' the day
is, or how 'still' the night. Yet there is no stillness in the sky, or
anywhere else where life and matter meet. The air is always
vibrant and aglow, full of volatile gases, staggering spores, dust,
viruses, fungi, and animals, all stirred by a skirling and
relentless wind. There are active flyers like butterflies, birds,
bats, and insects, who ply the air roads; and there are passive
flyers like autumn leaves, pollen, or milkweed pods, which just
float. Beginning at the earth and stretching up in all directions,
the sky is the thick, twitching realm in which we live. When
we say that our distant ancestors crawled out onto the land, we
forget to add that they really moved from one ocean to another,
from the upper fathoms of water to the deepest fathoms of air.*

The philosopher Alfred North Whitehead once called the phases of
education those of 'romance, precision, and generalization'. This
does very well not only for protracted disciplinary activity but for
pieces of writing as short as Ackerman's. Without 'romance'—the
engrossment factor—the demon of boredom takes over the management straight away; without 'precision'—names, dates, places,
numbers—we wonder, or should, whether somebody is just
making hypnotic passes; without 'generalization'—the mind in its
sweeping mode—it is not so much that we will feel stockaded in
among things smaller than ourselves, it is rather that any old

passer-by who throws us a few slogans is likely to capture our restive attention.

Whether by accident or by design, Ackerman's kind of writing offers a triple satisfaction. First, she romances, by way of the exotic and the various. All of us not cursed with unequivocal adulthood like to gape a bit from time to time, and for some the magicking force will attach to Colette's name, for some to the cumulus of scientific detail, for some to 'estrangement' as such—horizon at our feet, oceanic water meeting oceanic air, the great hand of gravity with all the atmosphere in its fist. Engrossment, too, can be reinforced by the switches from one rhetorical gesture or pitch to another—from command or appeal, through position and counter-position, to the proffering of one comprehensible detail after another. It all sounds animated, sounds energetic and appealing; listening to it, we know not only that something is going on but that someone is coming through.

As for precision, and besides the obvious particularities, Ackerman is up to one of the oldest intellectual games of the West, the imprinting of macrocosm and microcosm upon each other. The ancient saying that 'man is the measure of all things' can be construed in many ways, and among them is the sense in which we can gauge things partly by finding ourselves at home in them, as the familiar car clears the familiar gate-post, or the tall house-holder the low lintel. Careers, fortunes, masterpieces and night-mares have been made, of course, from a contrasting sense that we don't fit, aren't wanted, and will always be unspeakable, but that is not the only option, and is certainly not Ackerman's. *The Tempest* in airy nature, the washed dog in the sky, our very naming of any-thing and everything to which we turn our attention—this is a dovetailing of self into milieu, and a scanning, and a spanning. What is to be made of all this exercises as many people as ever, no doubt: but that something is to be made of it, and never without us, is one of the elementary givens of any humanism, whose fashionable enemies are inescapably parasitic upon it at every turn.

❂

And 'generalization ...' It interests us sometimes for straightforward reasons of codification, while we herd the genera of some realm or other; grown men and women can love taxonomy as small boys once loved toy soldiers, regiment by regiment. But I think that our taste for generalisation is also a sign of an appetite that is emotional, and ethical, and ontological. We hanker for the lot: that sky, that ocean, have got into our hearts. Autism is a dreadful affliction, though all of us flirt with it from time to time; the bid of generalisation is one of the ways in which we act against it. Generalisation has its own pathologies, and its own appalling complacencies—somebody could write a play about them, to be called *Waiting for Drongo*—but it is quite impossible to do without it, and at our best, as well as at our worst, we don't want to. It, too, is a way to 'inhale deeply', a way to keep a few strokes ahead of vengeful Poseidon.

1997

About the Contributors

DENIS BYRNE is a Sydney-based archæologist, currently with the NSW National Parks & Wildlife Service. His previous publications are in the field of archæological heritage conservation in Australia and Southeast Asia. He is currently working on a volume of essays about different conceptions of conservation in Asia-Australia.

BRIAN CASTRO is the author of six novels, numerous short stories and essays, and takes a special interest in the autobiographical form. He is currently working on some life studies and hopes to survive the revelations.

JOHN CLARKE was born in New Zealand and lives in Melbourne. He is a writer/performer, and adviser and comforter to the Government and people of Australia.

INGA CLENDINNEN is an historian and writer who divides her time between Melbourne and Magnetic Island.

BILL COPE is Director of the Centre for Workplace Communication and Culture and a former Director of the Office of Multicultural Affairs in the Department of the Prime Minister and Cabinet. He is the co-author of *Productive Diversity* (Pluto), *Mistaken Identity* (Pluto), *The Powers of Literacy* (Falmer Press), *Cultures of Schooling* (Falmer) and *Minority Languages and Dominant Culture* (Falmer).

ROBERT DESSAIX is a writer, broadcaster and literary commentator. He is editor of the Oxford *Book of Gay and Lesbian Writing*, the autobiographical *A Mother's Disgrace* and the novel *Night Letters*. He lives in Melbourne.

HELEN GARNER has worked as a journalist, reviewer and scriptwriter. Her novels include *Monkey Grip*, *Honour and Other People's Children*, *The Children's Bach* and *Cosmo Cosmolino*. She has also written a collection of stories, *Postcards from Surfers*, film scripts, *The Last Days of Chez Nous*, and *Two Friends*, and non-fiction, *The First Stone* and *True Stories*. She lives in Sydney.

KERRYN GOLDSWORTHY was born in rural South Australia, grew up in Adelaide, and taught in the English Department at the University of Melbourne from 1981 to 1997. She has edited three anthologies of Australian short stories, is a former editor of *Australian Book Review*, and author of a critical study of the work of Helen Garner and a collection of short stories.

PETER GOLDSWORTHY has published four collections of poetry and four of short stories. His first novel, *Maestro*, has been released on CD-ROM. His most recent books are the novel, *Keep It Simple Stupid* (Flamingo), and a collection of poems, *If, Then* (Angus & Robertson). A collection of essays, *Navel Gazing*, will be published by Penguin in 1998.

IVOR INDYK is founding editor of *HEAT* magazine and teaches English and Australian literature at the University of Sydney. He has written a critical monograph on David Malouf (Oxford) and on various aspects of Australian writing.

SHANE MALONEY is a novelist and columnist, and author of *Stiff* and *The Brush-Off*. He is Deputy Director of the Brunswick Institute, a weatherboard think-tank financed by his wife.

DAVID MARR grew up in Sydney, studied law and became a journalist. Between stints on the *Bulletin*, the *National Times* and 'Four Corners', he wrote biographies of Sir Garfield Barwick and Patrick White. In the last few years he has edited White's letters, presented on ABC Radio National 'Arts Today' and written for the *Sydney Morning Herald*.

LES MURRAY was born on the north coast of New South Wales and lives now in Bunyah. He is the author of many books of poetry, including a *Collected Poems*. He has also published four works of criticism, and, in 1997, a volume of selected prose, *A Working Forest* (Duffy & Snellgrove).

BARRY OAKLEY is literary editor of the *Australian*. He's author of the novels *A Wild Ass of a Man*, *A Salute to the Great McCarthy*, *Let's Hear It for Prendergast* and *The Craziplane*; plays, *The Feet of Daniel Mannix*, *Beware of Imitations* and *Bedfellows*; a book of short stories, *Walking through Tigerland*; and a collection of essays and articles, *Scribbling in the Dark*.

PETER PORTER is a poet and critic, and author of more than a dozen books of verse, the most recent being *Dragons in their Pleasant Palaces* (Oxford). He has collaborated with Arthur Boyd on four books, and in 1996 edited the *Oxford Book of Modern Australian Verse*. He was born in Brisbane and has lived in London since 1951.

PETER STEELE is a Jesuit priest, schooled in Perth, who has lived in Melbourne most of his life. He has a Personal Chair at the University of Melbourne and has published books of poetry and literary criticism, and writes extensively on these matters, and on various religious and cultural questions.

PETER WALKER was born in Wellington, New Zealand, and now lives in London. He is former foreign editor of the London *Independent on Sunday* and is currently working on a novel.

CHRIS WALLACE-CRABBE is a Melbourne poet and critic, and former Director of the Australian Centre at Melbourne University. His *Selected Poems, 1956–1994* won the *Age* Book of the Year Prize for 1995.

———————————— ✦ ————————————

A Note about Sources

Kerryn Goldsworthy's and Peter Steele's essays were commissioned for this volume. Publication details of all other essays are as follows: **Robert Dessaix**, 'Loitering with Intent', *Australian Book Review (ABR)*, Feb/Mar 1997; **Peter Walker**, 'Maori War', *Granta 58*, Summer 1997; **David Marr**, 'Windows '97', *Sydney Morning Herald*, 26.12.96; **Les Murray**, extract from 'The Best of Our Man in Bunyah', a column in the *Independent Monthly*, 1993–96, republished in *A Working Forest*, Duffy & Snellgrove, Sydney, 1997: pp. 100–2 (permission by Les Murray c/o Margaret Connolly & Associates); **Inga Clendinnen**, 'Reading Mr Robinson', *ABR*, May 1995; **John Clarke**, 'A Born Leader of Men', 'The 1989 Ashes Series', 'Gallipoli', *Great Interviews of the Twentieth Century*, Allen & Unwin, Sydney, 1990; 'The Hon. John Howard, Prime Minister of Australia', *Still the Two*, Text, Melbourne, 1997; **Denis Byrne**, 'Intramuros's Return', *The UTS Review*, vol. 1, no. 2, 1995; an earlier version of **Brian Castro**, 'Auto/biography', appeared in *Writing Asia and Auto/biography*, University College, Australian Defence Force Academy, 1995; **Chris Wallace-Crabbe**, 'Duncan Grant in New Haven', *Art Monthly*, April 1996; a shorter version of **Peter Porter**, 'Depth Soundings', appeared in *Eureka Street*, vol. 7, no. 6, Jul/Aug 1997; **Helen Garner**, 'Mr Tiarapu', *True Stories*, Text, Melbourne, 1996; **Peter Goldsworthy**, 'The Biology of Literature', *PN Review* (UK), 1997; **Bill Cope**, 'The Language of Forgetting', *RePublica 2*, Oct 1994; **Barry Oakley**, 'At the Third Stroke', *The Australian Magazine*, 2.12.95; **Ivor Indyk**, 'Atavism', *HEAT 1*, 1996; **Shane Maloney**, *Eureka Street*, vol. 4, no. 4, May 1994.

Many magazine, journal, book and newspaper editors, at my request, generously sent essays, making my task a companionable rather than an isolated one. I have been able to use only a tiny fraction of their contributions, but commend their publications to every lively reader. What follows is not an exhaustive list of sources but it will point enthusiasts and beginners alike in the right direction. *Australian Book Review*, *Australian Rationalist*, *Arena Journal*, *Arena Magazine*, *Art Monthly*, *Australian Cultural History*, *Eureka Street*, *Granta*, *HEAT*, *Island*, *Meanjin*, *New Scientist*, *Overland*, *Philosopher*, *Quadrant*, *Rolling Stone*, *Southerly*, *The Adelaide Review*, *The Australian Magazine*, *The Australian Review of Books*, *Good Weekend* (Fairfax), *Thesis Eleven*, *24 Hours*, *21C*, *UTS Review* and *Westerly*.

Australian Left Review, *Modern Times* (formerly *Australian Society*), *RePublica*, *The Independent Monthly*, *Scripsi* and *Voices* all ceased publishing between 1991–97, but can be found still in libraries.